THE IMMEASURABLE MIND

OTHER BOOKS BY WILLIAM R. UTTAL

Real-Time Computers: Techniques and Applications in the Psychological Sciences
Generative Computer Assisted Instruction (with Miriam Rogers, Ramelle Hieronymus, and Timothy Pasich)
Sensory Coding: Selected Readings (editor)
The Psychobiology of Sensory Coding
Cellular Neurophysiology and Integration: An Interpretive Introduction
An Autocorrelation Theory of Form Detection
The Psychobiology of Mind
A Taxonomy of Visual Processes
Visual Form Detection in 3-Dimensional Space
Foundations of Psychobiology (with Daniel N. Robinson)
The Detection of Nonplanar Surfaces in Visual Space
The Perception of Dotted Forms
On Seeing Forms
The Swimmer: An Integrated Computational Model of a Perceptual-Motor System (with Gary Bradshaw, Sriram Dayanand, Robb Lovell, Thomas Shepherd, Ramakrishna Kakarala, Kurt Skifsted, and Greg Tupper)
Toward a New Behaviorism: The Case against Perceptual Reductionism
Computational Modeling of Vision: The Role of Combination (with Ramakrishna Kakarala, Sriram Dayanand, Thomas Shepherd, Jaggi Kalki, Charles Lunskis Jr., and Ning Liu)
The War between Mentalism and Behaviorism: On the Accessibility of Mental Processes
The New Phrenology: On the Localization of Cognitive Processes in the Brain
A Behaviorist Looks at Form Recognition
Psychomythics: Sources of Artifacts and Misrepresentations in Scientific Cognitive Neuroscience
Dualism: The Original Sin of Cognitivism
Neural Theories of Mind: Why the Mind-Brain Problem May Never Be Solved
Human Factors in the Courtroom: Mythology versus Science

THE IMMEASURABLE MIND

the *real* science of PSYCHOLOGY

WILLIAM R. UTTAL

Prometheus Books
59 John Glenn Drive
Amherst, New York 14228-2197

Published 2007 by Prometheus Books

Inquiries should be addressed to
Prometheus Books
59 John Glenn Drive
Amherst, New York 14228–2197
VOICE: 716–691–0133, ext. 207
FAX: 716–564–2711
WWW.PROMETHEUSBOOKS.COM

11 10 09 08 07 5 4 3 2 1

Library of Congress Cataloging-in-Publication Data

Uttal, William R.
The immeasurable mind : the real science of psychology / by William R. Uttal. — 1st ed. hardcover.
p. cm.
Includes bibliographical references and index.
ISBN 1–59102–525–2 (alk. paper)
1. Science and psychology. 2. Psychology—Research. I. Title.
BF64.U78 2007
150.1—dc22

2007007859

Printed in the United States of America on acid-free paper

For Mitchan

CONTENTS

PREFACE

The guiding premise underlying this book is that it is possible to at least begin to inquire into the scientific status of psychology. To achieve this goal, we must start at the root assumptions of psychology and those endeavors for which there is agreement that they are natural sciences. We have to ask questions concerning the nature of science in general and psychology in particular. The need is great if we psychologists are to take our proper place in the hierarchy of modern sciences without promising too much or accomplishing too little. Make no mistake; psychology is at once the most important of all sciences and among the most fragile ones. It is a purpose of this book to evaluate its scientific strengths and weaknesses by comparing it against other "normal" sciences.

The history of science has identified a number of synoptic efforts that were specifically intended to transcend the details of laboratory experimentation, to examine the conceptual foundations, and to systematize one or another science. In those books that are amenable to mathematical analysis, the basic assumptions and axioms are made explicit, the logical rules formularized, and the conclusions or theorems that characterize the emerging science derived. It is clear at the outset of this discussion that this is more easily done for mathematics, biology, and the physical sciences than for psychology. Nevertheless, there is an opportunity and a need to at least ask the question if some comparable effort is possible for psychology.

Considering the long history of psychology, such programmatic reviews of the conceptual foundations have been relatively rare. The previous efforts that changed the direction of psychology havc usually been in the form of textbooks expressing a new point of view or an interpretation of a relatively limited ongoing research program. The eminent psychologists William James (1890), Edward B. Titchener (1899), John B. Watson (1914), and Ulrich Neisser (1967) all made their initial impact by compiling books that were essentially textbooks.

Of course there were exceptions. George A. Miller, Eugene Galanter, and Karl H. Pribram's admirable effort (1960) to organize psychological science and the prolific psychologist/philosopher Jacob R. Kantor's (1971) work certainly do not fall into the category of ordinary textbooks. Like theirs, a major concern of this book is the question, Are these differences merely reflections of different stages of scientific development or do they reflect something fundamental about the respective subject matters?

In the main, however, most of the milepost books of modern psychology were intended to be texts and, even then, tabulations of experimental findings rather than conceptual reorganizations of the field. There were and are few broad "theories" of psychology that transcend limited areas of psychological science. Therefore, there was little success in tying together the various chapters in each of these books beyond a couple of key ideas that often proved to be quite contentious. Why this should be so is not obvious and will be discussed later in this book. From the outset, it seems that psychology in some ways is intrinsically disorganized. However, so, too, was biology before Gregor Mendel's (1865) and Charles Darwin's (1859) great organizing themes.[1] Similarly, modern biological chemistry and genetics leapt from a collection of isolated ideas to an organized science with the determination of the structure of DNA by James D. Watson and Francis H. C. Crick (1953).

The question is—Are we on the verge of a similar breakthrough in scientific psychology? The answer to this question is—Probably not. However, there is much to be learned by at least considering the question as a guide for examining the current state of psychology.

The theme of this book is the idea of "Principles." By this I mean that I plan to seek out the most fundamental assumptions, principles, beliefs, and axioms that guide psychological research. I will only in passing be interested in the huge mass of empirical data that constitutes our profession's chief contribution to modern knowledge.

Furthermore, the subject matter I deal with in this book is almost exclusively designated by the terms *experimental*, *mathematical*, and *physiological psychology*. It is not well appreciated by the lay public that the word *psychology* is much too inclusive. It includes those whose humanistic goals are to help people with their mental problems from one end of the spectrum to cognitive neuroscientists at the other end who are striving to develop theories and explanations of how the brain produces the mind. My interests lie at the latter end of the spectrum. I only briefly entangle myself in the highly controversial subject matters of clinical, developmental, or social psychology. This is a book about what may or may not be a scientific enterprise. However difficult the task may be to resolve this issue for the hardier forms, it becomes even murkier when dealing with some of the fringe areas of what eventually might be considered to be a truly scientific psychology.

In many ways, this book is a summary of my thinking about various topics I have written about in the last few years. Because I have been working on similar problems during this time, I have deemed it appropriate to include some sections of previously written material in this present book. This is especially true for chapter 3, which deals with one of the most important issues of psychological theory—the applicability of mathematical thinking. This strategy is necessary to provide continuity and self-inclusiveness and to avoid leaving conceptual lacuna in some critical places in the discussion. In every case, the material has been updated as necessary to make the main points.

NOTE

1. We must not commit the usual sin of ignoring the usually overlooked Alfred Russell Wallace's (1858) independent, but near simultaneous, contribution to evolutionary theory. The two theories were not identical but were close enough so that Darwin had Wallace's paper read at a special meeting of the Linnean Society on July 1, 1858, and also expedited the publication of his book the next year.

ACKNOWLEDGMENTS

A Personal Note

This is the twenty-fourth book that I have written, edited, or collaborated on during my career. It is the tenth since my 1998 retirement from Arizona State University's Department of Industrial Engineering. I have an enormous debt of gratitude to my department for the support I received during this time. It is obvious to me that I could not have made any contribution without the facilities and support I received from my department chair, Professor Gary Hogg. Given the added complication that Gary was supporting a kind of scholarship that was wildly outside of the domain of his department, his support was especially appreciated.

Of course, there was an additional factor that has made my entire career possible. My dear wife, May, and I shared our fiftieth wedding anniversary in 2004 and it looks like we are well started on the next fifty years. May has always been the rock on which whatever I have done was based. Her love and companionship were, are, and, I fervently hope, will continue to be the foundation of my work as the years go by. I am not sure if she was serious when she asserted that she had married me "for better or for worse, but not for lunch!" Whatever her reasons, she certainly made this happy and productive last decade work wonderfully well by urging me to continue even when discouraged.

There is another acknowledgment that I should have made long ago but have deferred to this particular stage in life. There have been three people throughout my life who contributed especially strongly and perhaps uniquely to my professional, as opposed to personal, development. These three men appeared in my life at what turned out to be critical times. The first was a high school chum. The late Emil Taxay will never appreciate how much he influenced my life when he introduced me to what I can only describe as the possibility of an intellectual life. In the world in which I was growing up, I had no idea of the opportunity to think about some of the most important questions of human history. Emil turned me to books and ideas that were only obscure phantoms to me in those days and, without question, changed the course of my life. After the high school years, we went to college together but parted ways after graduation. I never saw him again and never had a chance to express the appreciation that gradually dawned on me about how influential he had been in directing my future career. Emil went on, I have been told, to be a physician and died young. I will always be angry at him for not giving me the chance to say "thank you."

The second person to whom I owe an enormous debt of gratitude has also died. John Rader Platt and I first crossed paths at the University of Michigan. At that time I had my PhD and was busily at work on a more or less conventional career as a laboratory researcher. I had dabbled with a little book writing, but it was John who was the role model for what was to be my real passion. John had been a distinguished biophysical researcher but abandoned his laboratory to write several very important and still well-remembered volumes, including his advice for rigorous science, *Strong Inference* (Platt 1964), the futuristic *The Step to Man* (Platt 1966) and the stimulating *The Excitement of Science* (Platt 1962). What I learned from John was that it was possible to spend a bit of one's time thinking "outside the laboratory box" and that books could be a meaningful part of a scientific career.

Since my retirement, books have become my sole media and mode of expression.

The third person to whom I owe an extraordinary debt of gratitude is my current colleague at Arizona State University—Peter Killeen. Along with his extraordinary intellectual stimulation, it was Peter who introduced me to the theoretical option of behaviorism. Previously, I had been a cognitive and neuroreductive psychologist. Peter, perhaps without actually fully knowing what he had done, was a role model for the behaviorist approach that had years before made Arizona State University known as "Fort Skinner in the West." The logic of his approach and the clarity of his thinking made me follow his orientation and, when the opportunity offered by my retirement arose, turn to what is clearly my current behaviorist orientation.

I have encountered many other friends and intellectual influences in my life, but these three stand out as the most influential. I am grateful to all three for making the last couple of decades among the most satisfying and productive. I am not sure what I will be doing next, but I hope to be able to continue the pleasure of making some kind of a contribution to scientific psychology.

Chapter 1

LEXICOGRAPHICA SCIENTIFICA

What Is a Science That It Might Be Called Psychology?

1.1. INTRODUCTION

Of all intellectual activities, perhaps none has wrestled more with the problem of its very right to declare itself a science than psychology. Over the centuries, whenever theologians, scholars, or modern students have considered the working of the human mind and/or behavior, questions have almost always arisen concerning the limits and constraints that inhibit our understanding. What kind of a science is psychology? Do we have access to the inner workings of the mind or are they unalterably private? Can mind be measured? Can mathematics and other logical methods be applied to mental processes? These are the kinds of questions that lurk in the background of every generation's attempt to analyze, control, predict, and describe mental processes.

The purpose of this book is to explore these questions from several different points of view. These questions are not easy to answer. They are posed in a historical context in which the mind was considered not to be a part of the material world. There is, therefore, a considerable amount of intellectual baggage that even the most modern approaches to psychology carry as a result. Thus, the salient issues remain open in spite of an imposing amount of research that is carried out under the assumption that these questions can be or have been answered in the affirmative.

Nevertheless, many psychologists deeply committed to the scientific role of their studies have struck out at their methodological, empirical, and theoretical status of psychology. It has almost become a cottage industry for psychologists to ask questions such as "Why hasn't psychology kept its promises?" (Schlinger 2004) or "Does cognitive neuropsychology have a future?" (Harley 2004) or "Why isn't psychology more effective as a basic science?" (Holth 2001). These critiques are not new, but their intensity and frequency has increased in recent times. Because of this increasing (as well as continuing) barrage of challenges to one of the biggest of the "-ologies,"[1] it seems timely to reconsider such questions.

The path to answering the question "How scientific is psychology?" is not going to be direct or easy. Materials relevant to answering this question are going to be found in related and unrelated fields of science as well as in classic and modern philosophy. Furthermore, there is no promise that a universal answer to such questions can be achieved. What is hoped is that by the end of this work, at least the questions will be clarified, even if they remain unanswered for the time being.

In this chapter, I consider the history of the critiques of modern psychologies. I then try to identify some of the major reasons likely to inhibit psychology from achieving status as a normal science. To be balanced, I next consider some of the counterarguments that support psychology's scientific status.

1.2. CRITIQUES OF PSYCHOLOGY'S SCIENTIFIC STATUS

It is fair to ask, Is this book the idiosyncratic view of one psychologist who has only lately come to appreciate the behaviorist point of view? In this first section, I seek some support for a negative answer to the question of the scientific status of mentalist psychology. As the following paragraphs show, mine is by no means a totally isolated point of view. For brevity's sake, I have tabulated these criticisms as a series of quotations that I believe capture the essence of each cited author's comments.

One of the earliest criticisms of psychology's status as a scientific enterprise came from a scholar who is considered the father of modern American experimental psychology—William James (1842–1910). James's (1892, 1948) oft-cited critical comment still rings true, as we will shortly see: "A string of raw facts; a little gossip and wrangle about opinions; a little classification and generalization on the more descriptive level; a strong prejudice that we have states of mind, and that the brain conditions them: but not a single law in the sense in which physics shows us laws, not a single proposition from which any consequences can causally be deduced. We don't even know the terms between which the elementary laws would obtain if we had them" (468).

Although we need not agree with each and every comment in this quotation, we will see that many of these condemnations still have some modern currency. Indeed, in this seminal comment, James highlighted the problem that a mentalist psychology had and still has in establishing its bona fides as a science. James was essentially asserting that there are no axiomatic foundations ("propositions") and no quantifiable laws or rules by means of which theorems ("consequences") can be derived ("causally be deduced"). As we see when we explore the nature of axiomatic-deductive science in the next chapter, these properties are the very essence of the great successes that many other sciences have enjoyed in the last several centuries. Several questions then arise. First, does this criticism hold for today's psychology? Second, if it does not, then what kind of an enterprise is psychology? Third, if it does, what then is the nature of today's scientific psychology?

This book, as noted earlier, is aimed at answering questions like these. However, before doing so, we must first examine just how broadly based are current criticisms about the nature of psychology. It is important to determine if James was just reflecting on the state of what was, in the late nineteenth century, a primitive science just recently separated from philosophy. Or, on the contrary, has psychology advanced so far in the century just passed that his comments can be relegated to the wastebasket of an outmoded and premature criticism?

For many years, philosophers have been especially critical of psychology's place in the hierarchy of sciences. A particularly fierce criticism comes from Ludwig Wittgenstein (1958), who asserted in this very context: "The confusion and barrenness of psychology is not to be explained by calling it a 'young science'; its state is not comparable with that of physics in its beginnings. . . . [Rather, it is characterized by] conceptual confusion" (232).

Psychologists themselves have been extremely critical of their own science.[2] There has been a continual, if unheard, commentary questioning everything from the applicability of the scientific method in psychology to its lack of convergence (or pending convergence) on a central scientific theory that unites and consolidates the ever-increasing mass of empirical data.

For example, several contemporary scholars have questioned whether or not psychology should be considered a science. Koch, a long-standing critic of "scientific psychology" expressed his view in the title of his critical paper "Psychology Cannot Be a Coherent Science" (Koch 1969). He detailed some of his ideas later when he (1981) described what he believed were the "limits of psychological science."[3] Koch (1993) followed up with a vigorous statement that the problems of psychology were so severe that they could not be overcome in the usual scientific manner. His argument was that psychology was not a coherent science but one that had to be considered as a chaotic collection of individual psychological studies.

Others have joined in the spirit of Koch's criticism in challenging the scientific status of their field for a variety of methodological reasons. Machado, Lourenco, and Silva (2000, 3–4) identified a number of these "flaws" of modern psychology including:

- Lack of a conceptual analysis.
- Triviality and illiteracy in the publication stream.
- Poor reliability and bias in the peer review process.
- Fragmentation of current knowledge and the disunity of the community of psychology.
- Overuse of the null hypothesis significance testing as a means to validate empirical propositions.
- The intolerance of mainstream cognitive psychology toward those who are not married to the system and steeped in its fashion.
- Its ineffectiveness in producing satisfactory solutions to practical problems in education and clinical psychotherapy.

Harley (2004), a critic of a relatively narrowly defined field of cognitive neuroscience—neuropsychology—came to some equally critical conclusions as he reviewed a newly published handbook of cognitive neuropsychology (Rapp 2001). These conclusions, which can be generalized to psychology as a whole, include:

- Lack of agreement among theories.
- Disagreement concerning what the relevant vocabulary means. (E.g., the word *word* has different meanings in speech and reading.)
- Imprecise specification of questions.
- The general complexity of brain organization.
- Overly simplistic models (e.g., box and arrow diagrams). (Harley 2004, 13–14)

Schlinger (2004), another modern critic, answers the loaded rhetorical question "Why hasn't psychology kept its promises?" by emphasizing the following failures:

- "The continued focus on conceptually vague mentalistic constructs." (123)
- Its "prescientific vocabulary . . . including such terms as mind, memory, thinking and consciousness." (125)
- "Psychologists' theorizing is often based on assumptions (about the existence of cognitive structures and processes) that can never be directly tested." (129)
- Overuse of ill-defined metaphors.
- Overuse of statistical testing of narrowly defined hypotheses.
- Inability to control experimental conditions precisely enough to permit "orderliness between independent and dependent variables." (137)
- Psychologists "do not receive the same degree of training or spend the countless hours in basic laboratory research that scientists in other disciplines do." (140)

Lykken (1991) has added additional criticism to the scientific aspects of psychology by clearly and courageously pointing out that:

- Psychology isn't doing very well as a scientific discipline and something seems to be wrong somewhere.
- This is partly due to the fact that psychology is simply harder than physics or chemistry, and for a variety of reasons.
- But the problems of psychology are also due in part to a defect in our research tradition; our students are carefully taught to behave in the same obfuscating, self-deluding, pettifogging ways that (some of) their teachers have employed. (3–4)

Some psychologists, for example, Hagen (1997), have directed their attacks specifically at psychotherapy and the particular use of clinical psychologists as expert witnesses in the courtroom.

It is an extraordinary fact that these attacks on the scientific credibility of a science come in substantial part from within its own ranks. That means that most of these critics are from the field to which each has dedicated most of his or her professional life and presumably is acquainted firsthand with its strengths and weaknesses. A special authority is given to their critiques by this simple fact. However, it should be noted that most of these criticisms are directed at the mentalist fields, those that accept the accessibility of mental events. The common targets are those areas of experimental psychology that seek to explain and reduce behavior to mental mechanisms as well as to psychotherapies that seek to treat psychological dysfunctions.

There is little in this chorus that speaks to behavioral psychology. Behaviorism, to the contrary, is criticized because of its "antihumanistic" properties: its tendency to "deny basic human nature," to make our concept of humanity "too mechanical," or because it "disparages religion." In the same spirit, behaviorism is often criticized because it is "too scientific" and neglects the humanistic aspects of life.

Thus, it seems undeniable that there is something deeply disturbing about the nature of modern psychology to a considerable, albeit a minority, portion of the psychological community. Nevertheless, it is a thoughtful group deeply concerned about the nature of psychology cum science. Many of these critics express a hope that many of these problems can be solved. However, there are some who believe there are deep and intractable problems facing psychology, particularly the mentalist approaches, that will have a substantial impact on its general acceptance as a standard or normal science. The suspicion is that some of these problems are so fundamental and embedded in the nature of the subject matter of psychology—the mind itself—that they may never be overcome.

However, to know if psychology is a science, we must know what a science is. Exploration of this issue is the topic of the next section.

1.3. WHAT IS A SCIENCE?

At the outset of this discussion of the nature of science in general, it is important to clarify one point that may only be implicit in the following material. Definitions of science, like definitions of mind, differ considerably from scholar to scholar. However precisely we may seem to be zeroing in on an acceptable definition, there may be as many controversies surrounding the question "What is a science?" as there are around the question "What is the mind?"

1.3.1. Some Definitions

If we are to ask the rhetorical question "What kind of a science is psychology?" with any degree of conceptual clarity, it is important to define exactly what the word *science* means to us. Science has been defined in many ways, varying from the most particular, specific, and exclusive, to the loosest and most inclusive. A typical dictionary definition goes like this:

> **1 :** the state of knowing **:** knowledge as distinguished from ignorance or misunderstanding
>
> **2 a :** a department of systematized knowledge as an object of study <the *science* of theology> **b :** something (as a sport or technique) that may be studied or learned like systematized knowledge <have it down to a *science*>
>
> **3 a :** knowledge or a system of knowledge covering general truths or the operation of general laws especially as obtained and tested through scientific method **b :** such knowledge or such a system of knowledge concerned with the physical world and its phenomena. (From *Merriam-Webster's Collegiate Dictionary*, online edition, accessed July 27, 2005)

Each of these three definitions leaves many loose ends hanging in the web we wish to weave about the meaning of the word *science*. The first simply makes science synonymous with knowledge. This definition is obviously far too loose; would knowing the way to the nearest grocery store be acceptable as scientific knowledge? Is the date of a historical event, such as the August 2 (not the July 4 date as popularly assumed) signing of the Declaration of Independence, science in the sense we generally mean it? Obviously, knowledge per se is not science.

Similarly, the second definition suggests that a science is any field of study that may be organized into an academic department. However, this also does not ring true. The "science of theology" is an oxymoron in which the two key words are mutually antagonistic in terms of strategies and foundation beliefs. Simply identifying a subject matter is not sufficient to define a science; the result can be nonsense. Not all academic departments are scientific enterprises.

The third definition comes closer to being useful. The idea that "science is a system of organized knowledge governed by laws" comes closer to the generally accepted meaning. However, when a science is defined only by its method, the results can be problematic. If something uses the scientific method, according to this definition, then it is a "science." However, such a definition quickly runs into trouble when the scientific method is applied to topics in which the subject matter violates the laws of other scientific fields. For example, the "science" known as parapsychology is departmentalized in a few instances in universities and also claims to use the scientific method to explore its subject matter—supernormal mental powers. Nevertheless, there is no acceptable body of repeatable evidence that justifies calling this activity a science.

Some other definitions of science include:

- Science is a process for evaluating empirical knowledge (the scientific method), a global community of scholars, and the organized body of knowledge gained by this process and carried by this community (and others). Natural sciences study nature; social sciences study human beings and society. (From the online encyclopedia Wikipedia)
- Science is a method of learning about the physical universe by applying the principles of the scientific method, which includes making empirical observations, proposing hypotheses to explain those observations, and testing those hypotheses in valid and

reliable ways; also refers to the organized body of knowledge that results from scientific study. (From NOAA Web site)

Psychology cum science, unfortunately, runs counter to the allusion to the "physical world and its phenomena." Just what is meant by the physical world? Do mental phenomena fail to meet this criterion given that they are not directly measurable with the units of the physical world? Or, to the contrary, are they manifestations (i.e., processes) of physical systems? Questions like these have perturbed both supporters and critics of the concept that psychology is a science.

The nature of science, therefore, remains elusive after looking at these lexicographical definitions. They do, however, suggest that there are two directions that we might go in our search. Science may, according to these hints, be identified by its subject matter or by its method. Unfortunately, neither of these characteristics satisfactorily answers our question. However, to the degree they interact, some further insights emerge.

1.3.2. Science as Subject Matter

Let's continue examining the possibility that science is defined by its subject matter. Using this approach, science can be defined in terms of the study of some aspect of the natural world. Accordingly, with this meaning, science is defined in terms of the susceptibility to the scientific method of what is being studied. Some subject matters are clearly amenable (e.g., physics) to scientific examination. Others are not (e.g., theology) and others, like psychology, are on the edge for some reasons already mentioned and others yet to be mentioned.

Debate will always rage over what is scientific if the subject matter criteria are strictly adhered to. For example, the use of psychoactive chemicals is widely touted as an example of a scientific field of study. However, there is no widely accepted theory of how these substances work to change behavior (beyond some demonstrated, but indirectly related, synaptic effects), and there are even a great deal of questions concerning the robustness of many of the experiments that have been carried out to determine their effects. Valenstein (1998), for example, details the absence of theory, the difficulty of formulating explanatory theories, and the almost anecdotal and fortuitous basis of this kind of medical "science." On close scrutiny, there is very little to distinguish modern psychochemistry from the anecdote-based claims of a primitive shaman. Nevertheless, the subject matter of psychoactive drugs is considered to be "scientific" because it is approached from a natural science perspective and, to the best of our current knowledge, does not obviously violate any laws of the natural world.[4] Clearly, however, defining a subject matter does not necessarily authenticate its scientific status.

1.3.3. Science as Method

It is difficult, therefore, to distinguish between "junk," or para-science, and a legitimate science on the basis of subject matter alone. The alternative is to accept the methodology criterion as a means of defining a science. Such topics as polygraphy, astrology, and jury selection all have large groups of supporters who claim that their studies are "scientific," since they purport to use (mostly unsuccessfully) the scientific method. To understand this argument further, we must examine the current view of the "scientific method."

One of the clearest statements of an ideal scientific methodology has been offered by Wolfs (2005):

1. Observation and description of a phenomenon or group of phenomena.
2. Formulation of a hypothesis to explain the phenomena. In physics, the hypothesis often takes the form of a causal mechanism or a mathematical relation.
3. Use of the hypothesis to predict the existence of other phenomena or to predict quantitatively the results of new observations.

4. Performance of experimental tests of the predictions by several independent experimenters and properly performed experiments. (1)

Here in a nutshell is a traditional and widely accepted observation-hypothesis generating-verification model of scientific research. It is the one that much of psychology has adopted and utilized in making its claim to acceptance as a science. However, hypothesis testing per se is not by itself a road to discovery. Cummins (2000), for example, points out that most hypothesis testing by psychologists is little more than showing that an effect exists. He argues that "a hypothesis isn't a law or anything like a law. The word 'hypothesis' as it is used in statistical analysis and the word 'hypothesis' as it is used to refer to a conjectured theory or law are little more than homonyms. They share the element of conjecture and little else." (2)

Another similar effort to define an ideal scientific methodology was suggested by Platt (1964) in his influential article "Strong Inference." Platt was specifically arguing for a more precise and powerful means of carrying out scientific studies. He proposed that the strongest means of proceeding to a solid scientific conclusion depended on the strict adherence to the following rules:

- Devise alternative hypotheses.
- Devise a crucial experiment (or several of them) with alternative possible outcomes, each of which will, as nearly as possible, exclude one or more of the hypotheses.
- Carry out the experiment in a way that produces clean results.
- Recycle the process to refine the remaining hypotheses. (Slightly rephrased from Platt 1964, 347)

Platt was a biophysicist and, therefore, conducted research in a field in which the complexities were much fewer than in psychology. However, some psychologists (e.g., O'Donohue and Buchanan 2001) have recently argued that such a rigid process is not applicable to psychology. Indeed, they suggest that it has rarely, if ever, actually been used by any scientist, past or present. Their point is that science operates in many ways, and this particular strategy does not define science.

The essence of this kind of argument is that, unfortunately, emphasis on the method also does not satisfy our search for an answer to the question of whether or not psychology is a science. The methods proposed by Wolfs or Platt do not take into account the fact that however compelling may be the desire to apply this kind of functional model to determine whether or not an activity is a science, in many instances, the steps in proposed method may simply fail for some science. For example, the observation or description of any introspectively reported phenomenon is hardly the foundation of a patently scientific inquiry. Observations of such isolated and often irreproducible phenomena are controversial, to say the least, and may be impossible. Furthermore, some statistically unlikely observations may have a further problem of inconsistency with normal science. Remote viewing or teleportation, for example, fall outside the rubric of science simply because they violate the laws of other sciences.

For a phenomenon to be observable and testable, measurements must be public and replicable; no private observation in the form of a unique (unreplicable) revelation is sufficient to provide grist to a methodological mill, however strongly the mill may turn. Unfortunately, both psychology and religious revelation are replete with unreplicable reports of private experiences that do not lead to empirical observations. I refer here specifically to the putative psychological effects of rare cases of traumatic brain injury, the topic of "sciences" such as the well-known, but idiosyncratic, field of psychophysiology.

The methodological step of "formulation of a hypothesis" alluded to by Wolfs is also inadequate by itself as a criterion for a "science." A wide variety of hypothetical explanations characterize many intellectual enterprises, some with reasonable plausibility and possibility, but many with no possibility of being tested and validated. Susceptibility to speculation is not a sign of science.

On the other hand, as we will see, the initial step in the most formal kind of science is the statement of one's axioms. Axioms are hard to distinguish from hypotheses; both are summaries of previous observations. Again, words fail to convey the precise denotation required in defining a science.

Finally, Wolfs's fourth methodological criterion of science is replicability. However, such a criterion may be more easily stated than achieved. It has been pointed out by many psychologists that few if any experiments are ever exactly replicated. Not only do psychologists shy away from repeating the work of others, but subject and experimental protocol differences based on random selection obviate efforts to repeat a study. For those few studies that are intentionally replicated, it is somewhat surprising to note that the higher and the more complex the cognitive phenomena under study, the more likely are the earlier results to be overthrown.

Because of the enormous variability of organic behavioral responses, the subject samples of environmental and experiential variability, and the diversity of measuring instruments, even experiments that are designed to be replications can often differ in critical ways. Some years ago, I (Uttal 1988) suggested what might still be considered as an inviolable law of psychological research: "Slight changes in procedure, stimulus material, or methodology often produce dramatic changes in the rules of perception" (289). Given this ubiquitous sensitivity to experimental conditions, psychology may have little claim to being a science that is characterized by empirical replicability and verification of its observations.

As a result of the intrinsic variability of human behavior, measures of central tendencies and other statistical measures (not only within an experiment but also between different experiments) have become necessary tools in the study. What we know, therefore, is more about groups than about individuals. Efforts to predict or explain individual behavior based on pooled data should, therefore, always be subject to special scrutiny, if not cynicism.

A further problem with behavioral variability is that it may be so great as to preclude any kind of verification or lawful understanding.

For all of our efforts to tame variability with statistics, there must come a point at which intrinsic variability cannot be distinguished from chaos.

1.3.4. Science as an Organized Body of Knowledge

Another way to characterize scientific activity is by the presence of a body of organized knowledge. I alluded to this criterion when I dissected the dictionary definitions. However, it is worth emphasizing that knowledge per se is an inadequate definition of a science. The question arises: Is any kind of an organized body of knowledge a science? In other words, does the subject matter define a science?

The answer to this question is obviously no! There are many institutions of learning that are dedicated exclusively to the study of theological issues that make no pretense of being "scientific." Many of the Madrassas and Jamia of the Islamic world, the yeshivas of Orthodox Judaism, and any number of different denominations of Christian parochial schools are explicitly and intentionally places of study of religion rather than science. Nevertheless, the training may be rigorous and organized on the basis of fundamental principles and assumptions in a way that is difficult to distinguish from the way science operates other than in terms of its basic supernatural assumptions.

The differences between any of these religious institutions and a school of science in terms of their foundation beliefs, however, are profound. Most notably, controlled observation and experimentation are usually absent in a parochial school but are present in a scientifically secular one. Another important difference is that the subject matter under study in a Madrassa or a yeshiva is very likely to be the contents of an ancient book believed to be the culmination of a divine revelation rather than summaries of observations of the natural world.

The point is that the organized study of some subject matter is not by itself a signature property of a science. Nor, for that matter, is the absence of such organized study an indication that some inquiry is not a science. One criterion that does characterize science (more than simply attentive study) is the willingness to grow and modify as new data and ideas emerge, the quest for those new data and ideas, and an objective analysis of observable natural phenomena. Of course, words like *objective*, *observable*, and *natural* raise their own problems of meaning and interpretation.

1.3.5. A Simple Definition of Science

Like many other efforts to define an elusive term, it may be that expecting any single criterion to do the job is demanding too much. It may be better to define science as simply and generally as possible and to assume that it is a multidimensional word subject to the whims of time and place. Based on these additional dimensions, one can cull out those unscientific anomalies from the all-too-inclusive conceptual net. One simple definition is that a science is a search for an orderly understanding of some aspect of the natural world—the key words being *search*, *orderly*, and *natural*. Although not very specific, such a definition incorporates methodology and subject matter as well as the concept of organization.

The method of science from this point of view is simply the search for knowledge in the most general way. The subject matter is, equally simply, the natural world. What is "natural" will differ, as I have already noted, from one authority to another, but the unnatural or supernatural eventually fails to meet some aspect of the scientific method by unobservability, unpredictability, or extensive unreliability (i.e., failing to be either coherent or consistent) implied by the word *organized*. Such a nutshell definition distills the various definitions that have been presented here to their essence. Both the method and the subject matter must interact for an enterprise to be considered science. The subject matter must be amenable to the application of the methods, and the methods must be effective in dealing with the subject matter.

It is, I must repeat, not always the case that such a pure and pristine definition adequately describes the way every science and every scientist operates. Scientists are not always completely constrained from allowing their personal beliefs, the reputation of predecessors, or vested financial interests from influencing interpretations or even polluting observations. Ideally, science must, to the maximum degree possible, be independent, iconoclastic, critical, and responsive to new ideas. Of course, this is more easily said than done, and loyalty-demanding "schools of thought" proliferate, particularly in psychology. It is terribly difficult, as many have discovered, to challenge a prevailing zeitgeist. Nevertheless, right or wrong, the role of a few critics in this profession is very important. As James Bryant Conant (1951) put it: "The stumbling way in which even the ablest of the scientists in every generation have had to fight through thickets of erroneous observations, misleading generalizations, inadequate formulations, and unconscious prejudice is rarely appreciated by those who obtain their scientific knowledge from textbooks."

Another key idea inherent in this definition is that science must be orderly and, by implication, converging. That is, science must proceed from the aggregation of a large number of observations to a small number of general and synoptic principles summarizing the meanings of those observations. There is implicit in the ideal of science that the simple collection of data or specimens without systemization and conceptual condensation is not scientific. Some effort must be made and some success achieved in organizing data for an enterprise to be considered scientific. A taxonomy showing causal relationships between different items in a collection is a sine qua non of a science. Furthermore, some success must be achieved in finding universal rules that help us to understand and explain.

One final and all-important property of a science is that it must be self-correcting. Past authority must always eventually succumb to new observations—if and when they occur. What is unnatural or incorrect ultimately falls by the wayside as the search for knowledge continues and as past observations are not repeated. The past must then regularly be acknowledged to be inadequate or incorrect as new ideas, theories, and assumptions are found. What is scientific is proven not by definition but by demonstration. Change is a fundamental criterion of a science. Perhaps this dynamic instability is as much a criterion of a science as any other.

1.4. SOME REASONS WHY PSYCHOLOGY MAY NOT BE A SCIENCE IN THE USUAL SENSE

So far, I have sought an acceptable set of criteria for what constitutes a science. Each of the suggested criteria helps us toward a clearer understanding of the meaning of this elusive term. However, it is clear that none is adequate to fully satisfy our need for an ironclad answer to the question "What kind of science is psychology?" We are beginning to see that psychology as a science of the mind has a number of frailties that have led a surprising number of our colleagues to question its scientific credentials and accomplishments. Almost certainly, psychology is subject to some contradiction and disagreement when tested against any of the general criteria of a science discussed in earlier parts of this chapter.

What are the reasons for this contentiousness? In this section, my goal is to seek out some of the underlying causes of this crisis of confidence. Before I begin, it is important to point out that none of these criticisms of psychology cum science are independent of any of the others. There are commonalities that link them together. It is not clear that any one of them is fundamental; I am not even sure which are effects and which are causes. Collectively, however, they represent a set of "in principle" characteristics of psychology that argue against its being classified as a science in the usual sense.[5]

Some of the most salient causal factors for the continued questioning of psychology's scientific credentials are among the most recalcitrant and have proven to be extremely difficult to resolve. The issue of the accessibility of mental processes—whether or not the mind can be assayed and measured in a way that makes it susceptible to a naturalist scientific examination—probably underlies and influences all of the other possible causes now to be considered. Certainly, the issue of the accessibility of mind to empirical study or introspective report is the crux of the great cognitive-behaviorist schism that continues to belabor psychology. For this reason, if no other, it is a good place to start.

1.4.1. Inaccessibility

Lying at the very foundation of mentalist psychologies is the presumption that, by means of introspection or experimental manipulations, it is possible to determine the nature of the covert mental processes or the mechanisms accounting for observable behavior. Their respective answers to the question of accessibility have been at the core of the great schisms that divided and bedeviled psychology since its origins. Nevertheless, at the present stage of the debate, on which side of the accessibility argument one falls is more a matter of a belief than an established scientific fact. There is no "killer argument" that has yet resolved the continuing disagreement over this fundamental issue, nor is there likely to be one in the future.

As sentient human beings, it is counterintuitive that we would not be able to convey our thoughts in a manner that would permit them to be understood, measured, and even dissected by a reader, listener, or shrewd experimenter. However, this assumption is based on the deeper assumption that my consciousness is pretty much the same as that of any other human. In point of fact, however likely or unlikely it may be that we all share common mental processes, there is no evidence (and there can be no evidence—see the discussion on behavioral neutrality and the one-to-many problem later in this chapter) that all of us function similarly at the behavioral level as a result of the same kind of activity at the mental or neural level. Indeed, there is evidence that not only is it impossible for another person to "read our minds," but that even individuals themselves also are unaware of the mechanisms and causes of their behavior.[6]

The most serious implication of the inaccessibility of mental processes is that relevant reductive theories or "explanatory" hypotheses simply cannot be tested. However plausible an inference may be, there is no way to constrain the research paradigm so that definitive tests can be carried out to exclude one explanation of a behavior from equally plausible alternatives. Since empirical tests that can either reject or confirm a putative explanation are a key part of the evaluation of scientific theories, the suggestion is that mentalist psychologies, in particular, may thus fall outside the realm of natural science. Behavioral approaches, on the other hand, do not suffer from this same limitation because they do not, in principle, seek to determine the nature of internal mental mechanisms and processes.

There are other ways to express the major problem created by mental inaccessibility. Inaccessibility is tantamount to the privileged privacy of the human mind. Only individuals are privy to their thoughts. One's thoughts are not available for public inspection. Indeed, the effort to probe the thoughts of another individual has many of the characteristics of the search for the validity of divine revelations.

Much of the blame for the current expression of angst among psychologists is clearly due to the fact that modern psychology is laboring under the umbrella assumption of historical mentalism. The central idea of all mentalisms is that the mind (whatever it is and however it may be defined) can be accessed by the accepted methods of science and thus represents a valid target of scientific inquiry. The acceptance of this assumption especially influences modern cognitive experimental psychology as well as an ever-expanding mass of psychotherapeutic "theories" and techniques.

It is a thesis of this book that the effort to read the minds of others or to determine internal mental structures is fraught with conceptual and methodological challenges. These problems are so overwhelming that it is likely, I argue, that any psychological science built on efforts to determine private mental processes is almost certain to fail. Rather, the only valid science of psychology must be some past, current, or future form of a behaviorism. The mentalisms exemplified by psychotherapeutics and cognitive mentalisms, I demonstrate here, do not meet the standards of scientific inquiry as we know it today. That does not mean that they will necessarily never achieve such a status, but only that at the present time their basic ideas and concepts are so flawed as to exclude them from the realm of the natural sciences. On the other hand, I also show that psychology does have some claims to being a science in the usual sense when it is restricted to a kind of behaviorism that enjoys only limited popularity these days.

To understand why some kinds of psychology pass tests of scientific validity and why others will not, it is necessary to distinguish between behaviorisms and mentalisms. A behaviorism, unlike a mentalism, is defined as an approach that concentrates on publicly observable events, eschews the inference of unobservable events, and seeks mainly to develop descriptive transformation rules that bridge between the stimulus inputs and the response outputs.[7] Behaviorisms make no pretense of unraveling the highly complex and dynamically changing internal mental or neural mechanisms that underlie those transformations. As shown later, for many reasons, behavior is actually neutral with regard to these underlying mechanisms. Behaviorists consider them to be unobservable and uninferable from the observations of external behavior. Mentalists, on the other hand, accept both the validity and the accessibility of hypothetical or inferred internal (i.e., mental) processes and structures. (I refer readers interested in a more complete discussion of the relationship of behaviorism and mentalism to my earlier work Uttal 2000.)

Defining exactly what constitutes behavior remains, nevertheless, a challenge. Simply put, behavior may be defined operationally as any response elicited by an organism that can be directly measured with the instruments and tools common to all sciences. An important property of "behavior" is that it is "third-person" observable. This means that not only must an initial observer be able to describe what was seen, but also that the original observation must be demonstrable to a third person (at least). It is for this reason that double-blind experiments are appropriate in solidly scientific studies.

The behavioral approach, therefore, eschews invoking, deriving, inventing, or inferring the existence of unobservable mental constructs. MacCorquodale and Meehl (1948) referred to these unobserved mental mechanisms as "Hypothetical Constructs," a term that I have frequently invoked in my recent books. Hypothetical constructs are the antithesis of behaviors, the former being the outcome of indirect inferences and the latter being direct observations. In a nutshell, this difference is the key to understanding the difference between behaviorisms and mentalisms. It is also the key to understanding what parts of psychology are indisputably scientific and what parts are fragile and fantastical inventions that differ little from prescientific "just-so stories."

Given the behaviorist view that mental processes are inaccessible, many questions arise. In several different ways, we want to ask, What are the logical, conceptual, and technical barriers that make mental processes inaccessible? In the following paragraphs, I consider a few of the reasons why I believe such barriers exist.

1.4.2. Poorly Defined Vocabulary, Concepts, and Questions

All agree that the vocabulary of psychology remains loosely defined, ambiguous, and redundant. Because of the inaccessibility and probable immeasurability of the "mind" and its components (if any), precise definitions of mentalist vocabulary terms are extremely difficult to specify in any operational sense without circling back from one closely related term to another. That is, every attempt to define a mental term depends on another equally vaguely defined mental term; definitions of mental terms are essentially analogs suggesting connotations rather than precise denotations. The problem is most evident when attempts are made to define the very essence of cognitive thinking—the mind. In the years I have wrestled with this problem, I have never achieved a satisfactory definition for myself, nor have I observed any other attempt that has succeeded. In this book, I have used the expedient way of referring to covert cognitive and mental activity by using the generic term *mechanisms and processes*. However, I must acknowledge the fact that, although I am confident they are real, I have no idea what they are. I suspect that most behaviorists join me in avoiding this kind of reductive analysis. I also suspect that mentalists do not appreciate the frailty of the hypothetical constructs they invent to fill this void.

The problem arises because mental terms are not governed by a taxonomic system that has simple, quantifiable dimensions. Instead, the meanings of mental terms vary from theory to theory and from time to time for reasons that seem to be related more to methodology than to taxonomic order. Psychological entities and phenomena, therefore, multiply endlessly as a function of the number of different experiments that have been carried out to observe some behavioral function. Because of this ambiguity and vagueness, a single aspect or property of cognitive functioning can appear in many different guises, guises that are likely to reflect the experimental protocol more than any real psychobiological process.

In my earlier work (Uttal 2001, 89–146), I reviewed the history of psychological components, faculties, and processes. That discussion made it clear that not only did the vocabulary of mental constructs vary from decade to decade in an irregular fashion, but also that there was no convergence on a more precisely defined taxonomy over the years. Mental entities that were popular a century ago have been replaced by equally poorly defined ones in the present. Indeed, the cognitive mechanisms that are popular today are not derived from early ideas in the cumulative sense of characterizing typical natural sciences. Rather, new mental processes and mechanisms just accrete to or replace earlier ones as new experimental protocols are invented or new measuring instruments are developed. Rather than psychological entities becoming more precisely defined, older ones simply fall out of fashion and are replaced by new concepts. Staats (1999) summed up the problem as follows: "A new theorist in physics would not be allowed to introduce a new term for mass, electron, quark, or other science products; the infrastructure of physics ensures that. There is no such infrastructure to prevent new redundant terms in psychology or to remove the huge redundancy that already exists and goes unaddressed" (8).

As an example of this redundancy, Staats points out the indistinguishability of the neologisms "self-concept, self-image, self-perception, self-esteem, self-confidence, self, and self-efficacy" (8–9). Clearly, slightly different experimental paradigms may be examining what is essentially the same cognitive process.

The severity of the situation is emphasized by the continuing controversy over an acceptable definition of what is the subject matter of psychology. Is it "behavior" or is it the "mind"? If it is mind, then seeking a definition is as elusive a task as is the search for a chimera, as I have already noted. Circular definitions in the dictionary define mental processes such as consciousness as awareness and then awareness as consciousness. The current enthusiasm for studying consciousness, the newest term for the process that has variously been called soul, psyche, ego, or mind in the past, does nothing to help us demarcate what it is that psychology is the science of!

There is no question, therefore, that the vocabulary of psychology is ambiguous and imprecise. However, it is not clear what kind of an infrastructure would be capable of regulating our vocabulary considering the disunity of the field and its many poorly communicating subdivisions. Certainly, as Staats also noted, the transition from behaviorism to cognitive mentalism did not contribute any such regulatory force. In fact, it made the situation much worse by magnifying the number of observed phenomena and hypothetical constructs. This was quite unlike the situation in physics in which competing theories and terms were weeded out over the years and the science converged on ever-more inclusive theories of the material world.

Psychology has shown little in the way of similar progress in weeding out our redundant vocabulary, concepts, and theories. The terminology has proliferated, rather than condensed, over the years. Likewise, theories have not been reduced in numbers as earlier ones are disconfirmed. Particular terminology and explanatory ideas come and go, not because of any logical or empirical rejection but rather because they become obsolescent in the context of some new methodology. Questions bubble to the surface of our attention and then disappear from the current literature, not because they are answered but because they become unfashionable or interest in them is lost. Rather than converging onto a smaller set of unifying ideas, the fractionation gets worse as our vocabulary, our empirical findings, and our theories increasingly diversify.

It seems as if there is something fundamental about the subject matter of psychology that precludes precision and consolidation of its language and its terminology. To the extent that this situation endures, psychology's status as a science will always be questioned.

The possibility of a grand unified theory in psychology, therefore, seems remote. Instead, we seem to be going in the opposite direction as the ideal of a scientific pyramid is replaced with a scattered, disorganized clutter of unrelated ideas and words.

A major implication of the difficulty of defining psychological terms is that meaningless questions can proliferate. Although it is easy to glibly formulate research questions, many of them are empty activities simply because the meanings of constituent terms are not specified. An example of such a meaningless question may be: How many different kinds of intelligence exist? Whether this question has any meaning at all depends on some other issues (e.g., the modularity of mind) that have not yet been resolved.

Among the most formidable critics of the weakness of vocabulary in psychology is Wittgenstein, as expressed in his famous book *Tractatus Logico-Philosophicus* (1921, 1947). He proposed that many of the questions asked by philosophers and psychologists were meaningless because the terminology was so poorly defined. Over the years his cryptic style has been interpreted in many ways but was renown for such quotations as "Philosophy is a battle against the bewitchment of our intelligence by means of language" and "The world we live in is the words we use."

Wittgenstein, the philosopher, believed that philosophy could not discover anything new but was limited to clarifying the logic of what we do. He considered any philosophical assertions based in words and sentences to be essentially nonsensical, leading to the "deep analysis" of "questions that are not really questions." Wittgenstein continued in this vein when he argued in his most famous quotation from the *Tractatus*: "What we cannot speak about we must pass over in silence."

Language continues to be one of the main problems of psychology. Many effects of the poorly defined vocabulary of psychology can be identified; one of the most damaging is the reification of hypothetical constructs. Rather than assuming that an inferred process or mechanism is just that—a metaphor, analogy, or rhetorical possibility—many become objects of study with no operational substance or reality. Reified inferences such as "intelligence" or "cognitive maps" become instantiated "objects" in research programs that treat these aides to thought as if they were material objects or entities.

Metaphors are sometimes substituted for definitions. What was originally a crude conceptual crutch can, if we are careless, become a substitute for a definition. Machado, Lourenco, and Silva (2000) emphasize that metaphors are a perennial source of misunderstanding throughout psychology. They cite a number of scholars (twenty-seven) who argue against the use of metaphors; their summary, however, is of special import. "In summary, we do not need to impugn the use of metaphors in science to recognize the dangers that may lurk when they proliferate without control. For if an approach that approves only of literal language stultifies our imagination, an approach that lingers on metaphors gives us only superficial looks of the thing itself" (30). Clearly, metaphors are especially treacherous when they take on reality by the process of cryptic reification. The massive problem they represent for psychology is that they are an example and a result of the extreme difficulty of defining mental terms.

1.4.3. The Many-to-One Problem—Many Behaviors Can Be Accounted for by a Single Explanation

The long-range impact of an ambiguous and uncertain scientific terminology (as well as an inadequate taxonomy) is that frequently many different words are used to describe what on reflection may better be considered to be a single internal mechanism or process. Once a multiplicity of experimental findings has identified what appears to be a collection of different behavioral responses, there is a tendency for each of those behaviors to be operationalized in the form of separate hypothetical constructs, distinct and separate internal processes, or mechanisms that are not themselves measurable. It is all too easy in such a context for these hypothetical constructs to be considered as the outcome of different underlying mechanisms and processes, not as separate manifestations of the same process.

The problem with such an uncritical approach is that different behaviors, each elicited by its own experimental method, may not correspond to separate psychobiological realities. Instead, they may be manifestations of the same underlying process. They may appear to have some unique properties but this is often a result of differences in the experimental method, not of any fundamental different modes of "inner" processing. Searching for distinct psychoneural equivalents for each behavioral finding may be no more possible than seeking artifacts of a totally fictional past.[8] In other words, the search for a mechanism of "need" or "drive" is no more likely to succeed than a search for a mermaid or archaeological evidence of the Exodus!

Thus, what appears to be a collection of "explanatory" mental constructs, each designed to explain a particular observation, may actually represent what are, in fact, different outcomes of a single process. I refer to this as the "many-to-one" problem—the idea that many different behavioral observations and measurements may, in reality, represent the outcome of a single underlying process or mechanism. Since the actual underlying process or mechanism is inaccessible, there is no constraint on how many such hypothetical entities may be invented. There are no constraints on allowing each behavioral observation to be "explained" in terms of a different source.

From this discussion, it may be fairly concluded that any behavioral observation is neutral with regard to whatever mental or neural processes may account for them. Explanatory (i.e., analytic or reductive) theories are not constrained by observations; it is only the imagination of the researcher that limits the number of inferential explanations. This is, to say the least, not a characteristic of a strong science. The proliferation of explanations, however, is a characteristic of psychology as we know it today.

The problem is exacerbated by the virtually unlimited number of experimental designs that seem superficially to be different and yet may all be influenced by the same inaccessible inner events. A particularly egregious instance of this false multiplication of entities can be found in the pages of the *Diagnostic and Statistical Manual of Mental Disorders DSM-IV* published by the American Psychiatric Association (Anonymous 1992; Anonymous 2000). This work is a more or less arbitrary collection of mental disorders that has accumulated over the years on the basis of anecdotal and intuitive reports by psychiatrists and psychologists. The included categories often overlap and are rarely based on the kind of research foundation that is acceptable in most other fields of psychology. What are seen as distinct diagnoses are more likely to represent minor variations of a single disorder. What is more likely to be a continuum is degraded to an arbitrary discreteness. The problems with the *DSM-IV* and its shortcomings are discussed extensively in Spiegel (2005) and Uttal (2005) and are briefly reconsidered on p. 244.

Nowhere is this "many-to-one" constraint on psychological theorizing more evident than in the proliferation of many different kinds of memory and learning. A substantial proportion of the research carried out by current psychologists deals with learning and memory. Since the underlying neurophysiological and cognitive processes are inaccessible, there is a compelling tendency to reify learning entities and endlessly invent different explanations and theories to explain them.

What is indisputably common to all of the tests of learning is the observation that behavior changes as a function of experience. What is likely to be common is that the same physiological mechanism—synaptic plasticity, number, or pattern or interconnection—accounts for all of these experiential effects. As obvious as these simple observations are, an immense research effort has been based on the suggestion that there now exists a variety of different kinds of learning mechanisms manifested in somewhat different behavioral responses.[9] The main finding guiding this multiplication of hypothetical psychological processes is that learning seems to have some slightly different properties when assayed by slightly different experimental protocols.

Modern cognitive psychology texts, following the lead of current and past research publications, often present a varied collection of learning types. The list presented here in a telegraphic form is organized along a dimension that varies roughly with the temporal dynamics (i.e., from the shortest to the longest term) of the experiments leading to each memory type:

- **Ionic or Sensory Memory**—The rapidly fading sensory image that fades in a fraction of a second.
- **Short-Term Memory**—Information storage that persists for a half minute or so and then is lost unless rehearsed.
- **Working Memory**—A special kind of short-term memory used to manipulate incoming information.
- **Long-Term Memory**—Information storage that persists for very long periods of time, often for a lifetime.
- **Episodic Memory**—A special kind of long-term memory that retains information about events in a person's life with the feeling that they have been personally experienced. (Also known as autobiographical memory; e.g., recollection of one's first date.)
- **Semantic Memory**—A special kind of long-term memory that retains information about specific facts without the feeling that they have been personally experienced (e.g., $9 \times 9 = 81$).
- **Implicit Memory**—Whereas both episodic and semantic memory both invoke conscious recollection, experiences can also produce changes in behavior that occur below the level of awareness.

Other categories of memory are defined by the subject matter being stored. Many psychologists distinguish between "verbal learning," "spatial learning," or "face-recognition learning."

In addition, there are other kinds of memory that are defined not in terms of their duration but rather in terms of the methods used to generate them. Most often, these are carried out on animals for which we are denied the verbal reports that are the usual bread and butter of human memory research. These include:

- **Classical Conditioning**—A method of associating previously ineffective stimuli with an effective stimulus, so the former eventually produces the same response as the latter.
- **Instrumental Conditioning**—A method of enhancing particular endogenously elicited responses by reinforcing them when they are spontaneously emitted by the person or the animal.

The critical question that pervades this collection of observed behaviors is just how distinct are they? Do these behavioral observations represent truly different mechanisms of learning and storage or are they all overt manifestations of what is actually a single unified activity—simply measured in different ways? There is a significant possibility that all of these behavioral types are actually the outcome of a single unified process (e.g., synaptic changes). Unfortunately, psychologists do not usually ask these questions as they go about adding to their collection of learning types.

There are other processes, usually considered as distinct, that may also need to be reconsidered. Related behavioral changes not included in the learning and memory rubric are dynamic changes in an organism's behavior by virtue of its evolutionary or developmental, rather than its experiential, history. Furthermore, changes in behavior due to fatigue and reflexes, although induced by experience, typically do not fall within the traditional rubric of learning. Similarly, many of the behavioral changes that occur over the life span of an individual that are attributable to growth are not usually referred to as learning.

However, the many-to-one problem suggests that this taxonomy should be reconsidered.

The many-to-one problem can be crystallized by this question: "Do these varied observations of behaviors that change with experience represent the effects of a collection of psychophysiologically distinct memorization mechanisms or are they just different manifestations of only one that is being measured with different methods and under different conditions?"

The answer to this question, I must acknowledge, is not easily determined. However, the concept of a considerable number of distinct psychobiological processes and mechanisms underlying these experienced induced changes in behavior seems ill supported by logic, if not by solid evidentiary links. Given the various problems with accessibility already mentioned, it does not seem extreme to suggest that, perhaps, like the proverbial elephant and the blind men, all of these examples of experience-based learning are the outcome of a single kind of synaptic memorization process. At the most molecular level, this may simply be the restructuring of the neural network by enhancement or diminishment of the effectiveness of existing synapses or, perhaps, by adding them. The observed behavioral differences may, on this perspective, be due to task differences rather than to any differences in underlying mechanisms. If this point of view is correct, then the body of theorizing about a cluster of different kinds of memory is an exercise in futility. Since there are insufficient constraints to resolve this issue, we are not in a position to either validate or reject the reality of any of the different kinds of "memory mechanisms" other than as behavioral observations.

The difficulties engendered by the many-to-one problem are also evident in many other kinds of psychological research. Perceptual research has its own examples. My own research on the time that a random field of dots was capable of masking a subsequently presented coherent line of dots (Uttal 1975) was actually assaying what, on subsequent analysis, was indistinguishable from Eriksen and Collin's (1968) study of the perceptual emergence of a combined percept from two temporally separate stimuli. However different the measured responses and the methods may have been, it is clear in retrospect that these two experiments were measuring the same psychobiological process.[10]

Here is the essence of the many-to-one problem. Different words, different methods, and different theoretical proclivities and prejudices may make what is actually a single psychobiological process become manifest in a number of operationally distinguishable behavioral responses. The impact on the fractionation of psychological theories by the many-to-one problem has been enormous.

1.4.4. The One-to-Many Problem— Many Explanations Can Account for a Single Behavior

Another major reason that psychology is subject to special problems in its efforts to provide scientific answers to questions of mental processing is that there are innumerable possible mental and neural internal processes and structures that can produce indistinguishable behaviors, just as there are single processes that can produce widely varying behaviors (the many-to-one problem).[11] This difficulty, which I designate the one-to-many problem, can be encapsulated in the postulate that there exist an unlimited number of possible (some plausible and some implausible) explanations of any one behavioral observation when one is dealing with a closed system. The one-to-many problem is also embodied in the philosopher's debate about the underdetermination of theories. By this is meant that no reductive theory or empirical observation in psychology is definitive; several, if not many, theories can equally describe the same data. In brief, this means that there is no way to choose among possible reductive explanations of behavioral responses.

An exceedingly important implication of the one-to-many problem, therefore, as I have strongly argued previously (Uttal 2005), is a fundamental neutrality of behavior (as well as of mathematics and all other kinds of theories, computational and otherwise) regarding internal processes in a closed system such as the mind-brain. Furthermore, the introduction of neuroanatomical (e.g., surgical or traumatic interventions) and neurofunctional (e.g., PET or fMRI imaging techniques) that may initially seem to offer some promise of opening the particular "closed system"—the brain—in which we are specially interested, in fact, do not do so. Although some theories and explanations may be so rejected, there always remain an innumerable number of possible alternative explanations that cannot be excluded by any number of experimental tests.

This interpretation of the one-to-many barrier remains a profound impediment to our understanding of the brain that has little to do with its complexity (that is another problem). Even a relatively simple closed system is subject to this same constraint. A major implication of this point of view is that it is impossible to know whether or not the mind-brain system actually operates in a holistic, as opposed to a modular, fashion.

Others have also called attention to the implications of the one-to-many problem. Cummins (1983), for example, makes the same point in a different way. In distinguishing between instantiation and reduction, he notes that "uniform instantiation is not sufficient for reduction, since a variety of modal truths will hold for the target property that does not hold of the instantiation" (24).

Shallice (1988) also makes the same point in his own fashion. First he carefully defines six different levels of functionally equivalent systems:

1. Modular systems
2. Coupled systems
3. Systems with a continuous processing space
4. Systems of overlapping processing regions
5. Systems of semimodules
6. Distributed and multilevel systems (249–53)

And then he points out: "Precise measurements that directly reflect significant aspects of the functional organization of the cognitive system do not exist. Hence any empirical procedure that stands a reasonable chance of helping to uncover the functional characteristics of the system is likely to involve as many assumptions as does the use of neuropsychological findings" (265). By this statement, I believe he meant that any effort to distinguish between these alternative systems is futile.[12]

The distinguished philosopher Willard Van Orman Quine (1975) was of the same mind when he said in support of his empirical underdetermination argument:

> If all observable events can be accounted for in one comprehensive theory—one system of the world, to echo Duhem's echo of Newton—then we may expect that they can be all accounted for equally in another, conflicting system of the world. . . . We may expect this because of how scientists work. . . . Scientists invent hypotheses that talk of things beyond the reach of observation. . . . These observable consequences of the hypotheses do not, conversely, imply the hypotheses. Surely there are alternative hypothetical substructures that would surface in the same observable ways. (313)

Quine (1970) also makes the same point in a slightly different manner when he refers to theories that are "logically incompatible and empirically equivalent." Although Quine was referring in this instance to the underdetermination of language translations, his argument holds for theories of the mind as well. Simply put, there are insufficient constraints built into language (or psychophysical data) to infer exactly what is meant by an utterance or what the underlying mechanism is.

In other contexts, Quine referred to the problem as the "inscrutability of reference and the indeterminacy of meaning." In mathematics, this kind of indeterminacy characterizes an "ill-posed problem," one that cannot be resolved with the data at hand and that requires certain additional assumptions or constraints that go beyond the raw observations be factored into the proposed solution. Whatever the phraseology, all of these authors are referring to the same constraint—the one-to-many problem caused by the fact that the observed empirical database is insufficient to provide a unique answer to the question "What is the internal mechanism accounting for the observation?"

The underdetermination problem, or one-to-many problem, has concerned philosophers for many years. It is disappointing that so few psychologists and philosophers are aware of its implications on the task they have set for themselves. A few have, however, understood the important implications this constraint has on the validity of any psychological theory. Frank (2003), for example, phrases it in a slightly different context—"Are there rationally undecidable arguments?"—in order to cover a much broader field of inquiry than psychology alone. Frank suggests that some conflicts may not be "rationally" resolved, by which he means that some deductive systems may not be capable of leading to theorems that are both unique and valid. From this perspective, truth may always be elusive, no matter how tightly controlled the relevant experiments and observations are. All of these ideas are manifestations of the basic difficulty in assigning a single theoretical explanation to a single observation—a goal inhibited, if not prohibited, by the one-to-many problem.

Other philosophers have also pointed out the barrier to reductive understanding that is posed by the one-to-many problem. Wimsatt (1974) cited Kauffman (1971) and Levins (1966) when he pointed out that "in complex systems, there are a number of possible decompositions and often no way of choosing between them" (74).

Another way in which the one-to-many barrier to scientific inquiry is exhibited lies in the individual differences of brain structures themselves. Clearly, the physical apparatus of the brain must be totally responsible for the many possible different cognitive processes that drive behaviors. However, this does not mean that the responsible brain structures are the same from one individual to another or from one instance to another. Recent evidence (Muotri et al. 2005) suggests, in addition to differences in neural representations generated by the genetic history and the experiences of individual brains, it may also be that bits of DNA can jump randomly from one neuron to another. Such a process would, to an unknown degree, increase the variability of individual cellular responses and permit a wide variety of different neural structures and arrangements to produce what appears to be the same kind of behavior. The implication of this discovery by Muotri and his colleagues is further evidence that no two brains are alike, no more in their specific wiring than in their genomes. This result represents a possible physiological proof of the one-to-many problem at its most basic level—neuronal variation! This result also adds to the argument that different underlying mechanisms may produce indistinguishable behavior.[13]

The implications of the one-to-many problem are enormous for explanatory theory building in psychology. Not only would it explain how cognitive mechanisms can exhibit such great individual differences, but it would be another formidable barrier to understanding the biological roots of mentation—mental activity—in general. Thus, even in the unlikely event that we were able to identify a specific mechanism for a mental activity in one animal,[14] there is no reason why it must be the same in another individual.

1.4.5. Neutrality of Theories, Models, and Behavior

One of the main results of the many-to-one and one-to-many issues, both of which are manifestations of the basic underdetermination of behavioral observations, is the fundamental neutrality of psychological theories. That is, however ingenious a reductive explanation of some phenomenon may be, it can be argued that, in fact, there is no way to "prove" a psychological theory in the same way as there is to prove a theorem in mathematics. Whereas mathematical theorems start from specific axioms and follow a well-established set of logical or mathematical laws, psychological theories are in the main often driven by loose inferences, weak analogies, and distant metaphors that do not have a sufficiently precise structure or clear definition to be grist for the mill of formal mathematical or logical manipulation. Psychological laws do not enjoy the axiomatic status of, for example, any of Newton's three axioms.

Thus, although theory building is ubiquitous in psychology, there are some fundamental limitations on its utility that have to be clarified. The problem has been alluded to in the previous sections, namely, that all psychological theories must be based on observed behavior. A necessary correlate is that human behavior, in particular, is incapable of being *uniquely* transformed into a robust reductive explanation because of a profound underdetermination generated by the inaccessibility of mental processes.

Although this general principle is well established throughout science, many psychological theoreticians behave as if they are completely oblivious to this serious limitation on the explanatory powers of their theories and hypotheses. To put it in the simplest possible terms, the proposal of a particular theory of mental activity never precludes the formulation of equally plausible alternatives. In short, theories are, at best, descriptive and completely neutral with regard to the underlying mechanisms.

The assertion that psychology has special problems in theory building because of its empirical neutrality can be discerned in a curious aspect of its history. From classic times until the present, there has been a proclivity for psychology to grab any and every new technology as a metaphor for explaining mind. There has been a tendency to seek explanations based on whatever machine happens to be currently available. This proclivity has currently culminated in the modern choice of the computer as the model of choice throughout cognitive psychology.

Cognitive psychology emerged as the predominant theoretical orientation of scientific psychology contemporaneously with the development of modern digital computers and information processing technology. This was not just a coincidence; the metaphor of the input-central processing-output machine was extremely stimulating to this new mentalism. The block diagram with its interconnecting and directing pathways, a useful tool for organizing the components of a digital or analog computer, became the prototype of a host of theoretical extrapolations to observed behavior.

It is now clear, however, even to most cognitive psychologists, that the standard digital computer is a flawed metaphor for either the brain or the mind. The information flowchart idea of the classic von Neumann computer became the embodiment of a kind of "boxology" that provided a fertile ground for a theory in which cognitive processes could be divided up into components or modules in the same way a computer was constructed.

The next evolutionary step in this metaphorical evolution was to grasp the parallel processing computer as a further metaphor for psychological function. McClelland and Rumelhart's influential works (1986) provided an intellectual foundation for this next step. Based on new ideas developed in computer theory, a link was established between parallel processing computers and what appeared at first glance to be comparable parallel processing neural networks. Although this computer–neural net metaphor also did not last (most current connectionist theories are framed in terms of functional cognitive modules rather than neuronal or simple logical components), the parallel processing idea still has a substantial following in current psychological theorizing. Indeed, it is almost certain that it is correct—in principle. Unfortunately, parallel processing systems of a complexity comparable to the brain represent intractable analytic and computational problems—in practice. I discuss this topic much more fully in Uttal (2005a).

Unfortunately, neither the parallel processing metaphor nor any other form of theory escapes the one-to-many difficulty. As a result, for all practical purposes, all observations of behavior, without exception, are neutral with regard to underlying neural or cognitive mechanisms. That is, psychological theories are limited to curve fitting (by an equally neutral mathematical formulation) or to selection under the influence of secondary considerations (e.g., Ockham's razor—the Principle of Parsimony) that may not be applicable to the highly redundant mechanisms that account for mind. In brief, the data of psychology do not sufficiently constrain theories to permit robust reductive explanations. At best, the models we have can only describe the process, not tease out its causes or underlying mechanisms!

Theoretical neutrality means that however elegant and however accurate as a description a theory may be, or even how well it may predict future behavior, it is indeterminate with regard to exact causal relationships at lower levels of analysis.

1.4.6. The Absence of Physical Anchors

Normal physical science (idealized by physics and chemistry) works because of a foundation of shared units and references to common physical phenomena. Each of these sciences is anchored to a material reality by a system of measurements and units that have their own independent standards. A gram is a gram regardless of the matter to which this measure is applied.

It should not be a surprise, then, that the most successful of the psychological sciences have been those that are most closely anchored to the units of the physical world—sensory and motor processes. Stimuli and responses can be defined and measured in terms of physical units shared with the other sciences. As long as one does not ask for complex judgments but only the simple evaluation of "same or different" (Brindley's class A responses, 1960), behavioral data are consistent, acceptably variable, and establish functional relationships between stimuli and responses.

On the other hand, when attempts are made to measure complex cognitive processes unanchored to the units and dimensions of the physical world, the task becomes much more difficult. The units and measures that psychology shares with physics that so successfully anchor sensory and motor processes to the material world are no longer available. Philosophers refer to the immeasurable mental events as "qualia"—the so-called raw feels of perceptual experiences. However, there are no direct measures of the temporal, spatial, qualitative, and quantitative dimensions or units of these experiences. Indeed, it is difficult to even define exactly what are "qualia." They are typically identified as the actual mental experience, perception, or awareness produced by some stimulus and exemplified by subjective terms such as *reddishness*. How "qualia" vary from one person to another is obviously impossible to determine; they are private and inaccessible.

Units of such psychological dimensions are not only harder to define, but there also is no direct way to measure them in the manner enjoyed by the physical sciences. There is no means of coordinating them with or directly transforming them into the common units of the physical world in the way that grams and pounds may be interconverted. "Mels," "sones," and "brils" have been proposed as the units of acoustic pitch, loudness, and brightness, respectively. However, these measures have fallen out of favor as it has become clear that there is no way to directly measure the subjective magnitude of an experience.

When psychologists attempt to measure some dimension or aspect of higher cognitive processing, the task of measurement not only becomes more difficult but also, some of us would argue, conceptually impossible.[15] Whereas a sensory experiment is at least linked to some measure of the physical world at its input, there is no equivalent physical dimension with which to measure such a process as decision making, attention, or greenness—or even to be sure that they are real psychobiological entities. All we can do is observe the overt changes in behavior associated with changes in the eliciting stimuli. The anchors to material reality are gone; therefore, there are no constraints on what can be hypothetically constructed or what dimensions or values those constructs may have. Without such anchors, these behaviors also become indeterminate in basic principle.

1.4.7. Numerousness and Complexity; Measurement and Quantification

Another reason that the scientific credentials of psychology must be questioned concerns the nature of the subject matter under scrutiny. The most likely theoretical explanation of the origin of the mind, as noted earlier, is that it results from the function of the complex network of many, many neurons.[16] However, the complexity of such a system is so great and the number of neurons involved in even the simplest cognitive process probably so large that this kind of theory suffers from well-known limits on mathematical analyzability and computability. Furthermore, it is also clear that behavioral variability is also enormous. Behavior, therefore, may also be subject to a similar kind of criticism based on response complexity. A strong argument can be made that many of the problems that psychologists attempt to solve are already known to be intractable. (I return to elaborate on this issue in chapter 3, where I consider the role of mathematics in greater detail as well as the problem of measurement and quantifiability of psychological phenomena.)

1.4.8. Physicophilia

Another argument against psychology's acceptance as a science may be that psychologists have been trying too hard. In their efforts to emulate physics, psychologists have not developed a paradigm of their own. Rather, they may have set an impossibly high standard by adopting a methodology that works well for a simple science but that is not appropriate for as complex an activity as psychology.

Psychology's fascination and emulation of physics is well known. Koch (1992), for example, has defined a new malady that has been epidemic among research psychologists: "Experimental psychologists have traditionally suffered from a syndrome known as hypermanic physicophilia (with quantificophrenic delusions and methodicoecholalic complications" (264). Stripped of humorous hyperbole and neologisms, Koch's obvious point is that psychologists have too readily adopted the strategies and methodologies of the simpler physical sciences as they have attempted to explore the much more complex mysteries of human cognition. A recent statement of the same problem phrased in slightly different words has been provided by Machado, Lourenco, and Silva (2000), who note, "the obsession of psychology with a narrow and mechanical view of the scientific method and a misguided aversion to conceptual inquiries" (1).

What can be made of these two statements? First, these authors suggest that psychology has made a major strategic error in reshaping itself in the previous century. Koch identifies the source of the problem as "physics envy," a simple desire on the part of psychologists to uncritically adopt the methodology that has served the physical sciences so effectively. The attractiveness of the physical sciences force is enhanced by another of Machado and his colleagues' suggestion. They proposed that there is a negative force at work—specifically, psychology's efforts to distinguish itself from its past in which philosophical speculation was the main methodology.

Thus, there are two forces at work here that cooperate to induce psychologists to overemphasize the empirical and underemphasize the conceptual. The first is a positive fascination with the methods of what many would consider to be the most successful science of all time—the empirical materialism of the physical sciences. By itself, this is a noble ideal. Science should stand as a bulwark against supernatural and untestable speculative ideas of nature of mind and behavior. It is understandable why psychology should have such strong ambitions to be viewed in the same light as physics.

The second force is a negative one—the apparent aversion to the speculative or conceptual studies from which modern psychology evolved. Many times I have heard a psychologist say, "Forget that, it is only a philosophical issue!" In so doing, these antiphilosophical types have not only attempted to cancel out our history but also to ignore some of the deep conceptual issues that psychology faces but physics does not. Many of the questions asked earlier by philosophers and theologians have their counterpart in modern psychological inquiries. Yet, as Machado and his colleagues point out, current psychological training programs relegate the past history of the study of mind to a minor role while overemphasizing the mechanics of experimental design. This is not to diminish the importance of these practical skills but to suggest that, without a deep appreciation of the conceptual foundations, controversies, and principles of a science, progress tends to stall and understanding is deferred.

Psychologists now not only tend to reject their distant philosophical heritage but also tend to ignore the results of the recent past. The kind of aversion to a predecessor methodology, or a finding (a phenomenon well known as "NIH"—**N**ot **I**nvented **H**ere—among many modern researchers), is particularly devastating to psychology. It tends to exacerbate the fractionation of psychology into a jungle of narrow, homegrown microproblems that defines the enterprise these days.

Thus, there are major forces, both attractive and repulsive, driving psychology toward an emphasis on empirical methods and away from consideration of the basic assumptions and concepts that underlie all modern research. These forces tend to distort what Machado, Lourenco, and Silva (2000) believe to be a proper balance among the three necessary, mutually supportive legs of modern science. They identify these three legs as factual, theoretical, and conceptual activities. Their argument is that in succumbing to a variant of physicophilia, psychologists have been hyperactive in collecting data using the experimental method and in developing a huge number of particular theories to explain those data.

Why has this inbalance among the three legs of psychology developed? Machado, Lourenco, and Silva identify a number of reasons in their call for a revival of conceptual studies and a reduction in the strictly empirical effort that dominates psychology these days:

- ". . . [A deeply] held suspicion of philosophical speculation." (2)
- An overemphasis on experimentation as the main source of knowledge with an overuse of the classic hypothetical deductive method resulting in a glut of meaningless empirical publications.
- The fragmentation of psychological knowledge because of an absence of global theory, adequate taxonomies, and solid conceptual analyses resulting in an artificial hyper-specialization on the part of researchers in the field.

- "An asymmetry between an advanced technology of data analysis [and means of collecting data] and a rudimentary state of conceptual and theoretical frameworks . . ." (4)
- The deification of tests of statistical significance as a criterion of meaningfulness and conceptual significance.
- The reward system of psychological and other kinds of science in the short run. Scientific eminence is mainly assigned for the accumulation of new knowledge rather than conceptual progress.

1.4.9. A Super-Abundance of Incompatible and Unrelated Theories and Trivial Data

William James's comment (cited on p. 19) still characterizes psychology. There is an enormous abundance of almost unrelated empirical observations, most of which are probably valid but each of which seems to operate in its own individual microcosm. Most of the relationships between stimuli and responses still seem to be highly idiosyncratic and dependent on particular experimental conditions. Theories of one level of formal sophistication or another abound. However, like the empirical findings, each theory is limited to a narrow range of observations. There are no grand theories linking different domains of psychology. A few special-purpose "laws" of performance have been discovered, for example, the Hick-Hyman law (Hick 1952; Hyman 1953) and Fitts's law (Fitts 1954), but it is not even certain whether they reflect the nature of the stimulus environment or a property of the cognitive system. For example, the germane issue is, Is the complexity of the stimulus simply driving prolonged reaction times or is the observer literally changing the strategy required to solve the problem?

Many other putative laws thought originally to pertain to cognitive processing such as Zipf's (1935, 1965) "law" relating word frequency of occurrence and rank order of usage are now know to be the result of inevitable mathematical and statistical forces rather than "psychophysiological" processes.

Hammond, Hamm, and Grassia (1986) summed up this state of affairs with the following frustrated general conclusion:

> Doubts about the generality of results produced by psychological research have been expressed with increasing frequency since Koch (1959b) observed after a monumental review of scientific psychology that there is "a stubborn refusal of psychological findings to yield to empirical generalization" (729). . . . Jenkins (1974) warned that "a whole theory of an experiment can be elaborated without contributing in an important way to the science because the situation is artificial and nonrepresentative" (794). Tulving (1979) makes the startling observation that "after 100 years of laboratory-based study of memory, we still do not seem to possess any concepts that the majority of workers would consider too necessary or important." (3)

Clearly, many thoughtful psychologists are deeply concerned that the fractionation of psychology is a symptom of its real nature and not just the effect of its primitive, underdeveloped state. If such a view is correct, then the idea of an integrative, converging science of the mind may be as elusive as the proverbial chimera.

1.4.10. Fragile Data

Despite the fact that most experimental findings of high-level cognitive processes are probably valid for the time and situation in which they are carried out,[17] many are eventually counter-indicated by subsequent experiments when replicated under slightly different conditions. The reason for this data "transitoriness" or "fragility" is obvious. No matter how well controlled the variables in an experiment may be, the multivariate complexity of psychological functions never completely controls all of the factors that can influence the nature of an emitted response. Sometimes the lack of control of the most incidental aspect (e.g., the background lighting) can turn out to be an influential variable in determining the outcome of an experiment.

Furthermore, the powerful adaptive cognitive powers of the

human may result in an experimental subject "not playing the game" that was intended by the experimenter. The more complex the cognitive processes being studied, the more likely it is that a subject will find some way to solve a problem that was not anticipated. Indeed, in many problem-solving challenges, this is exactly what happens; it turns out that different subjects invoke different strategies, some of which may have been entirely unanticipated by the experimenter.

Another source of difficulty in psychology is the rather soft criteria we have for accepting the results of an experiment to be valid (or, to be more precise, rejecting the "hypothesis" that our manipulations have no impact on the outcome). The .05 level of significance is a very modest one. Physicists typically demand a much higher criterion level for the acceptance of some unlikely event, such as a neutrino catch by a detector. As a result of the low level of "significance" accepted by psychologists, many experiments are published that do not stand the test of replication.

Finally, there is the mysterious "placebo effect." In psychology, as well as in medicine, suggestion is a significant influence on the outcome of an experiment. Such effects are especially significant when subjects are asked to self-evaluate their performance. For example, Gibson, Mascord, and Starmer (1995) have shown that subjective reports of the alertness and mood of fatigued truck drivers were equally good for those who had been given doses of caffeine and those who had been given an ineffective placebo. Objective tests of driving performance, however, showed that the drivers who had been given the caffeine did have much higher performance scores than the placebo group. So much for introspection!

Data and methods that are dependent on placebos or suggestibility, or that permit alternative strategies to be used, are typically confused and degraded. Although some research that may be subject to these kinds of degradations can sometimes be controlled by double-blind experimental designs, few of the published studies in our experimental psychology journals report the use of this important control.

1.4.11. Overemphasis on Methods and Metaphors

Closely coupled to the malady of physicophilia, and perhaps another manifestation of it, is psychology's emphasis on appropriating the tools and concepts of other sciences as metaphors for its own mysterious processes and mechanisms. Psychology has always faced a very serious problem, one that grew out of the inaccessibility criterion described earlier. Namely, how do we define and describe the processes and mechanisms that are the source of our mental activity? In the main, it is the intangible and elusive nature of the mind, spirit, ego, self, or soul (depending upon the moment in history) that led to an infatuation with the methods and ideas developed for other sciences and other purposes.

The result of this perennial search for a way to describe the mechanisms of the mind is that psychology has always been seeking models or metaphors for the mind from whatever was the popular and tangible physical theory of the time. The outcome of this need was that totally irrelevant physical processes became metaphors for the mind. These metaphors appeared to make tangible the intangible; their purpose was to provide a concrete, connotative equivalent for mind as a surrogate for an elusive, denotative definition of it. Unfortunately, the conceptual aide—the metaphor—was often reified and became more of a reality than what was originally intended. What had originally been a conceptual aide often became the driving force behind a particular kind of experimental strategy. The dividing line between conceptual aide and paradigmatic approach was just too delicate not to be subsequently breached.

Along with reified metaphors, ancient protopsychologists and modern psychologists alike have always been ready to adopt some new procedure or technique as a foundation of a new theoretical approach. This has been especially prevalent in recent times when machines of extreme sophistication promised to provide noninvasive means of examining the physiological processes going on inside the body. The invention of the EEG, the ERP, and, more recently, the modern PET and MRI imaging techniques have each stimulated a theoretical approach that depends largely on the specific kind of newly available data. For example, EEG recordings led directly to field theories of the mind, and fMRI images were the source of a reemphasis on an old idea—localized modular components of mind in the brain. The result of this inappropriate impact of methods was that the methods eventually tended to dominate the questions being asked and the theories being developed rather than the substance of the problem.

The impact of the material metaphors for the mind is enormous. Almost from its initial conceptualization, any newly available device, however distantly related to mental processing, takes on a theoretical life of its own. History is replete with such metaphors including, among others, fluids, clocks, telephones, as well as von Neumann and parallel processing computers. What was a remarkable technological development capable of solving a well-defined problem in physics, information processing, or medical pathology often becomes an entrenched paradigm of psychological research with all of the accoutrements of a scientific endeavor but without adequate consideration of the seductive call of what might well have been an ill-connected metaphor.

A related point has been made by Schlinger (2004) and also by Slife and Williams (1997). These scholars asserted that psychology has become a method-driven activity rather than one driven by important questions. Psychology, from their point of view, can be fairly accused of minimizing consideration of the conceptual foundations of the science while overemphasizing methodological considerations. Slife and Williams point out that psychology training is riddled with courses on methodology and phenomena but notably devoid of courses on its conceptual foundations. Very important topics of this kind are often relegated to low-priority curricula of psychological history or philosophy taught by aged or otherwise burnt-out professors. The fact that conceptual studies of psychology's history and concepts are hardly ever funded also exacerbates the low status of "history of psychology" courses. Today's students are diligently tutored in statistical or computer technology but less frequently in the root ideas of their science.

Historians from outside psychology also came to appreciate the hyper-methodological approach implicit in psychological research. Smith (1997), for example, noted that the behaviorists of the 1930–1960 periods came to believe that "observation, not logic or metaphysics, is the ground on which to build [psychological] science" (660). Since observations were far easier to come by than theories and theorems, this extolling of measurement as opposed to conceptual analysis continues to run amok in modern cognitive psychology as well.

Furthermore, the problem of overemphasis on method may be further exacerbated by the choice of inappropriate methods. A number of current authors (Loftus 1996; Nickerson 2000) have argued that significance testing of null hypotheses is a brute force and distracting, if not a meaningless, approach to science.[18] Nickerson makes the especially cogent point that a statistically significant result is not the same thing as a theoretically significant one. Loftus also emphasizes the discrepancy between statistical and theoretical significance by pointing out that some of the assumptions underlying significance testing are extremely artificial. For example, all such tests depend upon the assumptions of normality (i.e., a Gaussian distribution) of the data, equal variance for all conditions, and simple additivity (i.e., linearity) of effects (164). If we have learned nothing else about psychology, it is that its variance is unstable from subject to subject and its essential nonlinearity precludes simple additive models.

1.4.12. Questionable Assumptions and Principles

Finally, I turn to what is the most subtle, least appreciated, and yet most important influence on psychology's current state—its implicit assumptions and principles. Virtually every scientist operates on the basis of implicit assumptions. However, psychologists, perhaps as a result of their eschewing of philosophical or conceptual analysis, have been particularly negligent in unearthing these foundation assumptions. Most experimentalists rarely question the underlying propositions that guide their day-to-day activities in the laboratory. For example, much of modern cognitive psychology is based on the assumption that psychological components are (a) made up of semi-independent modules and (b) that the degree of independence of these modules is sufficient to permit them to be teased apart by appropriate experimental methods. Only a few of us (Fodor 1983; Pachella 1974; Uttal 2001) have attempted to consider the validity of the mental modularity assumption. Most cognitivists simply assume that the mind is compartmented like a computer flowchart, and they proceed from there. Whether or not the mind can be analyzed into components is still an open question, but the assumption that it is modular is hardly an adequate argument for plunging ahead as if it were. The major goal of this present work is to identify these usually ignored principles. Many of them, as we will see in chapter 4, turn out to be far more controversial than is usually appreciated by most psychologists.

1.5. SOME REASONS WHY PSYCHOLOGY MAY BE A SCIENCE IN THE USUAL SENSE

So far in this chapter, I have concentrated on the properties of psychology that raise questions concerning its identification as a science in the usual sense of the word. There are, of course, some compelling counterarguments to many of the antiscientific arguments I identify in the previous section. In this section, I deal with some of these counterarguments that support psychology's role as a science.

1.5.1. The Unknown

A perfectly legitimate counterargument to those who challenge psychology's role as a science is that we do not yet know the limits of knowledge of this field of inquiry. It is impossible to predict what can and cannot be known from the current vantage point. For this reason, it has been argued that we should accept psychology as a legitimate example of a science and plunge ahead to determine what can be known and where these limits exist. As discussed in the appendix to this book, the epistemological issues surrounding psychology are immense. In fact, they may be the core of this entire activity, and epistemology and experimental psychology may be two sides of the same coin. It can be fairly argued that the complexity and variability of mental processing and its underlying processes and mechanisms are so great that we should expect to be moving more slowly along the trajectory of understanding than did the simpler sciences, such as cosmology or genetic coding. To abort the effort now before we determine the limits of psychological knowledge may be to prejudge what lies on the other side of an as-yet-unexplored boundary between ignorance and knowledge. There is always the possibility that some new discovery, idea, machine, method, or theory will produce a breakthrough similar to the impact of the invention of the microscope, the discovery of radioactivity, or the expression of the principles of natural selection or relativity.

The argument here is that, whatever the current frailties that restrain us from dealing with psychology as a science are, the possibility of some future progress should not be denied prematurely. However scattered and redundant, the database of psychology only awaits its Leeuwenhoek, Becquerel, Darwin, or Einstein to make theoretically coherent that which seems opaque and elusive. The name of the search process is science; thus, we cannot and should not deny psychology this approach because it is suffering from the dysfunctional state known as infancy. Rescher (1984) summed up this point of view succinctly: "The cardinal fact is simply that no one is in a position to delineate here and now what the science of the future can and cannot achieve. No identifiable issue can be confidently placed outside the limits of science" (127).[19]

This argument goes on; prejudging now what we might learn in the future is unacceptable. Progress can be made even if we cannot achieve our ultimate goals and, indeed, it must be made since the questions of psychological science are so important for the ultimate goal of understanding human nature. Psychology is justified on this account by its importance, even if impenetrable barriers exist to its final fruition.

1.5.2. Accessibility

As I have already noted, the highly controversial issue of the accessibility of mental entities to experimental assay or introspection is the crux of the disagreement between behaviorist and mentalist psychologies. Unfortunately, there is no "killer" empirical argument yet available that can convince one side or the other that their cause is correct.

The argument for the accessibility of cognitive processes is largely dependent on the assumption that, although science cannot directly measure mental functioning, it is possible to infer from behavioral measures what the underlying structure and processes must be. This assumption asserts that there is a kind of transparency from observation to internal mechanism that is comparable to that found in any other science. Thus, proponents of psychological accessibility will argue that basic particle and cosmological physics suffer from the same barrier; there is no fundamental qualitative difference between these sciences. The differences are only quantitative and do not differ in kind or quality. Like those who study mental processes, physicists do not have direct access to their subject matter any more than do psychologists. Quarks, gluons, hadrons, and the other particles of the microworld, on the one hand, and the properties of dark matter, black holes, distant galaxies, and the other entities of the macroworld, on the other, are just as invisible to physicists as cognitive processes are to psychologists. Thus, psychology has nothing to apologize for. However limited its access to the "true" nature of the mind, its conceptual problems are no different than those of the other sciences. There is nothing special that should deny psychology its rights to be included within the pantheon of the sciences.[20]

1.5.3. Convergent Operations and Supplementary Assumptions

One way that an ambiguous, variable, or underdefined state of affairs may be clarified is to collect a body of evidence that may in the aggregate resolve what a single observation cannot. This process, known as "convergent operation," seeks to produce certainty in the same way that multiple measurements provide more and more precise estimates of some physical dimension. Convergent operations abound in our personal lives. It has been compellingly demonstrated that speech is better understood when a person both listens to the speech sounds and observes the lips of a speaker (Massaro 2004). Similarly, it is possible that our understanding of otherwise inaccessible psychological processes may be enhanced by integrating the findings of a number of experimental approaches. Collectively, they may point to a more effective estimation of the properties of some mental process than can be gleaned from a single experiment. Thus, what is not accessible in the simple case may, by processes of exclusion and inclusion, converge on a maximally plausible, if not unique, answer to some difficult question.

Closely related to the "convergent operations" approach is the use of plausible assumptions to add a degree of certainty to otherwise underdetermined data. Molecular structure is a field that faces this problem; x-rays are insufficient to determine exactly the shape of a complex organic structure. However, by making certain additional assumptions that are based on other observations, Rieping, Habeck, and Nildes (2005) found it possible to determine what is, at least, a very high-probability structure for a folded macromolecular chain of amino acids. This is very much like the method of regularization used by computer theoreticians to simplify what are otherwise incomputable problems to tractable levels.

Thus, it is possible that methods similar to convergent operations and supplementary and simplifying assumptions may also help us to overcome the inaccessibility of mental operations. The possible applicability of such methods again provides grist for the argument that, although primitive, psychology is fundamentally scientific.

1.5.4. A Science Need Not Be Quantitative and Materialist

A not unreasonable argument can be made that psychology can be a natural science even though it is not quantitative in the same sense as other sciences. Hatfield (1994) summed up this point of view well when he suggested:

> The equation of natural science with antimetaphysical, quantitative experimentation is problematic on two counts. As an approach to history, it partakes of the worst failings of "presentism" or "whig" history: it ignores the self understanding of earlier figures who considered themselves practitioners of natural science, and it redescribes their cognitive activity and intellectual products from the standpoint of the presently ruling party, in this case the community of experimental psychologists and their historians and apologists. Philosophically it takes the crude positivist assumption that all progress in science is progress in the quantitative description of natural phenomena. (186)

Thus, psychology may be a science even though it does not possess, to the same degree, some of the quantifiability and measurability properties of other, less controversial sciences.

1.5.5. There Are Many Open Questions That May Ultimately Be Solved by Pushing Ahead

Another argument for accepting psychology as a science is that, although there are many unresolved issues, many of them may yet be solved by simply continuing our explorations of the mind. It is, for example, too early to jump to the conclusion that mind is not modular when this may be a question that can eventually be solved by empirical research. Bechtel (2002), for example, argues that "it is through advancing and revising what is likely to be overly simplistic and incorrect decompositions that the goals of cognitive neuroscience are likely to be achieved" (229).

Palmer (2001) makes essentially the same point when he argues that science is a "convergent heuristic process" (201) and that any effort to abort an inquiry because of currently identified difficulties is "throwing the baby out with the bathwater!" (190).

Both are also essentially arguing that the future of science cannot be predicted and that surprises in technology and findings may provide an unexpected breakthrough that will make what seems to be impossible nowadays possible in the unknown future.

1.5.6. A Valid Psychology Is Fundamentally Behaviorist and Behaviorism Is Scientific

Although some parts of the psychological enterprise may eventually be deemed to be unscientific in the usual sense of the word, an argument can be made that most research findings are as good as those from any other science. That is, virtually all of experimental psychological research is carried out under conditions that mimic those in any other science. Stimuli and responses, if not the internal processes and mechanisms, are quantifiable and measurable, and the relationships between them can be described by mathematical formula or statistical analysis as well as any other science. Even efforts at prediction are often successful. From a certain perspective, as I have already noted, all of the empirical data collected by psychologists are functionally behavioral regardless of how they may ultimately be used. In the laboratory, all psychologists are behaviorists—there is no alternative.

Questions arise about the scientific status of psychology only when behavioral data is used to infer something about the inner structure of the mind. An astute comment attributed to Charles S. Harris asserts that "neurophysiological data are not psychological theories." From this perspective, it can be concluded that even the best and superficially most relevant behavioral data are not the same things as the mentalist hypotheses drawn from them. The point is that psychology has already demonstrated its objective, scientific bona fides and fails only when its findings are asked to do something they cannot do.

In summary, psychology should be considered to be a science in the usual sense, albeit a somewhat atypical one, because it has been considered to have been a legitimate scientific topic over the centuries. Indeed, mental processes have been the subject matter of inquiry for "natural philosophers" since classic Greek times. Furthermore, it examines a well-enough-defined subject matter, and its methodology is certainly comparable, if not superior, to many of the other sciences. Psychology, it is argued in its defense, is functionally objective and positivist despite its tendency to invoke unverifiable hypothetical constructs. Even though psychology may be subject to some special difficulties, they are not a priori insurmountable. There may be, on this point of view, some areas of psychology that are not scientific in the usual sense. Nevertheless, there is an identifiable core of scientific psychology. Why at this stage of the game should we stop including psychology among the sciences simply because progress has been difficult and accomplishments negligible? There is an entirely unpredictable future ahead.

1.6. INTERIM CONCLUSION

This brings us to the point at which the many issues discussed in previous sections of this chapter must be integrated into a tentative answer to the question of whether or not psychology is a science in the usual sense. At the outset of this concluding discussion, I must make it clear that none of the proposed answers to the question "What makes a science?" are satisfactory. These preliminary answers include:

- A science is defined by its subject matter.
- A science is defined by its methodology.
- A science is defined as an orderly body of knowledge.
- A science is defined by its use of mathematics.

To which I must add my own personal "simple definition":

- A science is simply the search for an orderly understanding of some aspect of the natural world.

All of these definitions, unfortunately, leave much to be desired and open the door for pseudoscientific activities to enter the halls of serious science.

There is another way to ask the same question that has not yet been considered. I have previously argued (Uttal 2005) that a science is defined by the nature of the explanations it provides of the phenomena it observes. That is, a science is a science to the extent that it provides integrative theories that meet certain qualifications. The qualifications include:

1. Accuracy
2. Consistency
3. Convergence, accumulation, and simplification
4. Synoptic breadth
5. Taxonomic order
6. Fruitfulness
7. Testability
8. Linguistically and methodologically naturalist

Each of these qualifications has some specific properties that upon examination help us evaluate psychology's putative scientific status. A brief examination of each of these ideas may help us toward a resolution of this contentious issue.[21]

1. Accuracy: Accuracy incorporates a number of the criteria previously discussed. The values of observed phenomenon to be incorporated into a theory must be measurable and the variability must be controllable to a degree that permits a modicum of replicability. At the very least, there must be some controlled effect of the manipulation of significant independent variables. If there is no effect or if there is a highly variable one, then accuracy in the sense used here is not achieved.

2. Consistency: Consistency requires that the phenomena and their measures must not violate any laws of other well-established sciences. Similarly, the theory must be internally consistent to at least a superficial degree. We now know, of course, that total internal consistency and completeness is not possible in any theoretical system (Gödel 1931). However, the axioms and deductions of a "good" theory must have some degree of internal agreement and external consistency with other sciences.
3. Convergence, accumulation, and simplification: A theory must be convergent in the sense that it must evolve toward a state in which smaller numbers of terms and concepts designate larger numbers of preliminary observations. An unsuccessful theory (and, therefore, by implication, an unscientific enterprise) would simply substitute terms at the same level of analysis for earlier ones with no generalization of meaning or condensation of concepts. A requirement for a science is the accumulation of knowledge in the nature of a conceptual pyramid. At the base of the pyramid of knowledge is a huge number of observations. At each successive level of the pyramid of knowledge, fewer and fewer ideas are necessary to incorporate the collective meaning of lower levels. At the pinnacle of the pyramid is a grand theory that explains, incorporates, and condenses the base of observations into a unified theory.[22]
4. Synoptic breadth: Almost above all other criteria, the theory of a science must incorporate a "substantial" portion of the observed findings into a coherent story. A plethora of theories that do not interact and that are restricted to the single database from which they emerged is not characteristic of a maturing science.
5. Taxonomic order: A science must be organized. Although there is no necessity that it be reduced to mathematical simplicity and obey all of the laws of such a formal system, simple data collection is not by itself scientific. Some orderly arrangement of the entities under investigation is necessary as a prior condi-

tion for theory building. Even so, a simple taxonomic scheme such as a typology begins to satisfy this criterion. However, it is much more useful to have some kind of a scheme that details the causal relationships that place entities in systematic order. A tabulation of correlations between two or more dimensions does not serve the need of identifying the causal interrelationships; it simply describes experimental outcomes.

6. Fruitfulness: To be candid, it must be admitted that fruitfulness is perhaps the least concrete of the criteria discussed here. However, the general point is that a "good" theory should propel a science toward new ideas, concepts, hypotheses, and insights in the hopes of building the intellectual pyramid of converging knowledge mentioned above. A theory that perfectly describes but provides no impetus to future understanding fails this criterion. Unfortunately, fruitfulness is always evaluated ex post facto and, thus, it is perhaps the weakest of these criteria.
7. Testability: Here, of course, is the sine qua non of a science—the ability for its hypotheses and concepts to be empirically tested, replicated, evaluated, and then either accepted or rejected. The key aspect of this criterion is that a theory that is incapable of being evaluated or compared against other ideas must quickly be rejected. An endeavor based on such an untestable theoretical or explanatory foundation does not deserve to be called a science. In general, we refer to many such nonscientific endeavors as spiritualisms, religions, folktales, or other forms of extranatural beliefs.
8. Linguistically and methodologically naturalist: Finally, the language and methods of a putative science must come from the natural world. That is, they must be anchored to physical measurements and concepts. Although this criterion will always be especially controversial, a sure sign of a pseudoscience is a vocabulary rich with neologisms and terminology from beyond the limits of natural science. However, the natural vocabulary

> cannot simply be appropriated from another science as camouflage for limited scientific content. An endless use of metaphors beyond their undeniable value as initial suggestions in the place of description and explanation is a good sign of a failed science. Similarly, the methodology must be one that can be applied to any natural subject matter and not be so specialized that it remains specific to the particular subject matter.

Two germane questions are now encountered:

1. How well (or poorly) do theories of psychology meet these criteria?
2. In light of the answer to question 1, is psychology a science in the usual meaning of the word?

Even the most cursory examination of this list of the characteristics of theories suggests some of the reasons that psychology's scientific status is so often challenged. The problems of psychology's credibility as a science are immense simply because its theories do not, as many psychologists have noted, accumulate from experiment to experiment. This absence of theoretical pyramiding may be the most important impediment of all to psychology's inclusion among the natural sciences.

In this context, it seems to me that psychology operates by a paradigm that is very different than some of the other sciences. The fundamental questions asked by earlier psychologies and philosophies about the mind and behavior are almost never resolved. Rather, after a few decades of frustration, they are cast aside in favor of newly formulated versions that differ little from the earlier conundrums. One cannot help being reminded when one reads a book like James's (1892, 1948) classic *Principles of Psychology* how few of the problems he enunciated have been solved and how many persist into the most modern of times. What has happened instead is an enormous accumulation of unrelated observations and data, many of which are simply forgotten and sloughed off like dead skin.

The failure of psychology's mentalist languages is an especially serious problem. Machado and his colleagues also quote Quine, who suggests that "the less a science has advanced, the more its terminology tends to rest on an uncritical assumption of mutual understanding" (Quine 1936, 90).

Much of psychology's "knowledge" depends on words for which there are no precise definitions (e.g., *mind*, *emotion*, *perception*, *personality*, *cognition*, *consciousness*, and even to a degree, *behavior*). These words are defined only as circular associations of what seem to be closely related or even denotatively identical concepts. However, this folk psychology language can (and indeed must) be used if we are to communicate at all with each other. It is useful because of a general, albeit imprecise, commonsense agreement that, while useful in our daily lives, does not serve science well. Certainly, the analytic methods and physical dimensions, which were evolved to describe well-anchored physical concepts, seem particularly inappropriate for a study of such ill-defined concepts as inferred consciousness. In general, it must be admitted that psychology's popular vocabulary does not meet the criteria for scientific utility.

Another formidable reason that positive answers to the question of the scientific nature of psychology are not more abundant is that psychology is not monolithic. There are psychologies and psychologies; it is worth a few paragraphs to consider some of the different meanings of the word *psychology*.

Although the word *psychology* is clearly intended to convey that it belongs in the pantheon of science (the subject matter is designated by the *psych* . . .—the mind—and the method is literally designated to be that of science—. . . *ology*), merely defining it as a science in this manner is not sufficient in meeting the theoretical criteria just enumerated. A finer dissection of the word is required. To do this, we have to distinguish between different kinds of psychology. For the purposes of this discussion, I choose to divide psychology into three subfields. This dissection is arbitrary but diagnostic of the current field. Such an approach greatly simplifies the following discussion by emphasizing the fact that the word has multiple meanings and may well have multiple answers to our two questions. The three divisions I propose are:

1. Experimental psychology from the point of view of behaviorism[23]
2. Experimental psychology from the point of view of cognitive mentalism
3. Clinical psychology and psychotherapy, another mentalistic approach

As a preliminary means of evaluating how scientific psychology is, let us consider how well the different characteristics of scientific theories just discussed are matched by these three divisions. The task may be most easily accomplished by constructing the matrix shown in table 1.1.

TABLE 1.1

	Behavioral Experimental	Mentalist Experimental	Mentalist Clinical
1.	Yes	Yes	No
2.	Yes	Yes	No
3.	No	No	No
4.	No	No	No
5.	Yes	No	No
6.	Yes	No	No
7.	Yes	No	No
8.	Yes	No	No

1. Accuracy
2. Consistency
3. Convergence, accumulation, and simplification
4. Synoptic breadth
5. Taxonomic order

6. Fruitfulness
7. Testability
8. Linguistically and methodologically naturalist

Examination of the scores in this matrix is not encouraging for many kinds of putatively scientific psychology. Although many therapists may dispute the points made here that clinical psychology does not meet any of the criteria of a science, a detailed examination of its general approach (with the exception of behavioral modification methods) suggests that psychotherapy has little fruitful theory, a poor taxonomy of mental illnesses, no evidence of convergence or simplification, and uses a terminology that invokes immeasurable and inaccurate concepts and an almost extra- (if not super-) natural vocabulary.

Similarly, because of the inaccessibility of cognitive components, any psychology that seeks to identify mental components comes close to failing to meet these criteria ab initio. It is only in the domain of the nature of empirical results (accurate and consistent measurements) that mentalistic psychologies do well in this analysis; it is at this level where all psychologists are essentially behaviorists. However, when cognitive mentalists begin to take their hypothetical constructs too seriously, they, too, enter a domain of untestable hypotheses and unnatural linguistic myths.

Finally, I raise another possibility. Perhaps we are asking too much of a single "science." The word *psychology* is so broad and inclusive that it captures too many activities within its far-flung conceptual net. It is often pointed out that a typical department of psychology in a medium- or large-size university contains scholars who have little in common. At the one end of a professional spectrum are the philosophers of science and at the other are computer modelers who cannot be distinguished from artificial intelligence engineers. In the middle are a variety of clinical psychotherapists, students of child development, social psychologists, and aspiring neuroscientists. Even within a narrower frame of reference (e.g., experimental psychologists), there are divisions into interest groups of one kind or another. All of these diverse activities, however, are currently collected under the single rubric of psychology. Many, if not most, however, have their closest intellectual contacts with people in other departments. What brings psychologists together is only a common history and a shared interest in what may in the end turn out to be the ineffable concept of mind. This may not be enough; some universities, especially newer ones, have divided their psychology departments into separate organizations.

Perhaps it is because of this unconstrained breadth that psychology is so terribly challenged. Too much is included within this rubric. The word *psychology* may actually mean something more like "engineering" or "biology," and specialized subdivisions should be encouraged. Perhaps many of the questions concerning the scientific status of psychology could be ameliorated if the target were much smaller. In such a case, many of the constraints that inhibit psychology's recognition as a science would simply fall away. "Behavioral science," I believe, would have a much easier time making its case as a science if it could shake off its ancestral mentalist accoutrements. If the problems and difficulties with the practical arts such as psychotherapy could be trimmed from the discussion, things would be much easier for all those concerned. Psychotherapists would not have to play at being scientists, and behaviorists would not have to justify to their brethren what is, from some points of view, an unrelated enterprise.

NOTES

1. The number of "psychologists" at work in the world today is not exactly known, but one statistic suggests that even as far back as 1991, the number was more than a half million. Furthermore, psychology is the second-most popular college major after business. Of course, not all of these psychologists and students of psychology are scientifically oriented. Still, it is quite a substantial number.

2. I am indebted to Machado, Lourenco, and Silva (2000) and to Schlinger (2004) for drawing my attention to some of the following items in this tabulation of critiques of psychology by psychologists.

3. Consistency not being a virtue, it should also be noted that Koch was the general editor of one of the most ambitious interpretive projects in psychology (Koch 1959a). In the introduction to this collection of handbooks, he detailed in a long list what a science "is not," concluding it was "all of these things and much else" (3). Part of this inconsistency may be due to the fact that Koch's (1969) work was mainly aimed at psychotherapy.

4. It might be noted in an aside that the problems faced in the current application of psychoactive drugs are not too different from those involved in using any psychotherapy. There is an absence of solid theory, experimental results are fragile and irreproducible, and systemization is minimal, if not absent. (See p. 44, where I discuss the mental health profession's diagnostic manual.)

5. A note to my readers: Please don't jump the gun and draw conclusions quite yet. There are two other considerations. First, this section will be followed by a list of reasons why psychology is a science in the usual sense of the word. Second, the final conclusion yet to be drawn will depend on what kind of psychology is being considered.

6. A full discussion of the evidence that we ourselves do not know the origins of our behavior can be found in Uttal (2000).

7. An important corollary of this point is that any mathematical accounts of these transformations do not explain or define internal mechanisms and processes but only describe what they collectively do.

8. The most salient example of archaeological misdirection is the search for evidence of what were clearly mythical civilizations. An especially clear-cut example of this can be found in the search for proof of Old Testament events and personages who may well have never existed. For example, there is at the present time no material evidence of the Old Testament patriarchs (including Abraham and Moses) or early kings (including David and Solomon) or of any of their adventures. According to a modern "minimalist" version of biblical history, these figures were invented to provide a history of the Hebrew people about the year 700 BCE, hundreds of years after they were supposed to have lived. An excellent introduction to this minimalist point of view can be found in Finkelstein and Silberman's (2001) fascinating book.

9. I defer any discussion of what are the neural correlates of these behavior changes. It is widely believed that all forms of learning are attributable to changes in the number of or conductivity of synapses. Variations on this theme suggest that synapses are eliminated or reduced in effectiveness rather than increased in number or effectiveness during the learning process.

However, these neural theories are totally unsupported by any direct comparison of synaptic and behavioral changes except in primitive model preparations such as Aplysia, the California sea slug. Whether or not these observed synaptic effects in Aplysia are true homologs of human learning has not yet been determined. The actual neurophysiological nature of human learning remains undetermined.

10. The difficulty was even further compounded by Eriksen and Collin's allusion to "sensory traces" and "psychological moments" as distinguishable phenomena.

11. The word *innumerable* is not chosen arbitrarily in this context. Moore (1956), for example, has shown that for any automata for which experiments are carried out to determine its internal structure, there is always an "innumerable" (i.e., unlimited, if not technically infinite) number of structures that cannot be excluded as possible alternatives. The defining properties of his "automata" are indistinguishable from those of the brain, according to many scholars in the field.

12. Surprisingly, Shallice immediately ignored his own admonitions concerning these methodological cautions and charged ahead with an effort to develop a particular modular and reductive model of human cognition based on behavioral data.

13. The one-to-many rule is comparable to the similar action of different computer programs. Programmers can produce the same output (behavior) with programs that are very different in the steps that intervene between the inputs and outputs.

14. In fact there is a strong argument that we cannot ever achieve this goal. See Uttal (2005) for a discussion of why neural net theories are unlikely to ever explain how brain activity produces mental activity.

15. As I discuss later in chapter 3, the most basic requirements for quantification—additivity and orderliness—may not hold for mental mechanisms and processes.

16. How large is "many" is not known. However, different estimates of the number of neurons in the human brain range up to 10^{13} when the cells in the cerebellum are included. We will probably never know even the approximate number because of cellular and synaptic variations throughout the central nervous system.

17. It should not go without notice that all experimental observations are of behavior of one kind or another. In the laboratory, all psychologists are

behaviorists. It is only when inferences are made about those observations that many psychologists cross the line into mentalism.

18. Loftus (1996) pointed out that this criticism is not new. On p. 170 of his article he lists twenty-one prior reports ranging from 1935 until 1996 also "decrying the enormous reliance we place on NHST [Null Hypothesis Significance Testing] . . ." Why this long-appreciated and repeated admonition has had so little impact may be attributed to a stagnant graduate educational system and a reluctance to accept some of the differences between psychology and physics.

19. Of course, as we see later, some ontological issues dealing with the stress between natural and supernatural explanations may never be resolved by science, however "identifiable" they may be. The failure lies not in science, however, but in its rejection by true believers.

20. I cannot resist a contrarian excursion at this point. Although the qualitative differences between physics and psychology may be small enough to say that both suffer from the same difficulty (the inaccessibility of their targets), it can be equally well argued that the quantitative differences in terms of complexity are so substantial as to make the problem faced by the two enterprises incomparable. Furthermore, the anchors that cosmological physics has to observations and measurements on this world may speak to a major difference between physics and psychology. Psychology does not have these anchors or the freedom to assert that the laws of the mind are the same as the laws of material world. Physics, to its great advantage, can assume that all of its laws work equally well in any part of the universe. However, I must also admit that this is one of the most difficult challenges faced by any exclusively behaviorist approach, and I am not utterly convinced that physics and psychology cannot be compared in this regard. Indeed, I am currently at work on a new manuscript that deals with this issue.

21. This is an expanded and updated list originally developed in my earlier book (Uttal 2005).

22. Of course, no science has yet achieved a fully unified theory of everything. Instead, it is the continued progression of ideas from low to high levels to which I allude here. My colleague at ASU, Peter Killeen (2005) has pointed out that "Falsification of the null [hypothesis], even when possible, provides no machinery for the cumulation of knowledge" (353). In this regard, psychology fails to meet even the criterion of accumulation, much less the stronger one of convergence.

23. It is very important to the thesis I present in this book to appreciate that many so-called behaviorisms (e.g., the work of Tolman 1932) were not behaviorisms in the sense I use the word here. Tolman and some other behaviorists were clearly seeking mental events and structures in a way that challenges the normative value of the term *behaviorism*.

Chapter 2

PRINCIPIA SCIENTIFICA

A Search for General Scientific Principles

2.1. INTRODUCTION

The study of human behavior and its causes represents one of the most complex and challenging human endeavors. As we learned in the previous chapter, psychology suffers from some serious handicaps that do not affect—at least not to the same degree—other forms of science. Indeed, psychology's scientific bona fides have often been challenged by those who believe that the "psyche"—the mind—is impenetrable to the methods of standard materialist science simply because it is of a different nature than the body. In order to understand the special difficulties faced by psychology, it is necessary to understand the paradigms used by other modern sciences, idealized though they may be. Currently, the ideal of a science is embodied in the observation-induction-axiom-deduction-theorem-verification method (known hereafter as the axiomatic-deductive paradigm), which has characterized natural science for centuries. This approach is similar to what John Stuart Mill (1843, 1874) referred to as "Induction, Ratiocination, and Verification" (book 3, chapter 11, section 3) and what Karl Popper (1902–1994) referred to as the hypothetico-deductive method in his book *The Logic of Scientific Discovery* (1959).

In this chapter, I consider the nature of axioms, the methods of induction and deduction, and the robustness of derived theorems. My major goal is to examine the structure of some of the best-known explicit attempts to structure and formalize particular sciences. It is not a priori necessary that a science follows this standard recipe, but the romantic ideal of what is the best in science is illustrated by the books reviewed here.[1]

In the previous chapter, I showed that all of the activities that we would consider scientific involve, at a bare minimum, empirical observation of events followed by a search for the causal relationships between different observations. Initial observations lead to inferences about the nature of the world by informal inductive methods. Based mainly on the accumulation of empirical observations, the conventional scientific paradigm then typically involves the generation (often by deductive methods quite different than the inductive ones that generated the basic axiomatic assertions) of synoptic theories (descriptions or explanations) or of theorems that represent generalities or laws about the realm being studied.

Ideally, therefore, a "good" scientific theory eventually transcends the individual observations and unifies them into a global statement that permits prediction and/or control of events that have not yet occurred. On this account, scientific process is circular. Inductively generated axioms are transformed into theorems that must be tested by new observations and measurements that may or may not validate the original induced axioms or the deductive logic that led to the theorems. This chain of observation-induction-axiom-deduction-theorem-verification steps is, as I just suggested, the archetype of a mature science.[2] Even problematic psychology regarded the failed work of Clark L. Hull in this mode as one of its proudest accomplishments. A major goal of this chapter is to analyze those sciences for which this approach does hold and seek the answers to why it progressively fails as the subject matter gets increasingly complex and disorderly.

To begin, however, I return to briefly review the minimum properties that define a science. There are two fundamental criteria that I believe represent the sine qua non of a putative science. The first is the necessity of public availability of the observations. If an observation cannot be made under common conditions by anyone with the proper tools, then I argue that the event does not fall within the rubric of science. If observations are private or restricted to a specially receptive observer or intermediary, the subject matter is beyond the pale of science. Theological revelations presented to a "gifted" prophet, for example, do not offer the opportunity for public availability (except through the intermediary "prophet") and, therefore, fall outside the scientific rubric, a priori. Nor, for that matter, is a "sensitive" who claims private knowledge of distant events within the realm of science.

The second (and closely related to the first) requirement of scientific activity is replicability or reliability. If a public observation is unique and can never be repeated, it is likely that, however interesting it may be, it does not meet the criteria required to be the subject of scientific investigation. So far, no form of so-called parapsychological activity has met adequate controlled tests of replicability and, therefore, despite its name, does not represent a branch of scientific inquiry.

The question before us now is, Do these two basic criteria permit or prohibit the inclusion of psychology among the sciences? A preliminary answer is that it appears that the privacy of our thoughts and feelings should exclude psychology. However, the situation is not that simple. First, psychologies come in many kinds, and it is never quite certain that the criteria defined for the simple, physical sciences are applicable to all kinds of psychologies. Furthermore, many different forms of research carried out by psychologists that do not utilize the strict axiomatic-deduction methodology probably should not be excluded from the domain of natural sciences. Such widely different activities as observing animal behavior in natural settings, observing the conditions that influence social intercourse, and manipulating the chemistry of the brain in order to change behavior, along with many other research strategies, are usually included within the range of activities that are generally considered to be scientific. There is no a priori means of excluding any particular "study" as long as the observations are replicable and public. An important goal of this book is to distinguish between psychological approaches that meet these standards and those that do not.

Although mathematical methods and thinking per se are not necessary components of every science, mathematics plays such a constraining and guiding role in scientific thinking that the least equivocal and most highly respected fields of science are almost always heavily mathematized. Mathematics controls the amount of verbal "hand waving" and makes precise what is all too often imprecise. By making what is vague, nebulous, or poorly defined into something sharp and precise, many propositions become clearly indefensible, and others take on a rigor not possible solely with verbal speculation. Science is increasingly a quantitative endeavor, and much of the following discussion deals with successes and failures in applying mathematical ideas to various kinds of science.

Since it is obviously impossible to survey all of science in our quest for understanding psychology's scientific status, I have chosen instead to concentrate on those works that explicitly set out to develop the foundation principles of a sample of particular sciences, physical and social. I concentrate on a group of books that seek to define their respective sciences by identifying key premises and axioms and then I attempt to use a formal system (e.g., logic or mathematics) to extend knowledge by a system of derivations. The question to be considered in this chapter is, How well does psychology fit this classic paradigm of science in the usual sense that has proven to be so useful and so powerful in the development of other sciences?

To begin, we have to consider the meaning of some of the terms that will arise in this discussion and the methods used to manipulate them.

2.2. AXIOMS, INDUCTION, AND DEDUCTION

The idea that *first principles* exist goes back to Plato and Aristotle—at least. Although we cannot know who was the first to propose that certain axiomatic or first principles governed all of reality, Aristotle's formulation of two fundamental principles seems to have summarized a view of nature on which both he and Plato had generally agreed. Aristotle suggested that everything in the world was accounted for by two fundamentals—the "One" and the "Indefinite Dyad." From these two fundamental principles was derived everything else.

It is clear, on reading the sections of Aristotle's *Metaphysics*, that these basic principles did not only refer to mathematics and numbers. The "One" was described as the essence of numbers from which all higher numbers emerge. However, the "Indefinite Dyad" combined with the "One" to produce numbers, forms, and, ultimately, sensible things, according to Aristotle.

These classical Greek philosophers and mathematicians set the stage for modern scientific and logical thinking by suggesting an epistemological paradigm for the accumulation of knowledge. Here we see the earliest origins of the axiomatic-deductive paradigm. First, for more or less "sound" and "self-evident" reasons, a set of axiomatic first principles is enunciated. Then, formal rules of argument, logic, or mathematics are applied to these axioms to produce certain derivations or theorems that themselves may not be self-evident but whose properties can be compared with subsequent empirical observations to verify the original axioms or the deductive processes. To the extent that the conclusions do correlate well enough with subsequent observations, this provides a kind of proof for both the axioms and the rules. Should they not conform to observations, one has to go back and change the rules or the initial axioms and try again.

The difference between this process and induction is that once the rules and the axioms have been agreed upon, everyone using them will presumably come to the same conclusions. Deduction, the process of applying the rules to the axioms, is a highly circumscribed process in which conclusions or theorems do not depend on arbitrary aggregations of observations, opinions, or intuitions but rather on a fixed process that should always arrive at the same conclusion.

As well structured and direct as the axiomatic-deductive system may seem in principle, philosophers have debated its efficacy as a scientific method and have raised questions about its relevance to many of the difficult-to-quantify sciences. The problem with this paradigm starts at the most basic level—the nature of axioms. Axioms are supposed to bc the self-evident statements of first principles on which the rest of the system is based. However, it has never been completely clear what constitutes an axiom. How can we be sure that axioms are at once true and self-evident, as well as irreducible? Even if they are true, can we always be assured that they lead to irrefutable theorems, given that they must subsequently be transformed by rules and procedures? Doubts about the "truth" of axiomatic statements still bubble along in the background of scientific reasoning even though it is generally assumed that one has to start someplace.

A major difficulty in accepting primitive ideas as axiomatic is that we can never be sure whether or not they are reducible to even more primitive concepts. The usually accepted nature of axiomatic assertions is that they are the inductive outcomes of the observation of many "instances" in which they do seem to work; in other words, they are more or less intuitive or insightful interpretations evolved from their repeated success in describing a reasonably large number of preexisting observations. Induction, furthermore, has been likened to pattern recognition or to the application of intuitions and insights that are not rigorous in the same sense as is deduction.

Inductive thinking has, therefore, been charged with being a particularly soft kind of scientific method. Indeed, it has been accused of being only marginally better than prejudices and intuitions by some philosophers. Some of the greatest names in philosophy including Hume (1888), Locke (1690, 1967), Kant (1965), as well as Newton, Russell, and Popper, dealt with the problems of first principles and innate axioms. All concluded that induction was inadequate as a rigorous scientific method. Their arguments that induction was fallible were based on the idea that inductive results are always exquisitely sensitive to refutation by the next contradictory observation, since they never are (and never can be) the result of consideration of all possible instances. Inductively generated axioms represent, these philosophers argue, a kind of gentleman's agreement rather than a robust proof that the world operates in the way the axiom suggests. Induction "goes gently" from observations to axioms. Deduction, on the other hand, is designed to constrain the steps from observations to theorems by means of robust and rigid intervening laws and rules. It is, as Coombs (1984) told us: "Axioms in mathematical systems are treated 'as if' true, and their consequences, deductively arrived at, are true. Truth in a mathematical (logical) system is a matter of deduction" (111).

On the other hand, as Medawar (1964) reminds us, John Stuart Mill argued that induction was the real pathway to discovery. Deduction, Mill's classic view went, "only uncovers, brings out into the open, makes explicit, information that is already present in the axioms or premises from which the process of deduction started" (Medawar 1964). In its place, Medawar suggests that our original hypotheses were developed by a process that was "imaginative and inspirational in character" and were neither induction nor deduction.

Medawar also distinguished between "discovery" and "demonstration or proof" as two different parts of the scientific enterprise. Discovery, the source of axioms, was for him a much less formal process in which "inspiration," exploration, and hunches all might contribute. The "demonstration or proof" could be provided by a consistent experimental proof or a hypothetico-deductive method, so idealized by Popper, Newton, and Whitehead and Russell, among others.

It should not be overlooked in highlighting this controversy that there is a third side that is very important in our discussion of psychology. Some philosophers of science have argued that neither induction nor deduction accurately depict modern science. Medawar hints at this position when he alludes to "inspiration," but it was developed most fully by Feyerabend (1975). Feyerabend suggested that there were no universal rules or methods that worked for all sciences all of the time or even some sciences most of the time. He championed a "theoretical anarchism" in which "anything goes." Induction, deduction, intuition, exploration, and even scientific prejudice all were useful methods with which to generate insights and, thus, in the long run, to guarantee scientific progress.

There is, nevertheless, a practical argument for accepting certain inductive statements as axiomatic; simply put, we have to start someplace in developing a compelling, elegant, and useful scientific system. If a starting point, however arbitrary, in an argument is not firmly established, then the scientist, mathematician, or logician is required to find even more primitive assumptions that can support the axioms on which a theory is based. This leads to what can be an exhausting, if not infinite, regress and throws a major roadblock into the upward development of interesting and useful theorems.

Axioms, therefore, probably should not be considered as totally basic first principles but merely as more or less convenient starting points. The hierarchy of the sciences reflects this practicality. Chemistry assumes certain summaries of observations as first principles. For example, certain kinds of chemicals are more likely to combine with certain kinds than others. Even though such axiomatic rules of combination may actually be derived from other even more basic concepts in physics (e.g., the attractiveness of oppositely charged objects), there is no advantage for the chemist to go that far down the explanatory tree.

Biology, in turn, accepts certain conclusions from chemistry as axiomatic first principles. For example, chemical reactions of a certain kind (the chemistry of macromolecules such as DNA) account for the continuity of species. Chemistry is also useful to explain neural activity. It is likely, therefore, that many of the axiomatic principles of sensory psychology in turn could be reduced to those of neurobiology. However, for practical reasons, it is not clear that it is necessary or even possible for psychology to make a reduction from neurobiology to chemistry. Like chemistry, psychology has its own problems. We can make the ontological assumption that mental events are the results of biological and chemical events without flooding ourselves with additional levels of what are likely to be irrelevant subaxioms. A salient analogy is the computer programmer who does not need to know anything about the hardware to successfully write a program. All that is necessary is knowledge of the available compiler-level language.

We must also ask, What does "self-evident" mean? The history of ancient mathematics and modern physics has made it clear that observations made at the human perceptual scale that are "obvious" and "self-evident" do not always persist as first principles. That which "seems obvious" to a person is inadequate proof that an axiom is either true or irreducible: observations at the human scale may be insufficient to represent reality at all levels. Nevertheless, the inductive process almost always depends initially on an amalgamation of observations into self-evident (i.e., obvious at some level) concepts by the human using logical methods that are not always obvious.

For example, it is "self-evident" at the human scale that parallel lines will never meet. No person has ever personally and directly seen a failure of this axiom and probably never will. Nevertheless, there are scales of measurement, both in the macrocosm and in the microcosm that violate this axiom. No matter how obvious an induced axiom may be and how many observations support it, raw human intuitions leave much to be desired as a foundation for an objective science. This has led some philosophers to deny the value of anything defined as "self-evident" in a rigorous science. Psychology is particularly vulnerable because of its illusions, hallucinations, distortions, and other forms of cognitive penetration.

The practical facts of the matter, however, suggest that it is necessary to start someplace, and what the starting point is, as I have just noted, may differ from one science to another. Economists may be happy to start with axioms such as "The purpose of production is consumption." Classical mathematicians such as Euclid started from the foundation of axioms such as "The diameter of a circle divides that circle into two equal parts." Newton's axioms are exemplified by the famous "To any action there is always an opposite and equal reaction."

Theologians accept the axiom "God exists." It is almost certain in each case that all of these statements are reducible to even more primitive ideas, but that is not the point. Each of these axioms represents a satisfactory starting point for the development of new ideas about the nature of our world by its respective theoretician. This book confronts the major question: Does psychology have some reasonable and comparable axioms from which it, too, might develop a similar coherent scientific system?

The axiomatic-deductive method described here has become the archetype of modern scientific reasoning. Without question, it has been enormously productive in helping us toward achieving both deeper understanding and better lives. Equally unquestionable is the idea that it is an idealization that rarely works in the social and psychological sciences. Indeed, there have been many disagreements with its validity in philosophical circles over the years. Recently, Popper (1959) denied that any such process could lead to confirmation of either axioms or conclusions, only to their falsification. Furthermore, Gödel (1931) has pointed out that such systems must always be incomplete and contain predictions, theorems, and conclusions that can never be verified.

Nevertheless, over the years, the axiomatic-deductive strategy still remains the idealized archetype of modern scientific methodology. There are few who would argue that an enterprise that is based on this methodology is not scientific.

In the following sections of this chapter, I review the history of the axiomatic-deductive method as it has shaped a number of sciences. First, I consider some of the historical milestones that have helped to shape modern physical science and mathematics. Then I gradually redirect the course of the discussion to consider fields of "science" that are far less sharply defined and whose scientific status is less obvious and more controversial. Finally, I examine one example of the application of the method to psychology (Hull's system), in particular, to see how well it may or may not fit this model of science. As already mentioned, it failed, but the reasons why are extremely instructive in our discussion.

In this discussion, I emphasize a number of the great works that over the centuries have explicitly been intended to follow the axiomatic-deductive paradigm. I believe that by carrying out this exercise, it will be possible to understand the strengths and weaknesses of psychology as a scientific enterprise. To continue, I consider the work of an extraordinary man from the distant past who, from some perspectives, may have been the original framer of the modern scientific paradigm: Euclid.

2.3. EUCLID

It is not at all certain where arithmetic and mathematics first emerged in human history, but there is no question that it was a part of life from the earliest times. Sarton (1952) describes the use of arithmetic and geometry in prehistoric times (10–15) and then examines the Egyptian and Minoan periods (113–16). However, there is little question that deductive mathematics and geometry reached their apex during the time of classic Greece. Pythagoras (569–475 BCE), universally acknowledged as the first great Greek mathematician, was mainly concerned with the relationship between numbers and geometry. Most famously, his expression of the Pythagorean theorem (i.e., the square of the hypotenuse of a right triangle is equal to the sum of the squares of the other two sides) formalized an empirical observation that had been well known to and used by many earlier societies.

The general idea of an axiomatic-deductive system, however, seems to have first emerged full-blown in the work of Euclid (325–265 BCE?), whose thirteen volumes of mathematics collectively titled *The Elements* (one fascinating translation of which can be found in Euclid 1714) would influence the rest of the world for more than two millennia. Although it is not known if Euclid was the first to propose such a strategy, his work survived and models the strategy of modern science.

Like his successors, Euclid attempted to define basic starting points and he used them to prove theorems like those of Pythagoras.

His initial "axioms" came in three varieties: definitions, postulates, and common notions, in his terminology. All of these would be considered comparable to the axioms of, for example, Newton.

Euclid's "postulates" consisted of twenty-three terms that essentially listed the entities or "things" with which his mathematics would deal. Examples of them include points, lines, right angles, circles, and other one- and two-dimensional forms. To these objects, Euclid added five postulates that manipulated the twenty-three defined objects. For example, he asserted in one postulate that it is possible to draw a straight line between any two points; in another, that all right angles are equal.

Next, Euclid added the third category of "common notions." These five notions can be compared to the mathematical laws or rules that were utilized later in the proofs of various theorems. It is here that the concepts of equality and congruence were introduced in the form of such universally accepted ideas as "If equals are added to equals, the sums are equal" and "The whole is greater than the part."

The nature of Euclid's postulates has been a continual topic of discussion among mathematicians. Modern mathematicians have suggested that Euclid also had other implicit assumptions that he adhered to in the development of his theorems. David Hilbert, for example, attempted a modern reconstruction of Euclid's work and suggested that as many as twenty such postulates were necessary for the development of the full range of Euclid's theorems. Furthermore, Ian Stewart, in his introductory discussion of E. A. Abbott's *Flatland* (1884, 2002), points out that some of Euclid's postulates may actually have been superfluous, specifically the one concerning parallel lines in which Euclid suggested that parallel lines would not meet even if extended indefinitely. That parallel lines will never meet is an intuitive idea that subsequently was shown to be correct only on the human scale. In non-Euclidean geometries, parallel lines can meet.

These, then, were the tools with which Euclid worked during his lifetime. Although the axioms of other sciences differ from topic to topic and from time to time, the germ of the axiomatic-deductive system is clearly evident in this approach. Based on this foundation of agreed-upon but unproven assumptions, Euclid went on to prove many of the most powerful and persistent truths of modern geometry. His proof of the Pythagorean theorem is still considered a classic application of geometrical deduction. His strategic model was to suggest a proposition (a hypothesis or a conjecture) and then prove it by applying his definitions, postulates, and common notions. This differs little in basic concept from any of the successful axiomatic-deductive systems that were to follow even thousands of years later.

2.4. RENÉ DESCARTES

The modern grandfather of applying axiomatic principles to the organization of science was undoubtedly René Descartes (1596–1650). Descartes was an amazing polymath whose contributions to mathematics, physics, physiology, and even psychology (in a rudimentary form, to say the least) were enormous. His book *Principia Philosophiae* (Descartes 1644, 1988) was influential in transforming the entire intellectual milieu from the Renaissance to what can be appropriately designated as modern times.

Principia Philosophiae is an extraordinary book by any measure. However, the aspect I would like to emphasize is that Descartes chose to isolate his discussions into components or fragments he designated as "principles." The first of the four sections includes parts of his *Principia* and deals with the general principles that should guide the acquisition of human knowledge. Although the "g-word" is scattered throughout Descartes' discussions, we read at the outset that skepticism is a desirable aspect of human intellect.

> That in order to seek truth, it is necessary once in the course of our life, to doubt, as far as possible, of all things. (part 1, principle 1)

Nevertheless, also being a reasonable man, Descartes almost immediately went on to express a commonsense principle.

> That we ought not meanwhile to make use of doubt in the conduct of life. (part 1, principle 3)

One wonders if this rule was truly felt or was simply a compromise being made to the then-dominant ideas of the church, since he went on to express another rule:

> That the existence of God may be again inferred from the above. (book 1, principle 18)

Unfortunately, there is no way to read Descartes' inner thoughts. It is not implausible to suggest, however, that he may have felt that if he embedded his heretical and skeptical scientific ideas in a covering camouflage of religion and avoided what were then dangerous controversies, his otherwise more objective and naturalist ideas might survive. As we see later in this chapter, this defensive cover has been part and parcel of many of the great scientific developments up until the twentieth century, when atheistic attitudes toward science became more acceptable.

The second part of Descartes' *Principia* dealt with principles of material things. However, his notion of "material things" includes much more than the usual meaning of these words. In this part, he concentrated on such matters as the relationship between the mind and the body. For example:

> That the perceptions of the senses do not teach us what is in reality in things, but what is beneficial or hurtful to the composite whole of mind and body. (part 2, principle 3)

Later, he deals with such ideas as the singleness of types of reality, a statement surprisingly consistent with modern monistic ideas.

> It also follows that the matter of the heavens and earth is the same, and that there cannot be a plurality of worlds. (part 2, principle 22)

This is an especially interesting idea that seems in sharp contradiction to his famous interactive dualism as well as to the religious ideas that pervaded his time. Was Descartes suggesting a monism for physical worlds but accepting multiple realities for the mind and body of the human world? Indeed, in another of his books, *The Passions of the Soul* (Descartes 1649, 1989), he argues strongly that the body and the mind (soul) are totally separate, and he emphasizes his personal commitment to this form of dualism.[3]

After a theistic interlude in which he considered the nature of God in the third part of his *Principia*, Descartes moved on to the fourth part titled "Of the Earth." Despite this title, it was here that he developed his principles of sensory perception, the main link between humans and the external world. Here, also, he made extraordinarily prescient remarks concerning the location of the mind (i.e., the soul) in the brain.[4] For example:

> That the soul perceives only in so far as it is in the brain. (part 4, principle 196)

It is also in this fourth part that Descartes made clear either his political sensitivity or his deeply held religious belief (we cannot tell which) when, in the final principle of his work, he said: "That, however, I submit all my opinions to the authority of the church. Nevertheless, lest I should presume too far, I affirm nothing, but submit all these my opinions to the authority of the church and the judgment of the more sage; and I desire no one to believe anything I may have said, unless he is constrained to admit it by the force and evidence of reason." Others will have to decide if the exception expressed by the term "force and evidence of reason" was actually a recantation of a recantation. Since we cannot read his mind, it will never be certain whether or not Descartes' obeisance to the church was sincere. There is certainly enough ambiguity in his writing to support either interpretation.

The problems faced by natural scientists during the dictatorial rule of a deeply entrenched and powerful ecclesiastical administration were as serious then as they are now. Nowhere did this become clearer than in the lives of such now-appreciated scientific pioneers as Galileo Galilei (1564–1642) and Andreas Vesalius (1514–1564), near contemporaries of Descartes, who both ran into serious troubles with the Inquisition in their later years. Descartes was obviously being very careful in his writings.

The important thing about Descartes' *Principia* was that it attempted to organize a collection of disorganized ideas into a coherent and explicit set of basic principles and assumptions within the context of his time.[5] It should not be overlooked, however, that he made other very important scientific contributions; he argued strongly for a particular experimental methodology. His "Methode" was spelled out in detail in another of his great books, *A Discourse on Method* (Descartes 1677, 1912). As a scientist, a mathematician, and a philosopher, Descartes had few equals in history. However, it remained for another great genius—Isaac Newton—to set the stage forty years later for the modern approach to organizing a science into a formal structure and to establish what has become the archetype of the ideal scientific methodology—deductive argument from inductively defined axiomatic principles to testable theorems.

2.5. ISAAC NEWTON

The grandest and most persistently influential of the great historical "Principias" is Newton's *Philosophiae Naturalis Principia Mathematica* (or *Mathematical Principles of Natural Philosophy*, Newton 1687).[6] Newton's (1643–1727) explicit and carefully circumscribed goal was to explain the mechanical behavior of objects (including the behavior of astronomical entities and fluids) when acted on by physical forces. It is thought by many that even the great Newton "stood on the shoulders of giants" and that he was particularly influenced by Euclid's approach to geometry. His monumental work, perhaps the most successful application of the axiomatic-deductive method in scientific history, started from the most preliminary rules and assumptions and derived mathematical expressions that accurately predicted the behavior of those objects. As Cohen and Whitman (1999) point out: "Newton put aside, for the moment at least, any considerations other than those directly related to mathematics and mathematical considerations of physics" (60). Included among these ignored "considerations" was the nature of the forces that affected the behavior of mechanical objects and the nature of their interaction with matter. Newton, for example, did not mention in his *Principia* whether the forces he alluded to were particles or waves in the "ether," even though there was a vigorous argument on this very topic in his time. He presumably considered such explanatory assertions as mere "hypotheses" that could not be validated with the instruments of his time.[7]

In a very important sense, therefore, Newton's theories were purely descriptive and not reductive. He described how material objects and forces behaved but did not delve into their underlying nature. From a certain perspective, Newton was a physical behaviorist, a characteristic that has been overlooked by many cognitive psychologists otherwise infected with physicophilia.

Newton's *Principia* set a high standard for scientific analysis. More than any other scientist, he embodied the transition from classical, medieval, and Renaissance speculation to an objective science that Descartes had initiated but never completed. Starting with fundamentals, he derived complex theorems of hitherto unexplained behavior of solid objects and fluids. The sequence that led to his enormous contributions passed through three logical steps:

1. General rules guiding his scientific thinking
2. Precise definitions of his terminology
3. Axiomatic assumptions: his memorable three laws of motion

Based on these three levels of analytic preparation, Newton applied rigorous mathematical techniques (some of which, e.g., including some of the preliminary ideas of the calculus, were of his own invention) to develop theorems (i.e., mathematical expressions that transcended the simple basic rules and described aspects of the system behavior not expressed in the axioms). In this sense of the word *explanation*, he provided links between basic principles and observed data that had not yet been previously discovered. Although these ideas may have been implicit in the axioms, Newton's accomplishment was to make them explicit. Furthermore, his work rejected the theorems or ideas that were not consistent with his mathematical development and thus resolved some of the controversies that had beset physicists of his time.

Perhaps the most important contribution of Newton's great *Principia* was to demonstrate that it is possible to develop complex understandings from fundamentals and mathematical procedures. One of the best examples of this was his proof that the orbits of planets could be derived from his three axiomatic laws of motion.

I begin this discussion of Newton's work by considering the general scientific rules that he championed as the foundation of science. At the beginning of the third book of the *Principia*, Newton asserted four general principles that he believed should guide science.

> Rule 1. No more causes of natural things should be admitted than are both true and sufficient to explain their phenomena. (794)

This, of course, is another version of the famous simplification criterion of William of Ockham (1285–1349), in which he (Ockham) asserts that "[w]hat can be done with fewer assumptions is done in vain with more." Now known as Ockham's razor, this criterion of simplicity has long been used to distinguish between competing theories that seem to describe phenomena equally well.[8]

The important point in the present context is that Newton considered this to be a primary rule of his science. Obviously referring to William of Ockham, he went on to expand on this idea: "As the philosophers say: Nature does nothing in vain, and more causes are in vain when fewer will suffice. For nature is simple and does not indulge in the luxury of superfluous causes" (794).

It is interesting to note that in spite of his assumption of the priority of this rule, Newton also invokes the most extreme of "superfluous causes." He notes in the final pages of the third and final book of the *Principia*: "This most elegant system of the sun, planets, and comets could not have arisen without the design and dominion of an intelligent and powerful being. . . . God is living, intelligent, and powerful; from the other perfections, that he is supreme, or supremely perfect. He is eternal and infinite, omnipotent and omniscient, that is, he rules all things, and he knows all things that happen or can happen" (940–41).

One can only wonder if this excursion into the supernatural—appended to the end of his naturalistic masterpiece—was just another example of the insurance taken out by so many of his predecessors to assuage the ecclesiastical authorities. We do know, on the other hand, that Newton was a devout Christian and was deeply involved in controversies concerning the nature of the Trinity. Perhaps it is best simply to accept the fact that, like Descartes, his physics and his theology, however internally inconsistent, were both deeply held simultaneous convictions.

Certainly, when he went on to expound his second rule, there was a strong commitment to the unitary nature of the forces operating in the world. Here, he exhibits the specific influence of Descartes (or the general influence of the then current zeitgeist) by asserting what seems to be the same unifying principle expressed by Descartes in his rule 22, part 2.

> Rule 2. Therefore, the causes assigned to natural effects of the same kind must be, so far as possible, the same. (795)

This rule makes the point that the natural world is united according to laws that are of a single kind. In other words, it is not necessary to invoke more than one kind of reality. Both Descartes' and Newton's separate expressions of this rule emphasized that the laws of physics studied in this world were also likely to be the laws of physics in distant worlds. The application of Newton's laws of motion to celestial objects, originally inferred from terrestrial sources, makes this point very explicit.

I believe that Newton was also expressing in the second rule, covertly if not overtly, a commitment to a kind of universal monism. An extrapolation of this rule (which he may not have intended) is that laws that work for the body should also work for the mind. However satisfactory this idea may be for modern philosophy and cognitive neuroscience, it was a revolutionary one for the seventeenth century. Cartesian dualism dominated thinking in those days, and Newton clearly was a Cartesian in his attitudes toward the mind. When Newton the physicist asserted this axiom, an internal contraction was set up for Newton the man. The idea that there were multiple kinds of physical realities operating according to different "natural effects" would have been anathema to Newton the physicist. Nevertheless, Newton the God-fearing Christian was quite willing to accept the idea that different kinds of realities and thus different "natural effects" might operate in the realm of the soul. Indeed, he is reputed to have actively sought to contact the "souls" of the dead in the later years of his life.

Furthermore, Newton's Christian denomination was Unitarianism. He actually wrote a book, *A Historical Account of Two Notable Corruptions of Scripture* (not published during his lifetime, perhaps because of his fear of the Church's disapproval), in which he challenged the tripartite nature of the Christian God. One can only wonder if his foundation physical premise of unified causes also influenced this aspect of his personal theology. Nevertheless, by expressing rule 2, Newton was providing an intellectual foundation, not only for the universality of his physics but also, ultimately, for the modern mind-brain monism.

Now let's consider his next rule.

> Rule 3. Those qualities of bodies that cannot be intended and remitted [i.e., qualities that cannot be increased and diminished] and that belong to all bodies on which experiments can be made should be taken as qualities of all bodies universally. (795)

In rule 3, Newton was expressing the idea that some of the properties of matter that could be measured in experiments were properties of the matter and not of their state of motion. He exemplified this rule by invoking the property of "hardness." He then suggested further that a part of an object must be inferred from the "hardness" of the whole object, and that the hardness of both the whole and the part had to be of the same kind.

Here is the germ of the idea that objects have certain constant properties (e.g., mass) as opposed to variable properties (e.g., momentum, force, and acceleration). It was not until the twentieth century that the idea that constant and variable forces such as mass and energy could be interchanged transformed our world from a Newtonian one to an Einsteinean one.

I interpret this rule also to mean that Newton assumed that the physical properties that remained constant as scientists looked up into the macrocosm also remained constant as they looked down into the microcosm. This rule, therefore, is another expression of the universality of physical properties and laws at all levels and scales.

His fourth rule deals with the controversial process of induction.

> Rule 4. In experimental philosophy, propositions gathered from phenomena by induction should be considered either exactly or very near true notwithstanding any contrary hypothesis, until yet other phenomena make such propositions either more exact or liable to exceptions. (796)

Here, Newton was considering the practice of inductive inference that condensed the manifold findings of empirical science. Data, accumulated from experiment to experiment, are the foundation of truth, and no hypothesis or theory unsupported by those data can ever take priority over the conclusions to which we are drawn by induction. However, I see this rule as implicitly complementing Hume's critique of induction. Newton is saying that induction is okay, but that it is always susceptible to change given a new contradictory observation. Furthermore, antagonistic theories (in the form of "contrary hypotheses") however sound and plausible they may seem to be, cannot contradict inductively constructed axioms without empirical evidence. On the other hand, in the absence of contradictory data, Newton seems to be arguing that we should accept our axiomatic inductions as being true enough for practical purposes. This seems quite consistent with the idea expressed earlier (see p. 92) that there are pragmatic reasons for operating from induced axioms even if they may be a bit fragile.

Rule 3 and rule 4 also make another very interesting and important point when considered together. With respect to rule 3, Newton argued:

> Certainly idle fantasies ought not to be fabricated recklessly against the evidence of experiments, nor should we depart from the analogy of nature, since nature is always simple and ever consonant with itself. (795)

In a similar vein, he suggested in explanation of rule 4:

> This rule should be followed so that arguments based on induction may not be nullified by hypotheses. (796)

To me, these two statements represent a strong argument for the supremacy of empirical science over speculation. This was a critical point of demarcation, as I have noted, between the philosophical and speculative mind-set of pre-Newtonian times and the modern scientific approach to considering the nature of the natural world. This interpretation highlights the fact that Newton, the great theoretician, was also Newton the experimenter. His work on optics (Newton 1704), which was primarily an empirical study, demonstrated his constant efforts to test natural phenomena directly.

In the final analysis, Newton was asserting the primacy of agreement between his mathematical formulae and observed measurements. To the extent that his explanatory expressions did not agree with observations, it was the expressions that had to be changed or rejected. Above all else, however, observations always remained dominant over speculations.

This did not mean that Newton was a slave to his data. He did not hesitate to "fudge" some calculations in the *Principia* to improve the fit of his theorems. Westfall's (1973) discussion of Newton's manipulation in the observed data concerning the moon's acceleration, the velocity of sound, and the precession of the equinoxes has become a classic example of scientific wrongdoing by the best of scientists. Apparently, Newton had more confidence in his theorems than in what may well have been the inaccurate data of his time.

It is obvious that it is not possible to solely credit Newton with this idea of the emphasis of observation over speculation and even derived theory. It was the nature of the times, and many of his predecessors and contemporaries (e.g., Copernicus, Kepler, and Galileo) were also thinking in the same way. Nevertheless, Newton was the one who embodied the transition between the past speculative and the modern empirical periods.

These four rules set the stage for Newton's scientific strategies. They described constraints and guidelines on scientific goals that are still timely and meaningful. None of us today could go far wrong if we adhered to these admonitions. However, they are very general, and Newton had to turn to a second set of fundamental ideas to pursue his particular program of explaining mechanics in an objective and logical fashion. This second set of ideas—precise definitions of the terminology he would use in developing his theorems—consisted of only eight entries, but they defined the mechanical world that he was to study for him as well as for future generations. I list them here as they are presented in Cohen and Whitman's (1999) translation:

1. Quantity of matter is a measure of matter that arises from its density and volume.
2. Quantity of motion is a measure of motion that arises from the velocity and quantity of matter jointly.
3. Inherent force of matter is the power of resisting by which every body, so far as it is able, preserveres in a state of either resting or moving uniformly straight forward.
4. Impressed force is the action exerted on a body to change its state either of resting or of moving uniformly straight forward.

5. Centripetal force is the force by which bodies are drawn from all sides, are impelled, or in any way tend, toward some point as to a center.
6. The absolute quantity of centripetal force is the measure of the force that is greater or less in proportion to the efficacy of the cause propagating it from a center through the surrounding regions.
7. The accelerative quantity of centripetal force is the measure of this force that is proportional to the velocity which it generates in a given time.
8. The motive quantity of centripetal force is the measure of this force that is proportional to the motion which it generates in a given time. (403–407)

In more modern terminology, Newton's eight definitions defined mass, momentum, inertia, force, centripetal force (i.e., due to gravity and magnetism), and the means of measuring the properties of forces (their magnitude, their accelerative effects, and their temporal properties). These definitions, therefore, provide the foundation for a theory of mechanical objects by specifying exactly which attributes of objects are salient and the methods by means of which they can be measured. It should be noticed, however, that these definitions are all strategic. Although they provide a means of doing so, they do not answer the question of how they are related to each other or to their magnitudes. Rather, they provide a conceptual framework within which experimentation can provide the data necessary to state specific relations or laws and values. This, in itself, was a substantial accomplishment.

Newton's organizational genius and precision of thought was illustrated by the next step in the logical chain of ideas he developed. Indeed, it is in this context that his influence was to persist for centuries. It was not until the twentieth century that some of his ideas of absolute time and space operating in a Euclidean space were supplemented by the work of non-Euclidean mathematicians such as Georg Friedrich Bernhard Riemann (1826–1866) and Nikolai Lobachevsky

(1793–1856) and relativistic physicists such as Albert Einstein (1879–1955).

In Newton's *Principia*, deviations from absoluteness were dealt with by emphasizing the fact that time, place, space, and motion are objects of sense perception and the admonition that "this is a source of certain preconceptions" (408). It was in this context that he stated:

> Absolute, true, and mathematical time, in and of itself and of its own nature, without reference to anything external, flows uniformly and by another name is called duration.

and

> Absolute space, of its own nature without reference to anything external, always remains homogenous and immovable. (408)

By expressing these concepts of absolute time, Newton was asserting that relative time and space were mere aberrations of our senses and not real physical entities. It is in this context, in particular, that Newton's ideas were later to be modified by relativistic physics. We now know that ideas of relative space and time are more applicable to both the microcosm and the macrocosm than are his ideas of absolute time and space. These were worlds with which neither he nor any of his contemporaries were familiar. In spite of this limitation, the theory he developed of his world continues to be used in ours. Newtonian mechanical principles still guide our excursions to the outermost planets of the solar system as well as our predictions of events in the solar system, if not in the entire universe.

Thus equipped with general scientific principles, well-defined entities, empirical strategies, and a precisely defined cast of entities, Newton was prepared to develop his theory of the mechanical world as he understood it. His method was to assert certain axioms, apply mathematical analysis, and develop explanatory and descriptive theorems of some of the grandest problems that had come to the attention of his predecessors and contemporaries. The beauty of his success was that the axioms and the rules together accurately predicted the behavior of objects. Thus were confirmed not only his axioms but also his mathematics.

Ideally, the axioms on which a theoretical development is based should be as few in number as possible. One of the most egregious faults of any scientific endeavor is to continuously add axioms, premises, entities, hypothetical constructs, or degrees of freedom to permit a theory to fit a set of observations. Each new degree of freedom provides an opportunity that is merely meaningless mathematical curve fitting (Nihm 1976).[9] One of the properties of his work that was so immediately attractive to Newton's colleagues was that virtually his entire system was based on only three fundamental axiomatic laws of motion:

> Law 1—Every body perseveres in its state of being at rest or moving uniformly straight forward except insofar as it is compelled to change its state by forces impressed.
>
> Law 2—A change in motion is proportional to the motive force impressed and takes place along the straight line in which that force is impressed.
>
> Law 3—To any action there is always an opposite and equal reaction; in other words, the actions of two bodies upon each other are always equal and always opposite in direction. (416–17)

The first law is considered to be the precise definition of mass and inertia. The second precisely defines the concepts of acceleration and force and is specifically formularized as $F = ma$. The third is an expression of an observation that can be formularized somewhat trivially as $f_a = -f_b$.

The inductive and intuitive processes underlying his enunciation of these three axiomatic laws were not explained by Newton. As axioms should be in any such system of thought, they were expressed without explanation or derivation. We do not know if they were inspired observations created prior to his work or the results of some kind of feedback from an ex post facto search for principles that provided the right answers when the rules were applied. They may either have evolved from contemporary thinking or have been intuitions and inventions by the master himself. They may, on the other hand, have been inspired inductive extrapolations from his previous definitions. They are presented by Newton with but a minimum of discussion and then only in the form of examples of relevant observations—as axioms should be. Whatever their source, they represent the primary components from which all of the other corollaries, lemmas, propositions, and theorems of Newton's *Principia* are derived.

Herein lies the enormous intellectual contribution made by Newton: he started from this very small number of axiomatic expressions, based on some general observations about the way science should proceed and careful definitions of the applicable terminology, to describe the nature of the mechanical universe as it was known at the time. One of the most important and persistent theorems to arise from his analysis was proof of the theorem that the gravitational forces had to be moderated by an inverse square law. This had been suspected but had not been proven prior to Newton's time, and other relations had been suggested. Many of the other laws of gravitational attraction also emerged from his brilliant work, as did our ability to predict trajectories of the objects in our solar system.

The *Principia* in which these ideas were spelled out was an enormous contribution that would have made Newton's reputation even if his other work in optics and mathematics had never happened. Its conceptualization and suggestions for how a science should be carried out remains the ideal, even if the specifics of his definitions and axioms are not immediately relevant to other sciences.

2.6. ALFRED NORTH WHITEHEAD AND BERTRAND RUSSELL

Another milestone "Principia" that continues to influence the course of other sciences is Alfred North Whitehead (1861–1947) and Bertrand Russell's (1872–1970) important work (Whitehead and Russell 1910–1913) deriving mathematics itself from its foundation axioms. Newton's overall goal was to use mathematical methods (some widely accepted and some novel) to derive the properties of mechanical systems. Whitehead and Russell's goals, however, were quite different. Their goal was to derive mathematics itself from logical primitives (axioms). However different these goals may have been, their strategic approach mirrored what Newton had established as the modus operandi of science two hundred years earlier.

The foundation premise of Whitehead and Russell's work was that all of mathematics is actually a part of logic. This led them to suggest and then demonstrate that mathematics can be derived from basic logical principles or axioms. Logicism, as this approach was known, had been championed by Friedrich Ludwig Gottlob Frege (1848–1925), the father of modern logical systems analysis. Predicate calculus, with its symbols for logical (as opposed to arithmetic) relationships, emerged from his pioneering work (Frege 1879, 1967). It provided a means of formalizing relationships among statements that might not be numerical or arithmetic. For example, the predicate calculus provided a means of codifying such relationships as "and" or "is implied by" that are not quantified in the same sense as "add" or "equal."

Frege (1893, 1964) had shown that such a logical approach could be used to define natural numbers. Whitehead and Russell (1910–1913) built upon this initial development and expanded it into a much more complete (but, by their own admission, still incomplete) derivation of many other mathematical theorems in their monumental *Principia Mathematica*. They extended the logicism approach to encompass areas of mathematics including set theory, number theory, infinite series, as well as basic arithmetic functions. Nevertheless, there were other areas of mathematics for which the logicism approach was not able to produce critical mathematical theorems. The reasons for some of these failures were twofold, one practical and one theoretical. First, for practical reasons, Whitehead and Russell did not complete their proposed fourth volume. Second, Gödel (1931) subsequently showed that no deductive system like theirs could be internally complete and, thus, the task Whitehead and Russell set out was unavoidably incomplete.

Whitehead and Russell's *Principia*, nevertheless, has been extremely influential in logic and mathematics. It also emphasized how powerful the general axiomatic-deductive method could be when applied to many other spheres of scientific inquiry.

Whitehead and Russell did not need to repeat the general Newtonian rules for "good" science (see p. 102). By their time, the scientific world had unquestionably incorporated those ideas into its most fundamental strategies. It is now taken for granted, for example, that laws that work in one place must be assumed to work in others.[10] It is also generally accepted nowadays that empirical evidence must take priority over speculative hypotheses. The naturalism and materialism that were expressed by Newton in his scientific work (if not in his religious beliefs) have also become an unspoken foundation for modern, twentieth-century science.

It was necessary, however, for Whitehead and Russell to spell out the axiomatic foundations and the rules by means of which their derivations of mathematics from logical primitives could take place. There were three parts to this declaration of fundamentals:

1. Specification of "primitive ideas"
2. Definition of "implication"
3. Enunciation of primitive "propositions"

Whitehead and Russell specified six initial primitive ideas that they believed could not be deduced from any more basic ideas. These are the axioms of their model and the foundation from which they attempted to derive so many of the rules of mathematics. I now paraphrase what they meant by each of these primitive ideas:

1. Elementary propositions: These are defined as statements that are highly specific and make no claim to incorporating other qualifiers such as "all," "none," or "some." In other words, an elementary proposition is a simple statement of reality or experience. Even if combined with other elementary propositions by the operations discussed below, the combined propositions are also elementary.
2. Elementary propositional functions: These are defined as relationships between elementary propositions for which the variables have not been defined. For example, Whitehead and Russell suggest that if p is an elementary proposition, not-p is an elementary propositional function.
3. Assertion: Statements may or may not involve the truth of what has been asserted. If presented in a way that they are only to be considered, then they are not assertions. However, if presented in a way that claims are made concerning their truth, then they are assertions.
4. Assertion of propositional functions: An assertion can be made of elementary propositions. If the propositions are not defined, then the assertion is also undefined or, at least, ambiguous. Such assertions can thus be applied without any specific meaning or intent other than the relation itself.
5. Negation: If p is a true proposition, then not-p must be false.
6. Disjunction: In an assertion such as "p is true or q is true," the relationship between p and q is referred to as disjunction. (Paraphrased from pp. 91–93 of Whitehead and Russell, 1910–1913)

The next part of the foundation they prepared for their enormous effort was a precise definition of what was meant by implication. That is, they sought to answer the question of the meaning of the manner in which primitive ideas could be "conjoined" by the rules of predicate calculus so that two or more low-level propositions could lead to higher-order propositions and theorems. Implication was defined, therefore, as the means by which they (or any other mathematicians or logicians) were able to concatenate elementary propositions to produce more complicated propositions.

Although Whitehead and Russell seemed somewhat apologetic for what seemed to be a truism, the notion of implication, they stated that "what is implied by a true proposition is true" (94). However obvious this may seem at first, without the axiomatic and rigorous acceptance of the validity of the concept of derivation and equality, the enterprise that they set out on would have been fraught with hazards. Errors may still occur in derivations, according to them, but the validity of the implicative process is a sine qua non of logical and mathematical analysis of all kinds. I believe they were entirely correct in highlighting this concept at the beginning of their project rather than letting it fester in the background as a potential source of weakness and criticism.

Finally, Whitehead and Russell fleshed out their axiomatic foundations by asserting a set of primitive propositions, statements of implicative relationships that expanded upon the primitive ideas. These operations essentially established the rules of their logical analysis and may be considered analogous to the three laws enunciated by Newton. The primitive propositions include:[11]

1. Anything implied by a true elementary proposition is true.
2. If q is true, then p or q is true.
3. If p or q is true, then q or p is true.
4. "p or q" implies "q or p."
5. If q implies r, then "p or q" implies "p or r." (95–97)

There it is: a few basic axiomatic concepts (primitive ideas) and some rules like these (primitive propositions) for manipulating them, as well as a definition of implication. From this skeleton, Whitehead and Russell developed a considerable proportion of mathematics as we know it today. From this impoverished set of ideas, they went on to derive a substantial number of more complicated definitions (see pp. 667–74 of their volume 1) and then proceeded to develop the concepts of numbers, series, and, perhaps most important, what we mean by measurement.

Although it was acknowledged by them to be incomplete, their work certainly stands as one of the, if not the, outstanding intellectual achievements in the history of mathematics. For our current purposes, their contribution once again illustrates the ideal logical method for science—postulation of certain basic axioms and the derivation of a theory based on the logical manipulation of those primitive, acceptable, but presumably unproven (unprovable?) axioms. Both Newton's (1687) and Whitehead and Russell's (1910–1913) great contributions, although different in content and certainly in linguistic style, established this strategy as the archetype of the modern scientific method. By implication, they also defined the idea of a science in terms of its methods rather than in terms of the content matter.

In brief, both of these important works dealt with the problem of how basic assumptions and rules of procedure can lead to derived theorems. The approach is synthetic in the sense that it works from the simplest and most self-evident axioms up to increasingly complex conclusions.

It is interesting to note at this point that this strategy is quite different than the analytic approach of most social scientists who seek to observe global or partial behavior and then analyze (or infer from) that behavior into the basic assumptions that seem to underlie it. Psychologists, in particular, collect behavioral data (regardless of their theoretical orientation) and offer analyses of how such behaviors might be generated from hypothetical basic processes. As such, psychologists are constantly confronted with the formidable challenge of "the one (question) to many (plausible and possible answers)," an analytic problem that synthetic sciences do not generally face. That is, analysis from a whole to a potential, even plausible, set of parts leaves too many degrees of freedom available to generating true statements in the sense of Whitehead and Russell's "primitive propositions." Whereas Newton started from the particular and generated the general, psychologists are constantly trying to reproduce the particular from the general when they seek unique cognitive and neural mechanisms for a behavioral observation. The fact that there are many possible and plausible inferences that can be drawn from an observation is a high challenge for psychology, if not a basis for rejecting its claims to any kind of reduction from globally observed behavior to primitive components.

2.7. PRINCIPIA OF ECONOMIC SCIENCE

At this point, it is entirely appropriate to ask, However appropriate the work of Newton, Whitehead, and Russell may have been for their highly structured fields, can such a strategy be successfully applied to "softer" sciences like economics, psychology, and their compatriots in what are sometimes called the social and/or behavioral sciences? To answer this question we have to examine how these activities fit the paradigm that Newton and Whitehead and Russell established. That is the purpose of the remainder of this chapter.

In the past, "social science" theories have been mainly narrative, and occasionally statistical, rather than formal derivations. Initially, therefore, they seem not to have the quantitative structure of physics or logic that was attributed to it by Luce (see p. 145). Therefore, we have to ask whether the strategy of making assumptions (i.e., establishing axioms) and then deriving outcomes (i.e., applying formal rules of math or logic) is appropriate for them. Furthermore, the question of the quantifiability and measurability of the "social sciences" is going to be exceedingly important in determining how hopeful any attempt to develop comparable "Principia" may be.

In spite of these and similar forebodings, the strategy of developing a coherent structure for psychology and other social sciences and humanities has been attempted from time to time. It is, therefore, worthwhile to consider the degree to which such efforts have succeeded or failed. I now turn to a consideration of several of these attempts. In preview, it seems likely that, whatever the degree of their success, there are substantial differences between the physical and social sciences that may make the axiomatic-deductive method inappropriate for the latter.

A major theme of past efforts to systematize social sciences has been directed at the "dismal science"—economics.[12] The reputed father of modern "economics" as we know it now (economists were known as "physiocrats" then) was François Quesnay (1694–1774), a contemporary of Newton. Quesnay was a physician who was so appalled by the poverty of his French contemporaries that he sought to develop an equalitarian theory that depended on what he considered to be a set of natural rights or principles that should guide human economic intercourse. His list of thirty basic principles (Quesnay 1767), mimicking the three laws of Newtonian mechanics, included inductively arrived-at expressions such as "a nation profits from foreign trade" and "a balance of trade is not necessarily advantageous."

Quesnay was also famous for his graphic model of the economy (Quesnay, 1758, 1972), in which he depicted the flow of wealth from producers to consumers. This milestone contribution has been fully analyzed by Eltis (2002). It is of special interest because of its role as what was perhaps the first flowchart model of economics, a method that continues to persist in many modern cognitive psychological models.

Although it is generally agreed that he was wrong on many of his principles and assumptions (e.g., that the only real producers of wealth were farmers), Quesnay is, nevertheless, credited with taking what was perhaps the first step toward a quantitative theory of economics. His work included calculations that were precursors for many of the more elaborate mathematical theories that were to follow. Not only were his ideas seminal in the historic development of economics, but many historians also have suggested that his equalitarian ideas provided a compelling intellectual foundation for the French Revolution.

Jean Jacques Rousseau (1712–1778), another early philosopher of economics, although not mathematically inclined, also attempted to establish a logical foundation for economic interactions. Rousseau was fond of expressing basic principles in the form of rules that were no less fundamental—though they were less quantified—than Newton's axioms. Rousseau is famous for "basic truths" such as "men in a state of nature do not know good and evil." Economists now appreciate that his concept of the ignorant "noble savage" was a straw man.

Based on the "noble savage" axiom, Rousseau argued that laws necessarily evolved as a result of the accumulation of property and social organization. His work was presented in one of the most prominent historical documents in economics: *Discourse on Political Economy* (Rousseau 1755, 1797).

Another early economist said to have been influenced by Quesnay was Adam Smith (1723–1790). Smith also believed that there were fundamental principles guiding economic behavior. He argued that self-interest, as one example, led inexorably to economic success for everyone in the system. His major contribution, *The Wealth of Nations* (Smith 1776, 1976), continues to be extremely influential in stimulating the thinking of modern economists. Like the other economists briefly surveyed here, he, too, attempted to start from some basic assumptions about human nature and commerce and then to logically develop their implications in the manner of Euclid or Newton. For example, he attributed improvement in labor conditions to be a result of the division of labor. From Rousseau's natural man to the factory worker, according to Smith, the improvement in a person's status followed directly from the fact that we are able to specialize in the work we do. Smith was also responsible for the introduction of evolutionary or dynamic ideas into economic theory, an idea that has only recently become a major subfield of psychology.

The economist David Ricardo (1772–1823) was directly influenced by Adam Smith; he alludes to *The Wealth of Nations* on the very first page of his book *On the Principles of Political Economy and Taxation* (Ricardo 1817). Ricardo attempted to establish a more precise set of principles that could account for the value of human products. One of his first principles dealt with the role of labor, a major target of the thinking of Quesnay and his contemporaries. Specifically, Ricardo (1817) asserted that "[t]he value of a commodity, or the quantity of any other commodity for which it will exchange, depends on the relative quantity of labour which is necessary for its production, and not on the greater or less compensation which is paid for that labour" (1). There is a quantitative tone that seems to resonate with the words of Newton in this axiom of Ricardo's economic theory. From assumptions such as this, Ricardo went on to develop a theory of the value of commodities based almost entirely on the amount of labor involved to produce the product. The logical sequence, although not mathematical, was not antithetical to the great principia of the past, in which primitive assumptions are acted on by rules of interaction to produce more complex ideas about the subject matter under study.[13]

The next significant economic theorist to be discussed is the much-maligned Karl Marx (1818–1883). *Das Capital* (Marx 1867, 1992) was an enormous and influential contribution to the development of the effort to systematize economic theory. Needless to say, his other efforts in the field of politics, most notably *The Communist Manifesto* (Marx and Engels 1848, 2004), probably were even more influential in the developing history of the twentieth century. However, the economic theory and the political policy strongly interacted.

Whatever one's attitudes toward the pros and cons of modern political history, *Das Capital* was an undeniable monument in the development of economic theory. It was among the first to explicitly use mathematical notations to describe the role of such variables as labor, value, and time. For example, chapter 18 of *Das Capital* begins with a specific mathematical-like formula.

$$\frac{\text{Surplus-labor}}{\text{Working-day}} = \frac{\text{Surplus-value}}{\text{Value of the Product}} = \frac{\text{Surplus-product}}{\text{Total Product}}$$

Elsewhere, Marx specifically alludes to the "rate and mass of surplus value," in a manner reminiscent of Newtonian laws. We can assume that this was not an unappreciated metaphor, since Marx was even more specific about the regularity of the laws of economic nature when he stated that "in the midst of all the accidental and ever fluctuating exchange relations between the products, the labour time socially necessary for their production forcibly asserts itself like an over-riding law of Nature" (section 4, chapter 1). Thus, Marx dealt with economic processes in what he believed was a regular and systematic scientific manner, championing the idea that there are laws of the social science known as economics that are as sound and predictive as those of physics.

John Maynard Keynes (1883–1946) should be considered to be the originator of the next critical step in the development of economic theory. His discussion of the economic system in his monumental *General Theory of Employment, Interest, and Money* (Keynes 1936) is replete with assumptions and mathematical statements of relationships between well-defined variables. For example, he noted: "Let Z be the aggregate supply price of the output from employing N men, the relationship between Z and N being written Z = f(N), which can be called the *Aggregate Supply Function*. Similarly, let D be the proceeds which entrepreneurs [*sic*] expect to receive from the relationship between D and N being written D = f(N), which can be called the Aggregate Demand Function" (chapter 3, section 1).

From this point, the mathematization of economic theory was on a roll. Indeed, with the initiation in 1969 of the Bank of Sweden Prize in Economic Sciences in Memory of Alfred Nobel (i.e., the Nobel Prize in Economics), the preponderance of awards has gone to theorists who were heavily into mathematical analysis. Gerard Debreu, recipient of the Nobel award in 1983 and author of the influential *Theory of Value* (Debreu 1959), reviewed the history of the mathematization of economics (Debreu 1991) in a highly illuminating article. In it he noted that "[i]n 1940, less than 3 percent of the refereed pages [of the *American Economic Review*] of its 30th volume ventured to include rudimentary mathematical expressions. Fifty years later, nearly 40 percent of the refereed pages of the 80th volume display mathematics of a more elaborate type." Debreu did not expect economics to be as mathematically fulfillable as physics, however. He went so far as to suggest that "theoretical physics had been an inaccessible ideal toward which economic theory sometime strove." He argued that economics had not yet achieved the breadth of physical theory for two critical reasons. (1) The complexity of the systems exceeded that of simpler sciences such as exemplified by physics. (2) Not enough resources have been dedicated to experimentation in economics. For both reasons, economists have had to deal with relatively uncontrolled "naturalist" observations. What modern mathematical economic theory does accomplish, according to Debreu, is to provide a formal means of detecting logical errors.

Thus, economics has over the years become a highly quantified science in which formal relationships between the many variables can now be evaluated in a manner that some suggest is somewhat comparable to the work of Newton and Whitehead and Russell. Many other economists, such as Kenneth J. Arrow (1953) and Herbert E. Scharf (1973), have also contributed to the development of mathematical principles for this science. Ideally, economics would use the same strategy as its predecessors, elucidating axioms and then deriving theorems. To a significant degree, others argue, this approach has worked. However, the model is not as well developed as in the physical sciences and mathematics. Economic axioms are nowhere as quantitative as those of Newton, for example. Thus, economic theory represents a partial application of the axiomatic-deductive model that has so successfully illuminated other, if I may, simpler sciences.

We must now ask how well this approach has worked for other fields of inquiry, some of which are even further from pure physics than economics in terms of the ambiguity, complexity, measurability, and accessibility of their parameters and dimensions.

2.8. PRINCIPIA OF SOCIAL SCIENCE

Efforts to structure the social sciences (other than economics) have not been promising so far. One of the first "Principias" of social science was Robert J. Wright's *Principia or Basis of Social Science* (Wright 1875, 1974). Wright's goal was to examine the social organization of society in general, not any particular field of social science. Even a cursory examination of this early work indicates that his effort to systematize social science in the same way that Newton had accomplished for mechanics did not succeed. Wright was writing from the point of view of a religious zealot and, somewhat curiously, as a champion of communal living. Although he constantly refers to "laws" and "principles," any such axioms or rules are so deeply embedded in an archaic and almost unreadable mixture of theology and politics that they are undetectable. The clarity and logical order of a Newton or a Russell is totally absent from this early failure to systematize the principles of social science. Whether this is a result of an intrinsic limitation of social science, his effort to overgeneralize, or a lack of ingenuity on his part is yet to be determined.

2.9. PRINCIPIA OF ETHICS

Even further afield from physics and mathematics is the philosophical study of ethics. Since the days of Pythagoras (560?–480? BCE) in the sixth century BCE, it has been a hope of philosophers that it would be possible to develop a formal foundation for ethics; that is, one in which the reasons for our judgments of what is good and bad could be derived from fundamental principles. As an early example, Pythagoras, with his mystical view of mathematics, believed that the "principles of mathematics are the principles of all things." In other words, he was committed to the idea that the fundamental nature of reality was mathematical. This suggestion implied that ethics could also be derived from basic principles. His philosophical speculations included the social and personal behavior of human beings. To the Pythagoreans, the foundation of ethics was quite straightforwardly derived from the simple axiomatic premise that what was good was orderly and what was bad was disorderly. They argued that the keys to achieving order were the rules of mathematics.

By the time of Socrates (470–399 BCE) and Plato (427–347 BCE), however, this somewhat mystical, but mathematical, concept of natural philosophy based on mathematics had largely been abandoned.[14] The enthusiasm for the protoscientific topics and the naturalist approach that had earlier guided the Milesian philosophers led by Thales (625?–546 BCE), as well as the Pythagoreans, was waning. In its place, a Socratic school of thought emerged that directed most of its attention to ethics and other humanistic issues, but with argumentation rather than mathematics as its methodology. As a result, a gap, which was to broaden in the years to come, developed between natural philosophy (science, as we refer to it these days) and moral philosophy (ethics, as we refer to it these days).

Thus, the Pythagorean ideal of mathematics as a foundation for ethics had largely dissipated by Socrates' time. It was only when Plato's student Aristotle (384–322 BCE) reignited interest in natural philosophy and the role of mathematics that Socrates' humanism was replaced by what we would today call scientific issues, and the search for a natural science explanation of ethics reappeared.

It is a continuing debate whether or not Aristotle actually believed that ethical principles could be derived from basic principles in the way that geometrical theorems could be proven. Herbenick (2005) suggests that "Aristotle saw no objection either to using mathematics as an aide to ethical decision making for a happy life, or to mathematizing at least some parts of an ethical theory of eudaimonism" (1).[15]

Aristotle, nevertheless, understood that the methods that might work for one kind of subject might not be appropriate for another. In a classic and oft-repeated quotation, he asserted, "It is the mark of the trained mind not to expect more precision in the treatment of any subject than the nature of the subject permits" (*Nichomachean Ethics*, 1:3). In so stating, Aristotle was among the first to raise a question that has bedeviled ethicists and, to a certain degree, students of other studies such as psychology, for millennia: Is it possible to formalize principles for the human sciences in such a way that they can be "proven" in the same way as a geometrical theorem? Or, on the contrary, are the principles of human behavior so arbitrary or so complex that there is no way to establish them in the same sense as mathematical theorems? Such questions have remained extremely contentious over the millennia. The best answer at the present time is that there is as yet no satisfactory axiomatic-deductive model of ethics or any other "social science" that enjoys wide support and credibility. This general issue will be expanded on in later parts of this book, but for the moment, let us continue with our discussion of this issue for ethics.

This is not to say that there has not been a long history of attempts to develop formal theories or quantifiable models of ethics or to identify basic ethical principles. One of the first struggling efforts in modern times in this direction was proposed by Jeremy Bentham (1748–1832) in his book *An Introduction to the Principles of Morals and Legislation* (Bentham 1780, 1907). Bentham suggested that pain and pleasure could be quantified into a "hedonic calculus" by scaling methods, and, thus, a mathematical model of ethical behavior was possible—in principle. On the basis of this suggestion, he proposed that a "moral thermometer" was available to distinguish the ethical from the unethical. Since, according to him, pain and pleasure could be quantified, Bentham proposed a basis for ethics that did not depend on arbitrary considerations but instead on something as quasi-quantitative as a rating scale.

Herbert Spencer's (1820–1903) *Principles of Ethics* (1892) was another effort to develop foundation principles for ethics.[16] First among the guiding axioms he identified as the basis of morality and ethics was pleasure, specifically the ratio of pleasure to pain, as it had evolved over the years. This "self-evident" axiom, he argued, was the result of evolutionary processes in the vein that Charles Darwin (1809–1882) had highlighted in the mid-nineteenth century in his great work on the origin of the species (Darwin 1859).

Another early attempt to formalize ethical principles in a book specifically titled *Principia* was George E. Moore's (1903) *Principia Ethica*. Moore's goal was to "discover the fundamental principles of ethical reasoning" (ix). He defined ethics quite scientifically, arguing that "[f]or it is the business of Ethics, I must insist, not only to obtain true results, but also to find valid reasons for them" (20). From this perspective, Moore was clearly arguing against an anecdotal, subjective, or intuitive interpretation of ethics. His fundamental ideal was the classical Newtonian methodology—to define a set of premises from which could be deduced the ethical standards of a society. However, the topic he chose to analyze was far less concrete and quantifiable than the one Newton chose, and his work remains another largely failed effort.

Moore suggested that ethics was the "science of the good," and establishing what is meant by "good" became the main theme of his book. He distinguished between "things" that are good in themselves (ethical axioms) and "things" that are derived from the basic axiom or assumption that some things are intrinsically good (ethical theorems). His goal was to determine the "causal relations [that] hold between what is best in itself and other things" (37). At first glance this seems to be exactly in the framework of Newton or Whitehead and Russell. At second glance, it does not work.

Moore made a determined but vain effort to lay out some of his basic axiomatic principles. Among the first: "there is a simple, indefinable, unanalyzable [*sic*] object of thought by reference to which it [ethics] must be defined" (21), by which we may assume that Moore was referring to his metaphysically opaque concept of good. Beyond that, unfortunately, Moore did not go. The "causal relations" he sought were never made explicit, and the rules by means of which ethical theorems are "derived" never came to clear exposition in his book.

It must be appreciated that this 1903 book was written before the idea of applying mathematical or logical analysis became widespread in the social sciences. Therefore, we should not expect to have found anything more than a primitive expression of the potential nature of fundamental principles and the hypothesis that rules by which they may exert their influence exist. Although we might have been led to expect more from a book that promised general principles and lawful derivations, they are not there.

Another even more recent attempt to mathematize ethics can be found in the work of the prolific philosopher Nicholas Rescher. His book, titled *Introduction to Value Theory* (Rescher 1969), is another attempt to apply the rules of formal mathematical notation and logic to ethical principles. Before beginning this discussion, I should point out that Rescher's use of the word *value* was broader than just ethics. Instead, he defined *value* as a composite term for all of the psychological and social forces that "rationalize" or drive human behavior. To the extent that the behavior is positive, its inferred motivation is a positive value—as opposed to a "disvalue." A person who uses a value to determine behavior is a "subscriber" to that value, and the recipient of the behavior is the "beneficiary."

Rescher argued that values can have dimensions of many different categories; thus, his concept of value was very broad. He suggested that values can be differentiated according to the following classification scheme, each item of which represents a "dimension."

1. Their subscribership
2. Their object items
3. The sort of benefits at issue
4. The sort of purposes at issue
5. The relationship between the subscriber and the beneficiary
6. The relationship of the value to other values (19)

Rescher (1969) continued his discussion by pointing out that most attempts to produce a formal theory of values have eventually turned into what he refers to as a "logic of preference," a tradition dating as far back as Aristotle. In such a context, weights could be assigned to alternative forms of behavior in a way that recalls (albeit dimly) some of the axioms of Newton's schema. The glimmerings of a logical notation system comparable to the propositional logic used by Whitehead and Russell also appear. For example, principles that apply to every situation are "better" (or preferable to) than those that are situation-specific. Specifically, this value may be denoted by $\alpha P \beta$ (α is preferred to β). Rescher then tabulated a long list (ninety-two) of preference principles of this kind.

The next step—the use of predicate logic to operate on these "axioms"—however, was not well developed by Rescher. According to him, one of the main goals of such a value system of principles should be to combine the personal values into a "social fusion." Rescher proposed "somewhat technical considerations by means of which a relatively simple solution can be found for this seemingly complicated problem" (145). The solution he proposed was to develop a huge matrix of individual values and then to assume that "the desired combination function F to be simply the average (arithmetical mean) of its parameters" (148).

This is obviously an untenable strategy. First, the matrix of human values is hardly going to be a linear system, thus average values are going to be misleading. Second, the gigantic equations with the manifold interactions of the many components, although an interesting metaphor, probably are intractable computationally. There are just too many factors and too many interactions for this kind of strategy to work. One is reminded of the similar expression by the mathematical biophysicist Nicolas Rashevsky (1948), who proposed a similar equation to represent the "entire organic world" (619).

Rescher fully appreciated the limits of such a simple linear approach to aggregating preference. He alluded to the famous work of Arrow (1953), in which Arrow demonstrated that if one assumed plausible conditions for social preference, some preferences would eventually turn out to be incompatible with others. This incompatibility precludes logical analysis, a smooth transition from initial conditions to final states. Sometimes, according to Arrow, this creates disastrous consequences; one example being that fusing individual preferences into a social consensus usually produces a dictator. This "impossibility conclusion"—preferences cannot be combined without huge social costs—therefore, implies that a formal analysis of values and its subset ethics may also be impossible.

In general, it appears that although there has been a long-term interest in applying the axiomatic-deductive paradigm to ethics, there has been little success. Simple axioms such as "it is unethical to inflict pain" are approximations whose similarity to any of Newton's laws of motion is severely strained. As much as we would like to find reasons for our ethical principles (i.e., derive them from such axioms), no one has yet achieved anywhere near the same degree of success as has been enjoyed by physics. In fact, this review suggests that there has been little success at all.

Indeed, there is a powerful resistance to any mathematizing of ethics in today's philosophical circles. Philosophers such as Jonsen and Toulmin (1988) have vigorously argued against the very idea of using a formal system comparable to that of Newton as a basis for laws and morality. Each real-life situation is so specific, they argue, that any attempt to develop a formal deductive system would inevitably lead to nonsensical conclusions. This argument against the use of mathematics in ethics is a modern version of the rejection of classical casuistry, the idea that it was possible to apply general rules and principles to determine specific ethical rules.

Jonsen and Toulmin (1988) argued that history so far has rejected both classic and modern casuistry as a satisfactory means of resolving ethical issues. No matter what principles one starts with, there will always be additional uncertainties generated by any attempt to formalize ethical principles. They gave, as one example, the following syllogism as being fraught with uncertainty and value judgments from the premises to the logical steps to the conclusion:

> Willfully terminating the life of a human being is murder;
> Early abortions willfully terminate the lives of zygotes;
> Zygotes are human beings;
> So, even early abortions are murder. (337)

The problems of applying this kind of formalism to ethical issues, they argued, are profound. First, the universal and absolute principles suggested by the first two premises are, in Jonsen and Toulmin's words, "attractive slogans," but not really fundamental or consensual axioms as they may initially seem. Second, the act of identifying zygotes with human beings is loaded with many other scientific and controversial issues. Whether it is "true" or not is a matter of one's criterion for defining a human being. Regardless of which side of the debate one is on regarding this issue, all have to agree that there is an argument here that cannot be resolved by a simple measurement, an inductive leap, a derived theorem, or a repeated experiment.

Despite this historical antipathy and logical frailty, Jonsen and Toulmin do not reject the idea of general principles driving our ethical behavior. However, their acceptance of such a possibility is of a far softer kind than any mathematical or logical system would allow. They conclude by noting: "At end of the day, then all reflective moral traditions keep it in mind that the kernel of moral wisdom consists, not in a hard line commitment to principles which we accept without qualifications, but in understanding the human needs and relations that are nurtured by a life of reflective moral action" (343). Obviously, this is not a recipe for a formal axiomatic-deductive attack leading from a "hard line commitment" to strong axioms through well-controlled steps to ethical principles. It is, quite to the contrary, an argument against the application of any such system to the definition of ethical principles. Embedded within this advice is the conviction that human behavior is too complex and too situation-specific to be guided by the methods of the simpler sciences.

Ethics is, therefore, closely entwined with epistemological issues. The question of what it is possible to know about issues such as what is good and what is bad probably will have to be answered before even a prototype logical or mathematical system can be developed. There is implicit in this entire discussion a point made long ago by Bertrand Russell (1945) suggesting that mathematics works on the syntax of symbols but not on the semantics. It thus becomes necessary to understand to what the axiomatic-deductive paradigm can be reasonably applied before attempting to apply it. Our next topic helps us to determine how physics and psychology compare on this critical point.

2.10. A NOBLE, BUT FAILED, ATTEMPT TO AXIOMATIZE PSYCHOLOGY

The application of the axiomatic-deductive method to psychology in a way that was originally hoped to emulate the physical sciences culminated in a grand, but ultimately failed, effort—the work of Clark L. Hull (1884–1952). Hull proposed a formal model of behavior that was obviously based on the classic Newtonian idea of axioms, derivations, theorems, and subsequent experimental tests.[17] His books (Hull et al. 1940 and Hull 1943, 1952) probably come as close as anything in the history of psychology in applying the classic axiomatic-deductive method to psychological processes. Their coverage was mainly restricted to learning (i.e., effects of experience on behavior) as explained by the unobserved hypothetical components of learning inferred from that behavior. For example, Hull identified two of these inferred mental processes as "habit" and "drive strength" and attempted to show how these constructs were influenced by stimulus conditions. His major axiom was that behavior was controlled and regulated by the reduction of these inferred internal states, a statement that defined his ideas as a "drive reduction theory."

Following the precedent set by Descartes and Newton, and implicit in the *Principia* of Whitehead and Russell, Hull (1943) also set the tone by enunciating a number of guiding principles of his pioneering theoretical effort. His initial chapter offered the following insights, some familiar and some novel:

- Science must be both empirical and theoretical. (Here Hull presaged criticism that modern psychology is too empirical and not sufficiently theoretical.)
- Science must be deductive, logically deriving (in the Newtonian sense) theorems from basic "postulates." (Here Hull expressed a fundamental assumption of his work that psychological activity is susceptible to the same kind of formal manipulation as are physics or mathematics and that these methods can be applied to it.)

- Science must be distinguished from argumentation. Hull stated, "The primary objective of argumentation is persuasion" (8). He also said, "The primary objective of scientific theory, on the other hand, is the establishment of scientific principles" (8). (Here Hull implicitly acknowledged that much of disputation in psychology is not based on the axiomatic-deductive system but on unstructured, ill-defined verbal conflict. The hope expressed by Hull in these comments was that, at least in some restricted fields, e.g., learning, it might become scientific.)
- For Hull, there were no absolutely true "axioms," only postulates that are proven by the eventual success of the derived theorems. (In this regard, Hull was not alone. There had been from the earliest times, as already discussed, an appreciation that axioms were fragile inductions that are always susceptible to change.) (Paraphrased and annotated from Hull 1943, 1–15)

With these fundamental attitudes about science as his guide, Hull went on to propose a system of many postulates, reminiscent of, but not identical in concept to, Newton's three laws. These postulates represented the starting points of his theoretical development. Unfortunately, the list of postulates is long (sixteen in Hull 1943, and seventeen in Hull 1952) and not identical in these two publications. For example, postulate 16 in the 1943 book deals with the relative likelihood of response for incompatible "reaction potentials," whereas postulate 16 in the 1952 book deals with the "extinction of responses." With the hope that clarity can be maintained, I concentrate on the more recent list.

Hull (1943), as just noted, claimed that his postulates were not comparable to mathematical axioms but were psychological in their basic nature. Certainly, they were far more complex than Newton's three simple, sharply defined axioms. However, I believe that there is little conceptual difference between the two sets of axioms beyond their number and complexity. What Hull's postulates reflected was the difference in complexity between mechanics and learning. Certainly, the "truth" of both Newton's and Hull's "axioms," or "postulates," depended on their success in deriving theorems that adequately represented or even predicted subsequent observations. Newton's accomplishments were widely appreciated because they successfully predicted the behavior of mechanical objects. As we will see shortly, Hull's did not achieve the same level of success in predicting human learning behavior.

The nature of Hull's postulates can be exemplified by the one he identified as number 4—the law of habit formation.

> If reinforcements follow each other at evenly distributed intervals, everything else held constant, the resulting habit will increase in strength [$_SH_R$] as a positive growth function of the number of trials according to the equation
>
> $$_SH_R = 1 - 10^{-.0305N}$$
>
> where N is the total number of reinforcements from Z [the absolute zero of the reaction potential]. (Hull 1952, 6)

It is obvious that such a specific postulate involving a number as precise as .0305 must have been based on some particular experimental observation.[18] It seems that this equation actually represented the outcome of some experiment rather than an intuitive or integrative leap of inductive thinking.

Others of Hull's postulates had quite a different and much less specific tone, which were more like Newton's f = ma. For example, Hull's postulate 3 asserted that

> Whenever an effector activity (R) is closely associated with a stimulus afferent impulse or trace (s) and the conjunction is closely associated with the rapid diminution in the motivational stimulus (S_D or s_G), there will result an increment (¢) to a tendency for that stimulus to evoke that response. (6)

Here, the general inductive nature of the postulate came closer to those expressed by Euclid, Newton, or Whitehead and Russell.[19]

Thus, Hull's postulates or axioms and their related corollaries represented something of a mixed bag of inductive conclusions and specific experimental results. Whereas there should be a deductive leap from the former to the latter, Hull mixed up the two in a way that seems to have hindered progress on his great project.

A fundamental source of difficulty preventing the long-term success of Hull's approach was that it leaned heavily on the inferential construction of what were actually inaccessible intervening variables (e.g., drive states) that he felt were necessary to implement his model. These processes could not, arguably, be directly measured. As emphasized by the "one-to-many" difficulty in chapter 1, there are always many more possible such intervening variables than there are experiments that could distinguish between the many equally plausible alternatives. This meant that, in practical mathematical fact, many of his equations could not be uniquely solved. Furthermore, with so many "free parameters" floating around (see his extensive glossary of symbols beginning on p. 357 of Hull 1952), almost any behavior could be simulated by hypothesizing different internal states, different values for constants, and even the different relations expressed by his extensive list of postulates.

Hull's goal of developing a unified theory of human behavior also fell victim to the fact that despite his extensive system, it was mainly concerned with the circumscribed field of learning and, even more specifically, with habit formation. Even in that restricted domain, however, the complexity of behavior (an issue that we now associate with the nonlinear and probabilistic nature of mental functions) meant that his goals could never be achieved.

Hull's emphasis on learning cum habit formation was clearly a result of the zeitgeist of the times. The dominant behaviorism of his time eschewed consideration of processes, such as thinking and perception.[20] Learning was the topic of choice because changes in behavior could be so easily measured. Nevertheless, as complicated as it was, ${}_{S}H_{R}$ was just too narrow a domain for the goal of establishing a grand theory of psychology.

The most cogent criticism of Hull's theory came from Koch

(1954).[21] Koch listed his view of the three main reasons why Hull's theory failed:

1. Secure anchorage [to observable and measurable conditions and events] either in a quantitative or qualitative sense, [did] not hold in a single case for the relations of systematic independent and dependent variables to their intended range of reductive symptoms.
2. No given intervening variable is securely and unequivocally anchored to its relevant systematic independent and/or dependent variables either quantitatively or qualitatively.
3. No given intervening variable is related to any other intervening variable in the chain with sufficient determinacy to permit quantitative passage from one to the other, nor are certain of the variables, and the relations connecting them, defined with sufficient precision to permit "qualitative" passage. (160)

I interpret this somewhat technical language to mean that the links between observed behavior and the intervening variables (i.e., the mental processes) were not adequately established in Hull's theory. I go beyond Koch to suggest that these anchors and links are not possible for mental events in general. I further generalize Koch's comments to also mean that no other formal axiomatic-deductive theory has yet broken the accessibility barrier to the mind and that the effort may well be futile. Although Koch may not have wished to be so categorized (he has been identified as one of the main instigators of the change from behaviorism to cognitive mentalism), he clearly identified himself as a crypto-behaviorist by these three statements denying mental accessibility.

Koch then went on in his comprehensive and astute critique of Hull's work to assert that "he [Hull] failed not *merely* because he aimed at comprehensive theory, or because relevant empirical knowledge is too painfully slim to justify even far more limited attempts. We have tried to show that he failed because he did not adequately meet concrete problems of *empirical definition*, of *measurement*, of *quantification, of intervening variable function construction*, and various sub-specifications of all of these. He could not meet these problems because no one else had met them, or currently can meet them" (161). To which I can only add my personal admonition that no one is likely to in the future.

In short, Hull's valiant attempt to model learning behavior in the classical Newtonian sense was thwarted by the complexity of the behavioral system; the limited field he chose to study; the inadequacy of available mathematics to handle the uncertainty, the complexity, and the nonlinearity of behavior; but, most of all, by the impossibility of uniquely describing private mental responses. Some observers suggest that if Hull had had even a modest version of a currently available computer, he would have been able to overcome the technical problem of what was for him mathematical intractability. It is not all certain that this is the case. The discussions concerning combinatorial complexity presented in chapter 3 will argue strongly that no conceivable computer could have solved Hull's equations.

It is questionable whether Hull's specific attempt to develop a comprehensive theory of learning left a trace in modern psychology. His grand failure has discouraged many who would be so ambitious as to attempt even a limited imitation of Newton's *Principia*. Although there is no question that mathematics continues to be applied to psychological functions, the particular Hullian approach seems not to have perpetuated itself. This may have been a result of Hull's mathematical version of neobehaviorism falling out of favor, along with all other forms of behaviorism in recent years.[22] More likely, his formal models of learning were devoured by the complexity of behavior. The mathematical methods he used were simply inadequate to represent all of the variables that were involved in even the kind of well-controlled animal experiments he and his students performed. Suffice it to say that Hull may even have had a significant negative impact on further developments in psychology by proposing an overextended and ultimately failed global theory of learning.

What did follow (but not as a direct result of) his work were two distinctly different genres—a probabilistic-statistical approach to learning and other topics and a continued study of sensory processes. Only a few examples of modern research seem to have been derived from his approach, and those that did are much more precisely defined and limited to unusually stable and simple patterns of behavior. Psychological research has been pursued that could be described by simple linear equations of the form proposed by Bush and Mostellar (1951). One of the best examples of modern Hull-influenced work research is the carefully controlled work of Bitterman (1988), Couvillon and Bitterman (1980, 1988, 1991), and Couvillon, Ferreira, and Bitterman (2003) over the last quarter of a century on honeybee behavior.

What has replaced the grand goal of a formal axiomatic-deductive system for a major chunk of psychology, therefore, seems to have been a plethora of theories of more modest goals—microtheories limited to a narrowly defined portion of the full range of psychological topics and a heavy emphasis on experimental methodology and empirical results. There still is nothing like Newton or Whitehead and Russell's *Principia* in the works at the present time.

Other themes of psychological theory have also flourished. Another can be discerned in the work of computer science–influenced psychologists. The fields of artificial intelligence (AI) and neural net theories have proliferated with the enormous improvement in available computer technology. However, little of this work is derivative of Hull's work or carried out in axiomatic-deductive mode proposed so long ago by Newton. Most of the work in these fields is better described as simulations designed to imitate behavior by use of whatever methods of computer systems are available rather than by the methods presumably used by the mind-brain system.

2.11. INTERIM CONCLUSION

In this chapter we have seen how the classic and prototypical scientific approach exemplified by physics and mathematics becomes progressively less successful as the subject matter becomes progressively more human-oriented and, thus, increasingly complex. Whereas physics and mathematics were "natural" applications of the observation-induction-axiom-deduction-theorem-verification paradigm, economics seemed less natural, ethics appeared to fail completely, and the major effort in psychology imploded because of complexity and mental inaccessibility. In general, as our discussion moved further into the domain of the social sciences, it became increasingly difficult even to define the basic axiomatic principles on which a discipline was based.

Having examined the successes of the standard scientific methodology in physics and mathematics in detail and its failures in psychology, there is an emerging suggestion that the classic explanatory approach involving deduction may not work for psychology. One of the main reasons for this inapplicability was highlighted by Cummins (2000). He pointed out that psychology, despite the continued discussion of theory, rarely attempts to "explain" anything. Almost all of psychological research is aimed at describing behavior, that is, describing *how* things happen, rather than explaining *why* they happen the way they do. Cummins pointed out that both hypothesis testing in psychology and statistical data analysis are actually means of describing data. Empirical laws in psychology are never truly and generally axiomatic but are descriptions of observations. Most of the laws of psychology, he argued, are simply restatements of the observed data or "specifications of effects." Indeed, he points out that they are "almost always conceived of, and even called, effects." They do not serve as the foundation for deductive systems to explain observations. Thus, Cummins concluded: "What, after all, would a successful explanatory theory of the mind look like? We can be pretty sure what it wouldn't look like. It wouldn't look like a *Principia Psychologica*" (6).[23]

Cummins believes that the main reason for the inability to apply the "standard" scientific method to psychology is that psychology is a "special" science. That is, its findings are always specific to the context in which they are observed and they do not generalize.

We are thus left with a residual question: Are there any general principles, axioms, and premises of psychology that might help us overcome some of the serious problems identified in chapter 1? A search for an answer to this question is the topic of chapter 4. However, before engaging that task, it is essential that we examine the role of mathematics in psychology. This is the focus of chapter 3.

NOTES

1. It must be remembered as one follows this discussion that the present book is a compilation of principles, not an attempt to apply the axiomatic-deductive method to psychology.

2. The interrelationship of maturity and simplicity should not be overlooked in this context.

3. The *Passions of the Soul* was written in the year before Descartes died. Was this another example of the strong influence that fear of death (see Uttal 2004) had on dualistic thinking in psychology's history? Or, to the contrary, was this just another expression of the ability of even the best of human minds to tolerate the deep contradictions between science and theology?

4. Attributing the mind to the brain was not, of course, a new idea. The concept that the brain was the seat of the soul-mind goes as far back as the Egyptian dynasties, Plato, and Vesalius.

5. This, I might somewhat immodestly add, is also the main goal of this book.

6. The most recent English translation of Newton's *Principia* was made by Cohen and Whitman (1999) and is the one that I referenced in the following discussion. (The page numbers of the quotes from Newton are from the Cohen and Whitman translation.) It is surprising to appreciate that this translation was only the second complete Latin to English translation since Newton's time. The only earlier one was made by Andrew Motte (1729), published shortly after Newton's death.

7. Newton's later work did consider this controversy. He came down

on the side of light, at least, as being corpuscular, i.e., being made up of discrete particles.

8. William of Ockham was not the only medieval philosopher to express this criterion. It has also been attributed to the French monks Durandus de Saint Pourcain (1275–1334) and Nicole d'Oresme (1323–1382).

9. In reality, the mythical Sue Doe Nihm is Michael H. Birnbaum of California State University at Fullerton, whom I once again salute for his insightful spoof of mathematical theories of psychological function.

10. Some modern physical theorists suggest that the laws of physics might be different in different universes, but this is a highly speculative concept. We have no data from other universes.

11. I have not included all of these primitive propositions, just enough to give the flavor of these laws or rules of logic that Whitehead and Russell assumed to hold. The full list can be examined on pp. 94–97 of their *Principia.*

12. In the following discussion on economic theory, I am not concerned with the specific economic philosophies or implications of each of the economists. Rather, I am interested in their methodology, specifically with the axiomatic assumptions and formalities of the relationships they use to model the economy.

13. It is interesting to note that the principle of the amount of labor, rather than the salary rate, is still the best indicator of living standard differences among modern societies. How many hours one has to work to buy some object is inversely correlated with the general standard of living.

14. This is not to suggest that Plato was ignorant or unsupportive of mathematics. He is reputed to have believed that mathematics was based on certain innate properties of the natural world that were not created by or manipulated by humans. He drew an analogy between mathematics and ethics, arguing that ethical principles, like those of mathematics, were not man-made. Therefore, they were not subject to arbitrary change by humans. However, the modern consensus is that he did not attempt to mathematically derive ethical principles in the same sense as did Pythagoras.

15. *Eudaimonism* refers to a philosophy that extols human happiness as the primary ethical concern.

16. The use of the word *principles* in a title was never so often used as by Herbert Spencer. In addition to his *Principles of Ethics* (1892), he also published *The Principles of Psychology* (1855), *First Principles* (1862), *The Principles of Biology* (1864), and *The Principles of Sociology* (1896), none

of which were particularly mathematical or derivational. All were collected into a set of books titled *A System of Synthetic Philosophy*.

17. Hull was reputed to have kept a copy of Newton's *Principia* on his desk as a reminder of the goal he set for himself.

18. For that matter, one becomes suspicious of the precision of any behavioral measurement taken to four decimal places.

19. It is of historical interest to note that this postulate also anticipated the synaptic reinforcement rule proposed by Hebb (1949), in the same way as did Wundt—see p. 217.

20. However, it should be remembered that sensory topics flourished at this time for reasons associated with their close links to physical stimulus measures and dimensions.

21. This notable book (Koch 1954) was intended to be a critique of five of the most eminent learning theories of the previous half century, those proposed by Clark L. Hull, Edward C. Tolman, Burrhus F. Skinner, Kurt Lewin, and Edwin R. Guthrie. Curiously, half of the book is directed at Hull alone.

22. It can be argued that Hullian neobehaviorism was not really a behaviorism. When he invoked internal psychological states such as "drive," he was pursuing a strategy that was indistinguishable from modern cognitive psychology, which seeks to identify and measure what some of us think may be inaccessible and indivisible mental processes.

23. I agree completely and remind my readers that I argue here that this cannot be done and limit my discussion to the establishments of modern principles arrived at by other means.

Chapter 3

MATHEMATICA PSYCHOLOGICA

What Is the Role of Mathematics in Scientific Psychology?

3.1. INTRODUCTION

It has often been asserted that one of the most salient cues to whether or not a field of inquiry is a science is the degree to which it has been mathematized. (See, especially, chapter 2, in which I discuss the role of the highly mathematized inductive-axiomatic-deductive-theorem paradigm that is considered by some to be the epitome of scientific methodology.) Although there are many legitimate and honorable qualitative (i.e., nonquantitative) studies of behavior,[1] mathematics is usually associated with the most robust "scientific" activities. At the outset of this discussion, it is important to make clear that mathematical notation per se is not by itself a defining characteristic of a science. Some overtly mathematical studies (e.g., Rashevsky 1948) applied mathematics in ways that were almost nonsensical, since the resulting pseudo-equations represented real-world systems that were inadequately defined, immeasurable, or intractable mathematically.

Another problem with the use of mathematics as a criterion of science is that many writers talk about mathematics rather than doing it. The mere insertion of a few equations does not a science make. This is particularly an issue in psychology when the = (equal mark) does not always imply quantitative equality and precision but instead a general trend. Indeed, most of the most famous psychophysical "laws" (Weber's, Fechner's, Stevens's, Fitts's, and Hick-Hyman's, respectively) are only gross approximations. Certainly, none of them is capable of predicting the precise individual values of the dimensions they propose to represent.[2] It is only when they are averaged or pooled that smooth-response functions appear, and these functions vary from subject sample to subject sample. The derivation of theorems from this kind of data is, therefore, less than deterministic and definitive.

Nevertheless, mathematics of many different kinds plays a powerful role in organizing and systematizing the structures of the simpler sciences, such as cosmology and particle physics. The success of mathematics in systematizing a body of knowledge, however, depends on the nature of that knowledge. There are many instances in complexity theory, neural net theory, and other fields directly relevant to psychology, among others, that remain intractable to formal mathematics. For mathematics to work, a regular structure of objects and interactions must be present. Furthermore, the structure must be simple and reliable enough to permit the rules of mathematics to be applied.

Perhaps the main question concerning the role of mathematics in psychology is the degree to which this particular subject matter can be quantified. In one of the most insightful considerations of the role of mathematics in psychology, Luce (1995) began his discussion of the rhetorical question "Why should mathematics play a role in psychology?" by expressing his conviction that "[n]o one holds that all true statements we can make about a person's behavior are independent of each other. Some propositions follow as a consequence of others" (2). Thus, Luce suggested that mathematics has a role in psychology simply because there is sufficient causal structure in psychological processes to answer his posed rhetorical question.

However, Luce went on to express his awareness of the fact that the situation is not quite so clear-cut as the raw assumption of an interrelated psychological structure might suggest. Since Luce is among the most eminent mathematical psychologists of our times, his words have special authority. It is especially important, therefore, to inspect carefully some caveats he raised to his original assumption of sufficient psychological structure. In particular: "The existence of psychological structure cannot be in doubt. But what that structure is, is another matter. . . . The existence of psychological structure means that mathematical theories are, at least in principle, a possibility in psychology. Nonetheless, such theories may not prove realizable in a deep sense; the attempt may prove to be a contradiction in terms, an oxymoron" (2).

In this paragraph Luce acknowledges the constraints and limits on his original optimistic assumption of the interrelated causes of behaviors. Implicit in his caveat is the idea that while behavior and the brain are in principle susceptible to mathematical analysis, their complexity may preclude the application of mathematics as we know it. Thus, what is possible *in principle* may not be achievable *in practice*.

It is problematic, furthermore, whether the psychological structure that Luce assumed as a prerequisite for the application of mathematics may, in fact, be there. Alternatively and very likely, the structure may be so complex that its analysis represents an intractable problem for any form of mathematics.

Certainly, there are many areas of psychological research in which the relations are so transient, so variable, so complex, or in which the salient dimensions are still unknown, that conventional determinist mathematics does not and cannot work. For example, we have no mathematical methods that work well in defining the global attributes of a form. Although there have been many attempts to develop a geometry of form (e.g., Leeuwenberg 1971), most of this kind of mathematics is aimed at defining and then manipulating the components of a form (e.g., feature models or the ubiquitous Fourier analytic model). No mathematics has yet been designed that captures the global nature of a form such as a face in the holistic manner in which the human observer apparently operates.[3]

Luce then went on to invoke the necessity for testability and refutability, which all agree are the sine qua non of any endeavor that we seek to designate as a science. Testability and refutability are obviously not features of activities, such as raw speculation or theological dogmatizing. However, these issues are separate and distinct from the problem of the applicability of mathematical reasoning to a putative psychological science. One can imagine a science that is empirical and testable but for one reason or another is not functionally mathematical.

One of the most important contributions of Luce's (1995) article, however, was his analysis of the various kinds of psychological theories. He accomplished this by defining four dimensions along which theories can vary.

1. Phenomenological versus process models: Phenomenological models are those that treat the organism as a black box, observing behavior "without asking about the underlying, internal mechanisms" (3). Phenomenological theories include those of classic behaviorism as well as a host of descriptive analyses of specific observations. A process model, on the other hand, "attempts to analyze the black box in terms of internal mechanisms of information flow" (4). Process models include both cognitive theories of modular components (illustrated by the ubiquitous "boxology" of cognitive theories), control system models, or neuroreductive theories that attempt to link behavioral data to neurophysiological findings.
2. Descriptive versus normative models: Descriptive models describe our cognitive processes as they actually occur. Normative models "describe how we *should* reason, draw inferences, and make decisions" on the basis of how a logically ideal individual would behave. Discrepancies between the two kinds of model have been well described by such psychologists as Kahneman and Tversky (1972) and Tversky and Kahneman (1973).
3. Dynamic versus static models: Dynamic models take in account the changes that occur over time. Static models, for

simplicity's sake, ignore temporal changes. Luce noted that most psychological theories are static and those conventional dynamic methods of "differential, difference, and integral equations—have not, so far, proved well suited to most psychological problems" (5).

4. Noise versus models of structure: Noise-based theories accept variability and use statistics as the mathematical tool of choice. Structural models, on the other hand, are typically more deterministic and use algebra, calculus, and differential equations rather than statistics. The discrepancy between the two approaches has required us "to tack statistics onto algebraic models" or "to develop probabilistic models of structure" (5). While the former solution generally does not work, as we will see later, stochastic or probabilistic approaches to modeling have played a major role in mathematical psychology. (Abstracted and annotated from Luce 1995, 3–5)

Luce then went on to provide specific examples of the four dichotomies and the tensions that exist among them. In doing so, he both implicitly and explicitly identified many of the difficulties and limitations involved in the application of mathematical methods to psychology, both with regard to the dimensions of these four theories and with regard to the formulation of mathematical theories in general. His thoughts are especially germane to the overall question of the role of mathematics in psychology and the relevance to its claim to be a science. A sampling of his verbatim comments includes:

- "Each approach [to dealing with variability] is to some degree unsatisfactory, and a fully satisfactory solution has not yet evolved." (5)
- "All behavior obviously must arise from some internal activity. But it has been difficult to establish plausible connections between standard information processing ideas and some types of regular behavior." (10)

- "A theory alleging only one mode of behavior may be easily rejected by a person having two or more available." (12)
- "Little comparable invariance [compared to physics and genetic coding] has evolved in psychology. It is moderately rare to find a psychologist who, when confronted by a new set of data, invokes already known mechanisms with parameters estimated from different situations." (13)
- "When each model is unique to a particular experimental situation, all of the model's free parameters must be estimated from the data being explained. Frequently, the resulting numbers of parameters outrun the degrees of freedom in the data. *This reflects a failure of the science to be cumulative, an unfortunate failure of psychology and social science that is widely criticized by natural scientists. I view it as one of the greatest weaknesses of modeling (and any other theory) in our science.*"(13, italics added)
- "Coupling our lack of knowledge about local dynamic mechanisms with these statistical difficulties, it is hard to be optimistic about our ability to test these nonlinear models effectively." (20)
- "I do not see a satisfactory solution for coping simultaneously with structure and error." (22)
- "Until they [dynamic processes] are pinned down in much more detail, one cannot view this approach as more than an interesting speculation." (23)

Luce's comments are well worth deep consideration. The telegraphic manner in which I have presented them here does not do justice to his extended discussion, and I strongly urge anyone interested in the role of mathematics in psychological theory to scrutinize it carefully. Despite his career as a mathematical psychologist, Luce raises many serious questions about the role of mathematics in psychology and, if one chooses to make its applicability essential, to psychology's role as a scientific enterprise.

Machado, Lourenco, and Silva (2000) also pointed out that conventional mathematics does not fit well with psychological constructs.

Comparing physical "forces" with psychological "expectations," they noted that vector calculus has a natural fit with the concept of force. However, "in the case of expectation, we are hard pressed to find anything [about conventional mathematics] that fits" (24). On this basis, they distinguish between the weak theories of psychology and the strong theories of physics. Strong theories, according to them, arise from systems in which the axiomatic-deductive model works, the axioms are clear, and the rules by which theorems are deduced are sharply defined. Weak theories are those that are "any set of loosely interrelated verbal statements about an empirical domain" (23), in other words, a mathematics-free explanation or description. This view may be extended to also point out that there are some weak theories that are not "mathematics free" but that still do not lead to the derivation of theorems or predictions.

3.2. MEASUREMENT AND QUANTIFIABILITY[4]

Looming in the background as a challenge to psychology's acceptance as a science is the problem of the measurability of mental processes. This is another facet of the problem of accessibility that deserves specific attention. Our guide in considering this issue is Michell (1999). His critique is based on the definition of measurement by Stevens (1951), a definition that has been virtually unchallenged since it was promulgated more than a half century ago. Specifically, Stevens states: "In its broadest sense measurement is the assignment of numerals to objects or events according to rules" (1), and, "It seems safe enough to say that measurement involves the process of linking the formal model called the number system to some discriminable aspects of objects or events" (22). Stevens then goes on to assert that these two definitions are synonymous with Bertrand Russell's (1937) statement that "[m]easurement of magnitudes is, in its most general sense, any method by which a unique and reciprocal correspondence is established between all or some of the magnitudes of a kind and all or some of the numbers, integral, rational, or real, as the case may be. . . . Measurement demands some one-one relation between the numbers and magnitudes in question . . . a relation that may be direct or indirect, important or trivial, according to circumstances" (Russell 1937, 176; quoted in Stevens 1951, 22).

The cryptic aspects of these definitions have to be teased out very carefully to understand their underlying assumptions and the potential difficulties they engender for modern psychology. First, despite Stevens's (1951) well-known and careful attempt to define different kinds of scales, there is an a priori assumption in these definitions of the idea that the cognitive dimensions are "quantitative" in the same sense that physical dimensions or number systems are. However, this is not now, and was not then, quite as self-evident as these persisting definitions seem to imply.

The problem is that the measurability and quantifiability of mental phenomena is nowhere as clear-cut as Stevens assumed. Michell (1999) went on to note two major discrepancies between Stevens's canonical definition of measurement and what Michell referred to as the "traditional" one—by which he (Michell) was alluding to the definition prevalent in ordinary mathematics. He argued that both couldn't be correct if these discrepancies can be authenticated.

The first discrepancy is that numbers or numerals are not "assigned" or "linked" (in Stevens's terminology) to objects in other fields of science. Rather, according to the "traditional view" of the physical sciences, Michell argued that numbers *are* properties of the objects that must be "discovered" instead of descriptors that are assigned. In other words, for physics, mathematics is a reflection of nature and not something imposed on nature by an observer—the latter being implicit in Stevens's own definition of psychological attributes. The role of measurement in psychology, therefore, is quite different from that of physics, according to Michell, especially as Stevens and Russell had so influentially defined measurement.

The second major discrepancy between psychological and physical measurement lies in the fact that, according to Michell, Stevens (as well as Russell) spoke of the measurement of objects or events when, in fact, the attributes of the objects or events are what is actually being measured. That is, a distinction is drawn between the attributes and the objects themselves. These attributes or dimensions are not the same as the object, on this view.

This, then, brought Michell (1999) to the crux of the issue at hand: How do we know when a dimension is quantifiable as opposed to being merely qualitative? (The obvious corollary, of course, is, Are psychological dimensions quantifiable?) Specifically, he asked: "How can the presence of quantity be detected?" and "What are the marks of quantity?" (19). Michell's answer to this question was an empirical one (which he attributed to Helmholtz). To be quantitative, an attribute must be tested to determine if it contains two kinds of properties—ordinality and additivity. Ordinality is determined by demonstrating that the measure used is characterized by values that are always arranged such that if a > b and b > c, then it must follow that a > c. Not too surprisingly, this is not always the case with psychological dimensions; pleasure and pain are among two of the most obvious exceptions to such an ordinal criterion. (See Bartoshuk, Fast, and Snyder 2005, for a recently appreciated example of how ranking can distort the order of sensory experiences.) Similarly, the shifting of temporal order in such phenomena as classic metacontrast and apparent motion effects suggests that mental responses do not follow in neat chronological order corresponding to order of presentation of stimuli.

Likewise, according to Michell, additivity must be determined by "the [empirical] discovery of a method of connecting or concatenating the objects that indicates the additivity of the attribute" (Michell 1999, 69). He continued on to discuss some of the methods that have been used to "discover" additivity. One of the least useful, of course, is quasi-exhaustive measurement—simply carrying out a sufficiently extensive, if not completely exhaustive, series of measurements. The general tendency toward nonlinearity in cognitive process suggests that such a series of experiments would find something other than the kind of additivity Michell sought.

Michell's critique may seem arcane and irrelevant to the problem of whether or not psychology is a science in the usual sense. However, if the measurements we make of mental phenomena are not quantifiable in the same manner as other sciences, then a serious question must be raised about the scientific nature of many aspects of psychology.

3.3. ON THE INTRACTABILITY OF SOME PSYCHOLOGICAL THEORIES[5]

Psychologists seem generally unaware of the limits of mathematical reasoning. If the relationships between variables or components of a problem are nonlinear, too complex, or just too numerous, then the problems of defining interrelationships may quickly become intractable. We do not yet know what the threshold of this kind of in-principle intractability may be for psychology, but it is clear that even relatively simple problems posed by psychologists may be beyond our analytic or simulation powers. These are serious limitations, indeed.

This section considers some of the problems of the mathematical intractability of neural network–type theories in psychology. There are two reasons for this emphasis on networks. The first is that the context in which the problems are clearest is the domain of computer-based neural net theories. We know more about computability and intractability in that area than in most other fields of mathematics. The second is that networks of this kind are most likely the psychoneural equivalent of mind rather than single cells, neuroelectric fields, or macromodular units of the brain. It is in this context, therefore, that most of my comments will be based. However, much of what is said for network mathematics is also true for other kinds of formulations.

3.3.1. Mathematical Intractability in General

It is now appropriate to consider the specific arguments for what I have only suggested before—that the search for underlying neural or cognitive mechanisms of the mind represents an intractable challenge for any research technique, be it computational, mathematical, behavioral, or neurophysiological. My thesis in this regard is based on ideas that are becoming increasingly well known among mathematicians and computational theorists but remain largely outside the ken of cognitive neuroscientists.

The problems of computational complexity and the intractability of what seem at first glance to be relatively simple problems have been of interest to mathematicians for years. Classic (i.e., pre-computer) problems relevant to this topic were mainly concerned with proving that some theorems are undecidable. The most famous of these undecidable problems was whether or not the Diophantine equation (i.e., an equation in which the solution has to consist of integers) of the form

$$x^n + y^n = z^n$$

had any nonzero integer solutions for x, y, and z when $n > 2$. The classic answer to this question was that it did not. However, this conjecture went unproven for centuries. Although it was originally suggested that a proof by the great mathematician Pierre de Fermat existed in 1637, this conjecture was not finally proven until the twentieth century by Andrew Wiles (1995) in a complex proof that spanned 108 pages and depended upon other proofs in what initially seemed to be unrelated fields of mathematics. The point is that proofs of what appear to be relatively simple mathematical questions to pose are sometimes very difficult to obtain. Even then, Wiles's proof was limited. It had been known since 1970 that there could be no general proof, like that of Wiles, that could resolve the issue for all kinds of Diophantine polynomial equations.

With the rise of digital computers, many other problems concerning the computational capacities of these powerful machines became of interest. One is the halting problem of how can we tell at the beginning of the computation if a computer will eventually arrive at a solution. That is, would a program converge to a solution or would it become caught up in an endless loop repeating over and over again? Turing (1937) had shown that it was generally impossible to predict whether a problem would terminate.

Another of the most important theorems concerning the computational complexity of programs was proposed by Meyer and Stockmeyer (1972). They described their work more fully and expanded it to probabilistic systems in a recent report (Stockmeyer and Meyer 2002). The point made in these highly important articles was that there were some relatively simple logical circuits (comparable to a neural or cognitive network composed of only a relatively few components) that could not be solved because of the enormous number of steps required for their solution.

Meyer and Stockmeyer (1972) showed that a relatively simple logic circuit consisting of only a few hundred binary input states would need *more than 10^{125} logical gates* to evaluate its input logical expression and produce the single bit of output information asserting that the input was true, that is, that the particular pattern of input states had been introduced! Since they also calculated that "the known universe could contain at most 10^{125} protons," obviously this device could not be built.

The point of this anecdote in combinatorial history is the general one being made here: superficially simple problems can demand such horrendous amounts of computer time or mathematical power that their solutions are either in practice or in principle unobtainable. The corollary of this assertion is that both neural and behavioral processes have all of the characteristics of the class of intractable problems that combinatorial and computational complexity theorists have dealt with in recent years. The practical impact is that many of the network models that have been proposed over the years are intrinsically incapable of adequately representing that which they are supposed to model. There is no deep mystery here; it is a matter of the number of nodes in a network, the complexity of their interactions, their intrinsic nonlinearity, and the dynamic condition under which all such simulations must be run. It is not a matter of the available computer power; no matter how big the computer, its powers would be quickly overwhelmed.

The intractability argument of mathematical models and theories is both a strong and a pessimistic generalization. Nevertheless, it is essential that those cognitive neuroscientists approach their work with an appreciation that mathematics is not omnipotent and is in many cases inapplicable.

This potential difficulty is exacerbated by the fact that network ideas have been applied to an enormous number of psychological problems. Computer and mathematical theories have been proposed that learn some appropriate response, recognize different forms, or solve some logical problem. The "problem to be solved," however, is special to each proposed neural network experiment. Despite this enormous breadth and the acknowledged dangers of overgeneralization, it is important to keep in mind as we proceed through the following discussion that the difficulties of combinatorial complexity and nonlinearity are universal whatever problem is being attacked and whatever theory is being invoked.

The question is, Why is this so? The answer is that the difficulty in solving a mathematical problem goes up with the number of variables.[6] For a psychologically realistic theory, the number of variables may be so large that the problem becomes intractable or unsolvable for practical rather than theoretical reasons. That is, although there may be no intrinsic barrier to the solution of a given problem (as there is in the case of Fermat's last theorem), it would take what is effectively an infinite amount of time to solve it. This combinatorial barrier is known by many names. One is the scaling problem; another is the NP-complete classification;[7] another alludes to the information content of the neural network. All fall within the general rubric of combinatorial complexity and all, ultimately, fall victim to either simple numerousness or nonlinear complexity.

3.3.2. The Scaling Problem

The simplest indication that a problem will be unsolvable or intractable is that its computational complexity (i.e., the number of variables) increases exponentially with an exponent greater than 1.[8] For any such exponential growth function, eventually the problem will become too complex or require too many steps to be solved. The tension then becomes a race between having a number of components or steps that is sufficiently large enough to adequately represent some realistic mental activity and the increasing tendency to computationally explode. What is not generally appreciated by neural network theorists and connectionists alike is that many, if not most, of the problems for which we seek solutions are "inherently exponential" (Stockmeyer and Chandra 1979).

For example, the effect of combinatorial explosions in neural networks for relatively modest numbers of neurons has been criticized for many years but without sufficient impact. Minsky and Papert (1988), for example, warned repeatedly that the jump from "toy" problems involving only a few synthetic neurons to realistically sized neural networks was not always feasible. They pointed out that there is a rapid progression from soluble simplicity to intractability.

For reasons that are both arcane and obvious, no one has ever run a computer simulation of a neural network that even begins to approximate the number of neurons assumed to be involved in even the simplest cognitive process. Depending on the particular problem, computers are capable of running a simulation consisting of a hundred or so neurons, each of which is interconnected to a relatively small number of other neurons. The reality of the human brain, however, is quite different—billions of brain cells, each with as many as a thousand interneuron interconnections, are probably involved in producing even the simplest cognitive process.[9] Computable neural networks, unfortunately, attempt to simulate the effects of this dispersed neural activity with grossly inadequate numbers of neurons.

The undeniable achievement of the computer network simulation approach has been to produce behavior that is sometimes comparable with the behavior produced by cognitive processes. The equally undeniable disadvantage of this approach is that there is no way to ensure that the simulation actually instantiates the same mechanisms and processes that account for the behavior produced by a full-scale biological system such as the brain.[10] The very fact that such simulations inevitably fail as the number of neurons increases, often very ungracefully, suggests that neural networks of the complexity level used by current theorists are, at best, process analogs and not true reductive explanations of mental activity. Thus, a major problem inherent in this kind of theorizing is that only very small or "toy" problems can even be attempted.

Toy problems may be useful and may provide interesting insights and heuristics, but they are in no way definitive, no matter how similar their overt behavior may be to a seemingly related psychobiological response. This problem is exacerbated by the fact that there is no guarantee that the rules and axioms programmed into a particular "toy" neural network will prove to be the same as those that might be effective in a full-scale system. The much more usual outcome is that virtually all such toy simulations collapse when attempts are made to increase the number of units to a level comparable with real systems. This may be due to a rapidly increasing number of interactions as the number of nodes increases. In addition, simply increasing the number of input stimuli typically leads to a collapse of even those successful models that worked for small numbers of test stimuli. In general, it is certain that the "toys" will not scale up in a way that becomes meaningful before they collapse for combinatorial reasons.

This brings us to another issue. In principle, mathematicians know that it is possible to solve any problem by exhaustive search techniques: However, Minsky and Papert (1988) pointed out that, in practice, the number of steps necessary to carry out such an exhaustive search for anything other than a much-reduced problem quickly becomes enormous (262). They further noted that the possible number of interactions (moves and countermoves) in such a relatively simple game as chess prohibits an exhaustive search and a determinist solution to the problem of beating an opponent.

The formidable obstruction to valid psychological theory construction faced by neural network aficionados is that their algorithms also tend to diverge so quickly that the proposed tests would quickly require a number of steps that would be indistinguishable from the number required for exhaustive search. Minsky and Papert (1988), therefore, expressed their conviction that neural network theorists have a responsibility to be sure that the scaling issue would not make their own favorite model collapse under the weight of its own proclivity for intrinsic exponential growth. Furthermore, even the use of randomized or Monte Carlo procedures is not certain to overcome the scaling problem. They address this issue as follows:

> Moving from small to large problems will often demand this transition from exhaustive to statistical sampling, and we suspect that in many realistic situations the resulting sampling noise would mask the signal completely. We suspect that many who read the connectionist literature are not aware of this phenomenon, which dims some of the prospects of successfully applying certain learning procedures to large-scale problems. (264)

Minsky and Papert emphasized, despite the superficial biological relevance of neural networks and despite the preliminary successes some small "toy" problems have had, that efforts should always be made to determine the effects of scaling. They argued that this should be done before leaping to the conclusion that a particular toy theory was going to be upwardly scalable and thus represent a realistic model of some psychological function.

An important corollary of this admonition is that it is not only the engineering capability of computers that is the issue. Rather, it is often the intrinsic nature of the problem that blocks a successful solution. Simply seeking another model or theory is not likely to overcome the "in-principle" barrier to a solution exhibited by many problems of this genre.

3.3.3. NP-Completeness

The same limit on the solvability of some classes of neural network models arises under a different name—NP-completeness. Combinatorial complexity theorists have suggested a taxonomy in which mathematical problems can be classified in terms of their intrinsic difficulty and amenability to solution. "P" problems are those that can be solved by an exhaustive search in a determined amount of time;[11] "NP" problems are those that probably can be solved but only in an undetermined amount of time; "NP-hard" problems are those that are at least as hard as NP problems but may be more difficult to solve; and "NP-complete" problems are those that cannot be solved in any determined amount of time. NP-completeness is signaled by the fact that a problem is both NP and NP-hard. NP-complete problems are, therefore, problems that cannot be solved, not because they are in principle unsolvable, but rather because they would take a length of time that is, for all practical purposes, infinite, even if not literally so. The point being is that neural nets have a strong propensity to scale up very quickly to become NP-complete problems even though they may be P problems in their "toy" state.

The difficulty strikes close to home when we consider problems that are specifically psychological. Speaking specifically of the problem of loading information into a neural network (i.e., learning), Judd (1991) made the same general point about the intractability of a particular kind of problem that network theorists repeatedly attempt to solve. He said: "The learning (memorization) problem in its general form is too difficult to solve. By proving it to be NP-complete, we can claim that large instances of the problem would be wildly impractical to solve. There is no way to configure a given arbitrary network to remember a given arbitrary body of data in a reasonable amount of time. This result shows that the simple problem of remembering a list of data items (something that is trivial in a classical random access machine) is extremely difficult to perform in some fixed networks [comparable to the brain]" (7).

Judd went on to prove the NP-completeness of several different versions of the learning problem for several different kinds of logical interconnection schema. He also proceeded to show that many problems of this class remain intractable even if some kinds of constraints are applied. For example, it does not help to simplify the problem by limiting a neural network to two layers. Reducing the complexity in this way only introduces other impediments to "solving" a neural network problem, a caveat that was also pointed out by Minsky and Papert.

Orponen (1994) surveyed a wide range of different neural network theories and also came to the conclusion that many of the neural network algorithms that have been proposed so far by ambitious neural network theoreticians have already been determined to be NP-complete by mathematicians. He reports, for example, that it is not possible to determine if a "given symmetric, simple network" (12) of the Hopfield type has more than one stable state, a property that would preclude its solution.[12] In this example, a "stable state" means a single deterministic solution. "Multiple stable states" alludes to ambiguity, false minimum solutions, and, ultimately, intractability, which are properties that contribute to behavioral complexity and insolvability of neural network systems.

Orponen additionally points out that the task of synthesizing a neural network by comparing its inputs and outputs as would occur in a back-propagation system is in many cases (depending upon how the problem is formulated) also an NP-complete task. This is an important observation providing formal proof of the dictate that both mathematics and behavior are neutral with regard to internal structures and mechanisms.

Parberry (1994) provided a formal treatment of the challenge created by combinatorial complexity specifically in the context of neural networks. Although he notes that not all neural network problems are NP-complete, the fact that so many instances of familiar psychological theories are should be a strong warning to those who would seek to model mental functions with neural networks. Among the many instances of what are usually considered to be standard problems that Parberry found to be NP-complete are:

1. "Simple" two-layer logical structures in which the two layers either perform AND or OR logical functions, but not both (the

layers are alternating in function) and for which there is considerable convergence (i.e., fan in) from one layer to another.

2. Most forms of neural networks with feedback such as the Hopfield model (Hopfield 1982). Such systems are referred to as "cyclic" and may be unstable or fail to halt in any reasonable amount of time.
3. The problem in which the computer must learn a sequence of input-output pairs (the loading problem) even when the number of nodes is relatively small.

Parberry did acknowledge that some problems could be simplified to the point that they do become solvable, that is, in a determined amount of time. For example, he points out that "[o]ne way of avoiding the intractability of learning [demonstrated earlier] is to learn only limited task sets on simple architectures with limited node function sets" (239). However useful this advice is, it appears to be merely a recipe for testing "toy" problems, and it leaves open the challenge faced when attempts are made to scale a problem upward beyond "limited task sets" and small network sizes. For those interested in the history of the complexity problem, an interesting rendition of the story is told by Karp (1986).

Furthermore, there exist other compelling proofs from mathematics or other sciences that certain goals that psychology and neuroscience have set for themselves have already been demonstrated to be impossible in other contexts. Hilgetag, O'Neil, and Young (1996, 2000), for example, have shown that it is not possible to determine the hierarchical structure of a heavily interconnected network, no matter how many observations have been carried out.[13] Moore (1956) has shown just as certainly that no inference from stimulus-response relationships can ever uniquely determine internal processes and mechanisms. For that matter, there will always be innumerable remaining alternatives about the organization of a complex network, no matter how many experiments are carried out according to them.

Complexity and intractability signal their presence in another way—nonlinearity. Many of the processes of human behavior and its underpinnings are best represented (if they can be represented at all) by nonlinear equations, where the various forces interact as functions of each other. Mathematically, this means that the signal and its derivatives are cross-multiplied with themselves and with each other. One result of this nonlinearity is that the various equations of a model cannot be added together in the manner called linear superimposition. A serious result of nonlinearity is that the equations representing such a system are not generally solvable without extreme simplification or by simulation rather than an analytic solution. Thus, some situations exist in which a mathematical representation is possible, but it is sterile; the representative equations are intractable.

Thus, psychology or at least some parts of its domain are simply not amenable to explanatory mathematical theory in the reductive sense that is so longed for by many of its practitioners. It is very important to point out that the fact that some of its problems are intractable does not by itself deny a subject matter the right to claim to be a science. Physics, for example, deals with comparable limits (e.g., the irreversibility of time, the impossibility of perpetual motion, and the speed of light) in a way that does not retard empirical or theoretical progress in the field. However, psychology's limitations must be understood and dealt with in a way that does not lead us to waste our time trying to build our own psychological version of a "perpetual motion machine." Although not reductive or explanatory, a mathematical formulation can often be very useful in describing and even predicting the nature of a system's performance.

The meaning of this digression into the limits induced by combinatorial complexity or by other mathematical constraints is that many of the explanatory tasks that psychologists have set for themselves are manifestly impossible. They are no more likely to solve some of their stated problems than a theologian is to prove or disprove the existence of God.

3.3.4. The Limits of Computational Simplification

Current efforts to use neural networks as theories of mind have had to be turned to the use of simplifying constraints. The most successful have been simplified lattices in which all of the components were identical and the interconnections between components all functioned in the same way. The earliest successes in neural network modeling (e.g., the work of Ratliff and Hartline 1959) were for models of this kind. Happily, the model accurately represented the simple nature of the eye anatomy of the *Limulus polyphemus*—the horseshoe crab. Each ommatidium (visual receptor cell) was identical to each of its neighbors, and each interconnection exerted only a simple, reciprocal, and inhibitory effect on its neighbors. This simple, regular, almost crystalline arrangement could be well simulated by a relatively simple computation structure. The model was successful in predicting the neural responses when stimulated and was confirmed by neurophysiological studies. As such it had a profound, but ultimately misleading, influence on subsequent thinking.

However, most of the neural networks proposed so far are not of this highly simplified and regular genre. Nor are we able to take full advantage of the simplification based on homogeneity used by the gas dynamicists or the cosmologists, because the networks used in the brain are intrinsically irregular and heterogeneous. Indeed, the goal of most of the learning-type networks is to modulate the weight or strength of the connections between nodes in a dynamic way that is dependent upon the inputs. The trend is, therefore, toward increasing structural (i.e., synaptic weight) diversity and, therefore, away from the kind of simplification that even simple forms of regularity would offer. In other words, it seems increasingly likely that most of the proposed neural network theories simulating the learning process are NP-complete.

In some cases, it is possible to develop shortcut mathematical techniques that can take advantage of this regularity. For example, Fast Fourier Transforms have been developed that permit the application of this powerful technique by compartmentalizing the calculations to avoid high-level and long-distance interactions. But, even then, complex problems can still overwhelm these shortcut techniques.

What else can be done to permit solutions to some subset of the seemingly intractable problems attacked by network theorists? One possibility is to apply the method that was originally proposed by Rosenblatt (1958, 1962)—apply random or Monte Carlo techniques. Although randomness is not a universal solution, it can overcome some obstacles to a correct solution, such as the false energy minimum. Random excursions could sometimes lead to a solution accidentally "popping out" of a false minimum solution and thus have a "chance" to find the true solution. Nevertheless, there remain barriers to the glib application of stochastic methods. For example, Stockmeyer and Meyer (2002) showed that their theorem demonstrating the impracticality of deterministic logic circuitry also applies to randomly interconnected logical units.

Another simplification strategy that is ubiquitous, but fraught with its own problems, is to break up the problem into a set of component modules, in other words, to partition it into subtasks. This has the possible advantage of simplifying the task at hand by solving parts of the mind-brain problem independently. Dayanand (1999), for example, working in my laboratory, developed a surface reconstruction method that works by breaking up the whole task into a series of small, tessellated triangles. The triangles were then interconnected by assuming that the slopes of the triangles must be identical at the points of intersection. What had been an enormously difficult problem of many variables, nodes, and interconnections had been reduced to local and almost trivial computations. Of course, the combinatorial problem still remains. There is a practical limit to the number of triangles that can be dealt with for any given surface. Another strategy is to deal with a coarse-grained version of what is in reality a fine-grained problem. This already-mentioned strategy was used by Bornholdt (2005) in dealing with genetic networks.

Finally, another means of simplifying a complex problem is known as regularization. The modeling of a complex process with even a relatively modest number of variables can, as we have seen, typically become very complex, very quickly. One way to think of regularization is as the imposition of an artificial requirement for a smooth solution. One kind of regularization helps to reduce complexity by adding a cost factor that increases with the deviation of a particular value from a smooth or locally average function. In some cases, this artificial smoothing may permit a solution to be obtained where none had been possible before.

Using parallel computers has also from time to time been considered to be a means of solving some very difficult problems. Judd (1991) dealt with the value of parallelism in computational models, per se. He pointed out, however, that, in many cases, it just will not work. His argument goes as follows: "This [intractability] is true whether the algorithm is conceived as a nodal entity working in a distributed fashion with other nodes or as a global entity working in a centralized fashion on the network as a whole" (43). He goes on: "The parallelism inherent in most neural network systems does not avoid this intractability. An exponential expression (c^x) cannot be contained by dividing it by a linear expression (cx). In many connectionist approaches to learning, there is a strong reason why large numbers of computing elements will not accomplish the loading problem in feasible time. . . . Naïve attempts to exploit parallelism can actually be counterproductive" (43).

The key in all of these approximation methods used to solve "intrinsically difficult problems" (Stockmeyer and Chandra 1979) is adequately constraining the problem under attack to a simple enough condition to be computable. However, it must be appreciated that whatever gains one makes in simplification comes at a cost. The cost may be in accuracy of the solution, uncertainty in the produced probabilities, or in approximate rather than deterministic solutions. There is no free lunch! At the worst, one may lose the essential nature of the problem under attack!

Clearly, we do not yet have a coherent and complete proof of the tractability or intractability of neural net theories of mind. The suggestion, however, is that they are similar to other problems that are demonstrably intractable. As Karp (1986) pointed out in his Turing Award Lecture: "The NP-completeness results proved in the 1970s showed that, unless P = NP, the great majority of the problems of combinatorial optimization that arise in commerce, science, and engineering are intractable: No methods for their solution can completely evade combinatorial explosions" (105). The fact that such an explosion can happen with relatively few nodes and that, in many if not most cases, simplifications or approximations cannot be applied without losing the crux of the problem argues strongly that neural network models, although the most relevant ontologically, may well be epistemological dead ends for psychology.

3.4. WHEN IS A LAW NOT A LAW?

Even within the domain of psychological studies that are amenable to mathematical analysis, there are further general constraints on what can possibly be considered as a law or a feasible theory. Falmagne (2004) has reminded us of several of these in a very important paper that, although mainly directed at the physical sciences, can be easily interpreted in terms of the laws and theories of psychology.[14]

Falmagne first notes, from his special point of view, that a scientific law is an "equation in which the variables represent physical quantities such as mass, length, (absolute) temperature or time duration" (1341–42). Such a law, he argues further, must be "invariant with respect to changes in the units of its variables" (1342). If one changes the units of the equation and the equation changes in some fundamental way, then the law is not valid, and any theory deduced from it may be invalid. Falmagne refers to this kind of unit invariance as "meaningfulness."

For example, a ratio whose significance depends upon the units used would not be meaningful. Suppes and Zinnes (1963) pointed out the ratio of two temperatures as an example of a meaningless relation.

The significance of the ratio (i.e., whether it is large or small) depends on the units, be they centigrade, Fahrenheit, or Kelvin, as well as the absolute values of the measurements in whatever scale is used. On the other hand, the ratio of the differences between high and low temperatures on two days will be the same regardless of the units used. (The size of the units essentially cancels out in this case, but not in the first.) Thus, this would be a meaningful measure.

The point is that, given the problems psychology has with its ill-defined units of mental activity, many of the mathematical relationships proposed to describe internal mental interrelationships may prove to be meaningless! Although superficially mathematical (the notation may be mathematical), the designated relationships may be unrelated to the actual processes and mechanisms of mental activity.

Second, Falmagne goes on to propose that to be a law, an expression must also be "order invariant." That is, transformations of various kinds of the independent variables must not affect the dependent variable. If the dependent variable is dependent upon the order (or other kinds of transformations) of the independent variables, then it is said not to be "order-invariant."

Should a putative law not obey the meaningfulness and order-invariance criteria, then there are significant prices to be paid in its formulation and in any derived theorems. However, if it does, there are some advantages. Falmagne (2004) spells out these costs and benefits in detail.

1. Permitting non-meaningful laws would foster the establishment of a scientific Tower of Babel in which the mathematical form of a model would depend upon the particular measurement units favored by a community of scientists, promoting confusion.
2. More importantly, any empirical mechanism is by essence unit free, and so can never be regarded as a model (in the logical sense of the term) of a non-meaningful scientific law. Non-meaningful expressions are poor expressions of reality.

3. . . . formulating meaningfulness as one or more of the axioms of a scientific theory may result in a weakening, or at least a reformulation, of other axioms. This may produce a refocusing of the theory, and conceivably, a better understanding of the basic processes at work. (1380–81)

Although Falmagne's study was aimed at the physical sciences, it seems quite clear from considering the implications spelled out in his list that the putative scientific laws of psychology may well be seriously compromised by a failure to satisfy the principles of meaningfulness and order invariance. The history of psychological theory, to say the least, is not unfairly characterized as a "Tower of Babel." Beyond the sensory inputs and motor output, the relation to units of measurement of cognitive processes is so fragile that the idea of a "meaningful" psychological law is barely imaginable for mental constructs. Data obtained in scaling (i.e., rank order) studies, as I mentioned earlier, often do not even approximate the conditions necessary to be called meaningful, and many other experimental protocols are poorly linked to measures that can be called order-invariant. Not the least of these curious results are the causal effects of later stimuli on earlier ones as exemplified by apparent movement and metacontrast phenomena.

Indeed, the basic problem of what measurement means in psychology has remained a continuing problem for mathematical psychologists. As Suppes and Zinnes (1963) also pointed out early on in the history of modern mathematical psychology, two problems confound psychological theorists:

1. . . . justification of the assignment of numbers to [psychological] objects and phenomena.
2. . . . specification of the degree to which this assignment is unique. (4)

Given that these problems still represent unsolved challenges for psychology, in particular (see, e.g., Michell 1999 and the discussion on p.

149), it is difficult to accept the concept of meaningfulness or invariance of the units and dimensions of psychological science. Difficult, of course, does not mean impossible, but we should be forewarned; nothing may be as simple or obvious as it may seem initially.

Rarely are the transformations and units of a psychological experiment explicitly considered and made a part of the initial formulation of a theory. Thus, there is a plausible argument that psychological theories often do not meet either the meaningfulness or the order-invariance criteria necessary for the generation of feasible scientific (i.e., mathematical) theories. This may mean that it is going to be difficult to go beyond the qualitative theories typical of so much of psychology to the quantitative ones so ardently desired. Of course, this is an interpretive leap from the rigor of Falmagne's criteria to the domain of psychology. Others may draw different conclusions. The bottom line is that mathematics cannot be uncritically applied in psychological theorizing.

3.5. ON STOCHASTIC VERSUS DETERMINISTIC MATHEMATICS

Much of what I say in this chapter and in later chapters concerning the applicability of mathematics to psychology is based on a comparison with the classic Newtonian model. From a certain perspective, I must acknowledge, this is not entirely fair. As we shall see, one of the universally accepted ontological principles of psychology is that its findings are highly variable and can be best explained on a probabilistic rather than a strictly deterministic or analytic basis. Indeed, the greatest successes of mathematical psychology have been in its use of stochastic rather than deterministic models. Although variability is present in all sciences, special attention to it has been forced in psychology by the widely dispersed values of measurements taken in almost any conceivable experiment.[15] Studies of choice behavior and the grand signal detection theory that are so widely appreciated in psychology are actually based on a priori assumptions of probabilistic distributions of potential stimuli, decisions, and responses. Rather than specifying the precise deterministic relationships between the stimulus and response, many of the most successful models of behavior have probabilities of both stimuli and responses scattered at all levels of their analysis.

In general, simple deterministic theories have not served psychology very well. Because of the very large number of factors that may influence any behavior, measurements always vary from trial to trial and from experiment to experiment. Thus, precise representation or prediction of a particular individual behavior is unlikely. Only in the sensory or motor fields of inquiry do simple functions of the form R = f(S) seem to provide useful predictive models. Even then, such a simple functional relationship is usually the statistical distillation and condensation of a substantial body of moderately variable experimental outcomes. The data from virtually every sensory experiment are usually best described by a psychometric function in which the independent variable may be precisely specified but in which the dependent variable scores are either probabilistically distributed or summarized as central tendencies. Rather than R = f(S), the modal relationship is p(R) = f(s) (where p indicates "the probability of" and = represents "is strongly influenced by" rather than equality) for virtually all psychologically relevant experiments.

The practical implication of the intrinsically stochastic nature of psychological data is that, although probabilities may be assigned, it is unusual to obtain the same result from trial to trial or from experiment to experiment. Actual behavioral functions are, therefore, intrinsically complex, driven by a plethora of unknown forces.[16] The net effect is that they appear to be distributed (to a greater or lesser degree) on the dependent variable axis. The spread of this distribution may actually be determined by a complex of factors. For this reason, stochastic mathematical techniques are typically used to model behavioral data.

Unfortunately, any model based on random influences and variable effects is not predictive in the same sense as a deterministic description. Improbable things occur and probable ones sometimes surprise us by their absence. The model may perfectly describe the statistics of the ensemble of responses but completely miss the value of a particular response.

Thus, stochastic models describe the ensemble of possible behaviors and may even indicate, within some limits, a range of their expected values. However, they are useless in predicting the occurrence of specific cases. In the present context, the emerging question is, Is a stochastic description the equivalent of scientific understanding? Clearly, this is also a question that has beleaguered physicists. Many, including the universal hero Albert Einstein, were unwilling to accept probabilistic models as complete descriptions. Einstein apparently always believed that quantum mechanical theories, based as they were on probabilistic assumptions, were incomplete because of as-yet "undiscovered principles."

On the other hand, many modern quantum physicists assume that the stochastic nature of microparticles is fundamentally just that—stochastic. It is not a matter of missing information or hidden variables; rather, randomness and probabilities are the essence of their true nature. Psychologists have their own analogs of these theoretical differences, and they are related to the same underlying issue: Is behavior intrinsically stochastic or is it intrinsically deterministic? The answer to this question will ultimately speak to the future of psychology in the same way it has motivated physics for the last half century.

Clearly, this debate is not yet concluded, and the scientific standing of stochastic models is still controversial in psychology as well as in physics.[17] The residual issue is, Are the stochastic theories of psychology just a temporary expedient, as quantum mechanics was originally thought to be in physics? Or, to the contrary, are they the best that we can do given the nature of both physical and mental activity? These questions speak directly to the kind of mathematics that should be used by psychologists to develop their theories.

The history of modern mathematical psychology is mainly the history of stochastic models. It is rare to find a deterministic model, law, or expression based on conventional analytical mathematics that is more than just a gross approximation.[18] Those that promise or imply more are usually limiting cases actually based on highly specialized observations. These include some of the most famous, apparently deterministic equations, such as Weber's (1834, 1942) law of just noticeable differences, Stevens's (1961) power function law of sensory magnitudes, and Rescorla and Wagner's (1972) law of classical conditioning. It is now well known that such models are always incomplete and inaccurate in the same sense as stochastic models. The problem is that the causal factors in determining behavior are always complex and multideterminate. Simple laws or limiting cases like these three always obscure the fundamental complexity of the underlying mechanisms and processes.

It is interesting to note in this context that classic Newtonian physics ignored probabilities. It was not until some years later that such advances as quantum theory introduced the concept of probability into mechanics. The reason for this development was that physics was driven to probabilistic models when new observational tools made it clear that uncertainty was a property of the microcosm.

Psychology, on the other hand, has been faced with this problem from its inception.[19] Most of the major developments in mathematical psychology in the last half century, including Estes's (1950) stimulus sampling theory, Tanner and Swets's (1954) adaptation of signal detection theory for psychology, Luce's (1959) work on individual choice behavior, and Tversky's (1969) preference intransitivity theory, have involved stochastic methods. Unfortunately, none of these models offer precise control or prediction of individual behavior. The suggestion is that they probably cannot "in principle" do so.

3.6. INTERIM CONCLUSION

The conclusion to which I am driven by these comments, and by other issues discussed in this section, is that psychology still has not demonstrated that conventional analytic mathematics is a necessary and sufficient tool for our science as it is in some of the other natural sciences.

Many of its applications are superficial or questionable, if not erroneous, with a superfluity of free parameters used to provide a fit between the model and the data. In other cases, there is little more than a mathematical notation to provide a link between mathematics and ill-defined psychological variables.

The mathematical techniques that have been most successful are the stochastic, probabilistic ones that assume some sort of random processes are influencing the outcome. Whether these models work because that is the way behavior is or because they provide a means of finessing the problem of multiple causation is not known. The characteristics of psychology that are usually raised as impediments to deterministic mathematics are complexity, hidden processes, nonlinearity, testability, and variability, among others.

This brings us to the question of what psychologists can hope for from mathematics. The answer to this question is implicit in the discussion just presented. I argue that at the very best, mathematics can never be more than a descriptive representation of our findings. In other words, mathematics (including statistics) provides a powerful means of condensing observations and demonstrating some of the relationships that exist among different observations. However, mathematics, like behavior, is essentially neutral concerning the causal forces that define those relationships. It is no more able to peer into internal cognitive mechanisms to discern underlying causes than is behavioral data. Both are neutral with regard to internal structures. Therefore, neither can resolve an overall response into a unique set of functional cognitive or neural modules. Functional analyses of this kind are intrinsically speculative and inferential, but not definitive. What stochastic procedures accomplish is to provide an approximate means of working around these difficulties.

Furthermore, it may be that, because of the intrinsic complexity and variability of behavior and its mental and neural roots, neither conventional nor stochastic mathematics can ever be applied to control or predict individual human performance. The particular shape of an equation representing a law or a tendency may be nothing more than an artifact of pooling "noisy" (i.e., multiply) determined nonlinear data. That is, pooling a collection of functions that are generally, but irregularly, monotonic produces what appears to be a lawful, smooth monotonic function for the group. However, that function is unrepresentative of individual human behavior. It is, as I have discussed elsewhere (Uttal 2003), more a result of natural mathematical manipulations than a specification of psychobiological reality.

NOTES

1. One excellent example is Lynet Uttal's (Uttal 2002) study of employed mothers, which provides deep insight into the behavior of families in the modern world utilizing a qualitative analysis rather than a quantitative one.

2. It should not go unmentioned that this variability and imprecision also holds for neurophysiological data even though it is much less encumbered by subjective judgments. We have known for years (e.g., Kiang 1965, Luce and Mo 1965) that the response dynamics of individual neurons were as varied and idiosyncratic as the judgments of sensory magnitude.

3. I have discussed this problem in detail in an earlier work (Uttal 1988). Some current computer methods aimed at recognizing faces are based on a vector or set of measurements between some prespecified local points. These are also essentially feature models. In any event, they don't work very well once removed from the laboratory. The small sets of faces used in the laboratory do not scale up to practical face-recognition tasks.

4. Material in this section has been abstracted and updated from Uttal (2003) and is used with the permission of the original publisher, Lawrence Erlbaum Associates Inc.

5. Portions of this section on mathematical intractability have been abstracted and updated from my earlier work on neural theories of mind (Uttal 2005). I have included them here because they are essential to the present discussion. They are used with the permission of the original publisher, Lawrence Erlbaum Associates Inc.

6. The term *variable* should be construed to be synonymous with a number of other equivalent words. Variables are also known as parameters, dimensions, factors, independent measurements, nodes, or operations. The

point is that, whatever they are called, there is a vast increase in the number of calculations that must be made for even relatively simple problems or for neural networks with relatively few units.

7. It should be pointed out that it has not yet been proven that an NP-complete problem is necessarily intractable in a formal, in-principle sense. In all likelihood, however, mathematicians agree that intractability and NP-completeness are synonymous, for practical if not for theoretical reasons.

8. However, any other growth function in which the dependent variable grows faster than the independent variable will also exhibit this combinatorial explosion, albeit at a relative speed that will be determined by the power of the exponential function and the other growth function, respectively. The traveling salesman problem, for example, which seeks to find the minimum-cost travel schedule for a given number of cities, explodes at a rate determined by the factorial expression as *n*, the number of cities, increases (Karp 1986).

9. The widespread activity of the neurons in the brain exhibited in all functional magnetic resonance images (fMRI) attests to the truth of this assertion. Single-cell theories and simple "toy" neural net theories ignore this fundamental fact.

10. Even more fundamentally, no neural net model is capable of determining whether or not consciousness is present. The simulated behavior could always be that of an automaton that only analogizes behavior but is not sentient.

11. A "determined amount of time" is also referred to as "polynomial time," i.e., the number of steps that is a polynomial function of the size of the problem.

12. Hopfield (1982) networks are those that incorporate feedback from their output levels to their input levels for their solution.

13. The hierarchical structure of a network is a description of its inputs and outputs and the order of the interconnections between the nodes. In other words, how the network is organized. In the absence of a defined hierarchical structure, it is not possible to say in what order steps occur and whether a region is inhibited, excited, or even disinhibited by another region.

14. What was, perhaps, the initial discussion of the meaningfulness criteria for psychology can be found in Suppes (1959).

15. It is interesting to note that the domain from which modern statistical analysis emerged—agriculture—was also plagued by wild variability.

16. This is not to say that almost all measurements made in any science or the engineering field are not also basically stochastic in nature. The problem with psychology is that the variability is usually relatively greater than in most other fields. Furthermore, most cognitive parameters are not anchored to the units and dimensions of the material world.

17. The successes of quantum mechanics have tipped current thinking toward acceptance of that which Einstein abhorred—the idea that our world may be fundamentally stochastic rather than deterministic. Perhaps, in retrospect, "God does play dice with the world."

18. By "conventional, deterministic mathematics," I am referring to models based on calculus, differential, and integral equations—the kind that works so well for engineering and physics.

19. I am grateful to Peter Killeen and Jim Townsend for informative discussions on this section.

Chapter 4

PRINCIPIA PSYCHOLOGICA

A Search for the Fundamental Principles of Psychology

4.1. INTRODUCTION

So far in this book, I have inquired into the nature of psychological science using three strategies. The first is based on a comparison of psychology with standard definitions of science. The second is concerned with psychology's fit with the standard observation-induction-axiom-deduction-theorem-verification paradigm (abbreviated as the axiomatic-deductive method) that seems most closely to define the well-established natural sciences such as physics and chemistry. The third considers the role of mathematics in psychology. We have seen that none of these strategies provides us a satisfactory answer to the question of whether or not psychology is a science in the usual sense of the word. Psychology and other social sciences appear to have some fundamental differences with the natural sciences and their use of mathematics. None of the simple definitions or comparisons made so far resolves all of the uncertainties about psychology's scientific role. Thus, we have what is at least a preliminary appreciation of how difficult it is going to be to define psychological laws and principles.

Global psychological principles seem especially elusive in spite of the persistent historical tendency of psychologists to title their texts *Principles of Psychology*. There obviously is a deeply felt need for the scientific status that would come if psychology could be shown to have successfully used the same axiomatic-deductive strategy typical of other sciences.

In this context, the question posed in this chapter is, Do unifying and foundational principles of an axiomatic nature exist for psychology? A positive answer to this question would provide a basis for the development of a more robust psychological science. A negative answer would require some rethinking about the nature of psychological research and what the ultimate goals of this activity should be.

Before beginning this search for basic axiomatic principles, there are some preliminary matters concerning my personal perspective that I must make explicit. I am convinced that if psychology is ever to claim full scientific status, there are two basic principles that must be accepted at a bare minimum. They are:

- Principle 1. Mental functions exist. We all have a first-person existence proof of our own mental activity and sentience. From this fact must follow the not-unreasonable assumption that others are equally sentient and not automata. Accepting the existence of mental activity means that, however imprecise and vague it may be, we must use mentalist language and subjective concepts to converse. Otherwise, no human communication would be possible. Indeed, there would be no sentient entities to communicate.
- Principle 2. All mental functions are produced by the material activity of the nervous system. The mind is a process of the brain and in principle, if not in practice, is fully explainable as a function of a material thing. Without the thing—the brain—the mind cannot exist. No other nonnatural forces or processes are necessary to account completely for our mental lives.

These two principles are essential for us to even consider attributing normal scientific status to psychology. If we are only mindless automata or if the mind is an illusion or some kind of epiphenomenon, then the entire policy of studying and understanding psychology, in any of its forms, is misguided. This admonition holds true regardless of the accessibility or inaccessibility of mental processes.

Similarly, if mental processes are not completely associated with a material mechanism, then the task of physiological psychology (or cognitive neuroscience, as it is now known) is equally untenable. These are the minimum conditions for including psychology in the scientific pantheon. Unless we accept these principles at the outset, the game is over.[1]

It appears that most psychologists with a scientific bent do accept these two basic principles. However, they are only the barest beginnings of a set of axiomatic principles for psychology and do not provide the foundation of a comprehensive and acceptably scientific theory. For this reason, I have set out in this chapter to identify the basic principles of psychology. My goal is to identify the principles from both sides of the many contentious arguments that have both stimulated and divided psychological thinking concerning these basic issues over the years. Furthermore, I make an effort to classify those principles in order to add some clarity concerning their interrelationships. I now report the results of this quest using four different strategies.

1. An Internet search
2. A search through the classic and modern textbooks of psychology, both at the introductory and advanced levels
3. A survey of my colleagues
4. My own experience as an iconoclastic critic of scientific psychology

4.2. AN INTERNET SEARCH

A search on the Internet for "Psychological Principles" turned up 5,600,000 entries. However, most of the citations were popular and pre-scientific recipes for applied fields of human activity, such as advertising, education, sports, salesmanship, the promotion of travel, personnel management, group psychotherapy, and a host of other practical applications that are based on quite different tenets than those characterizing a rigorous science. The principles encountered were statements of popular, intuitive advice instead of being derived from formal, empirically well-founded axioms akin to Newton's three laws. Few, if any, seemed to have been based on any directly relevant research. Intuition, anecdote, wishful thinking, and commercial opportunity seemed to motivate and guide authors to propose these advisory "principles." Illustrative examples of the broad generalizations encountered on the Internet included:

- Learning results when meaningful goals are pursued.
- People strive for consistency in their behavior.
- Positive thinking is a powerful force for success.
- Define metaphors clearly when giving a speech.
- Higher-order strategies for selecting and monitoring mental operations facilitate creative and critical thinking.
- Keep it [your presentation] short and simple (KISS).
- Practice makes perfect.
- All human functioning and activity of any kind involves an affinity between subject and object.
- People feel obligated to respond positively when positive behavior is received.
- Education should be directed at the left brain or the right brain specifically.

Professor John Reich of Arizona State University also provided me with a supplemental list of these popular but scientifically unsupported principles.

- Humans are able to decide what their behavior will be. In other words, they exhibit "free will."
- The heart is the seat of emotion.
- Opposites attract.
- Winning a lottery is always a good thing.
- It is always good to receive help.
- It is always good to look deeply into one's past and one's motives to understand the causes of one's current emotional states.
- Financial rewards always improve performance.[7]

However noble, wise, obvious, and useful these "principles" may be in smoothing human intercourse and helping us achieve some practical goals for daily life, they do not provide the foundation for a deductive science of either behavior or the mind in the usual sense. Whatever the validity of these pieces of advice, most of them are devoid of any empirical foundation. They are, in the main, the results of informal intuitions and somewhat distant extrapolations from esoteric laboratory results. This fact has much to say about the human proclivity to generalize on the basis of very flimsy evidence.

One has to dig far deeper, therefore, in the scientific literature of psychology to find principles or laws that are comparable to those of other sciences. To extract putative scientific principles from this literature, a more detailed examination of the text and treatise literature was, therefore, required. I began by looking back at some of the most significant documents in psychological history that also were involved in the search for basic principles.

4.3. THE SEARCH FOR PSYCHOLOGICAL PRINCIPLES IN THE CLASSIC LITERATURE

From the earliest consideration of psychology as a subject worthy of a scientific approach, the prototypical title of general and, often, specific textbooks has invoked the word *principles*. Classic titles sometimes seem a little dated, but modern texts continue the trend with the prototypical title, *Principles of Psychology.* Often this basic label was modified with allusion to special fields such as *comparative*; *developmental*; *social*; *gestalt*; *physiological*; and so on. This proclivity apparently was the result of a long-term tradition in which psychologists and protopsychologists believed that basic principles should characterize a science and serve as a framework for the analysis of psychological thinking. For example, some of the earlier tomes discussing psychological concepts include:

- *Inquiry into the Human Mind on the Principles of Common Sense* by Thomas Reid in 1764.
- *Introduction to Principles of Morals and Legislation* by Jeremy Bentham in 1780, 1907.
- *Essays on Phrenology; Or an Inquiry into the Principles and Utility of the System of Drs. Gall and Spurzeim and into the Objections Made against It* by George Combe in 1822.
- *Principles of Psychology* by Herbert Spencer in 1855.
- *Principles of Mental Physiology* by William B. Carpenter in 1877.
- *Principles of Physiological Psychology* by Wilhelm Wundt in 1874.
- *Principles of Psychology* by William James in 1890.
- *Psychological Principles* by James Ward in 1920.[3]

Psychology's historical concern with "principles," therefore, is a rich one. The basic idea is the traditional scientific one—any system of thought should be based on a relatively small number of underlying laws or assumptions from which can be derived the larger numbers of empirical details. It was argued that this had to be both the starting point of any system of knowledge as well as the outcome of deliberations about it. As it turns out, however, the basic assumptions or principles underlying psychological thought have rarely been made explicit beyond the titles of these books.

Modern scientific thinking in what was to become psychology can be traced to a group of philosophers or protopsychologists in the eighteenth and nineteenth centuries who initiated the modern perspective.[4] Herbert Spencer (1820–1903) contributed to this sea change in thinking with his remarkable *Principles of Psychology* (Spencer 1855, 1892), in which the material origins of the mind (including especially fervently and innovatively the concepts of evolution) were emphasized. Without question, he was one of the major players in separating psychology from philosophy and theology during its early years.[5] Spencer was clearly within the associationist school, an idea he found eminently compatible with the new Darwinian ideas then shaking up nineteenth-century society. Indeed, much of his writing was based on a general discussion of evolutionary biology rather than on the nervous system. The linking of neurophysiology and psychology, the foundation of a major portion of modern thinking, was more typical of the orientation of other writers of his time, most notably Alexander Bain, who is to be discussed shortly.

Spencer's idea of intelligence, especially as emphasized in the following quotation, illustrates the enormous impact that Darwin had had on him: "That intelligence has neither distinct grades nor is constituted of faculties that are truly independent, but that its highest manifestations are the effects of a complication that has arisen by insensible steps out of the simplest elements . . ." (1: 388).

However, perhaps the most quoted idea in Spencer's multivolume work on the principles of a wide range of scientific topics—his "universal postulate"—might be considered to be antithetical to this materialist premise. In his search for a single foundation assumption on which to base his work, Spencer suggested what to many nowadays is a woefully incorrect idea. His universal postulate states that "[w]e must accept as true anything that it is 'inconceivable' to reject." Given the frailties of human thought, the widespread acceptance of otherwise acceptable "inconceivable" ideas and the unwillingness to reject even blatantly incorrect ideas, this seems to be a frail foundation on which to base a science. Nevertheless, Spencer played a very important role in naturalizing psychology and can, without question, be considered the father of modern evolutionary psychology.

Many historians consider the first major treatise emphasizing experimental rather than introspective psychology to have been written by a contemporary of Spencer, Alexander Bain (1811–1877). His two seminal volumes, *The Senses and the Intellect* (Bain 1855) and *The Emotions and the Will* (Bain 1859), are acknowledged as the first works to develop a synthesis of the British empiricists' associationism and the late nineteenth-century developments in brain science. Unlike Spencer's foundation concept of evolution, Bain emphasized the new brain sciences and, from some points of view, can be considered to be the father of modern cognitive neuroscience, a science once known as physiological psychology.

In the present context, however, his work did not promise general principles, not even in the title. That was left to Wilhelm Wundt (1832–1920) and William James (1842–1910), both of whom emulated Spencer's use of the "Principles" title. Both were also strongly influenced by the new developments in brain science of their times as well as by the materialist philosophies of the origins of mental processes suggested by Spencer and Bain.

Although subsequent psychologies became increasingly materialist and thus should have been easily included among the natural sciences under the tutelage of Spencer or Bain, not all historians see it happening in that way. Hatfield (1994), for example, points out that the usual suggestion that materialist psychology evolved from dualist and immaterialist philosophy and theology in the manner of biology and physics may not be correct. Instead, he suggests: "In point of fact, of all of the major eighteenth-century authors who made contributions to the development of psychology, only Erasmus Darwin allowed that the mind might be material; nineteenth-century founders of psychology, including Wundt, Helmholtz, R. H. Lotze, Hermann Ebbinghaus, William James, Hugo Munsterberg, and Alfred Binet, banished the very question from scientific psychology" (218). Nowhere is this antimaterialism made clearer than in chapters 5 and 6 of James's (1890) first volume, wherein he first attacks the idea of automaton theory and then asserts the essentially dualist idea of a separate reality of the soul:

". . . to posit a soul influenced in some positive way by the brain-states and responding to them by conscious affections of its own, seems to me the line of least logical resistance, so far as we yet have attained" (181) and "Such a mere admission of the empirical parallelism [of mind and brain] will there[fore] appear the wisest course" (182).

In spite of this widespread early dualism, psychology accelerated its separation from philosophy in the late nineteenth century under the influence of Wundt and James. Wundt opened what many consider to have been the first laboratory in experimental psychology in 1879 in Leipzig. At that time, William James in the United States was virtually the only person teaching what was to become his kind of scientific psychology.[6] Both published milestone books, *Principles of Physiological Psychology* (Wundt 1874, 1910) and *Principles of Psychology* (James 1890), which were to influence scientific psychology well into the twentieth century.

Let's consider Wundt's milestone contribution first. One of the first things that one encounters on reading this remarkable work is that Wundt expressed a strong disagreement with Immanuel Kant (1724–1804), who thought that psychology could never be a science simply because the inner mental processes could not be measured. Wundt, to the contrary, designated mental processes as the subject matter of psychology in the vein of modern-day mentalist and cognitive psychologies. He argued: "Physiological psychology is primarily psychology, and therefore has for its subject the manifold of conscious processes, whether as directly experienced by ourselves, or as inferred on the analogy of our own experiences from objective observation" (11).[7]

Wundt continued by asserting that the purpose of physiological psychology is to act as the "mediator between the neighboring sciences of physiology and psychology" (13). He listed some "general principles of central function" in the concluding chapter of volume 1 of his work. These principles, along with some of my comments, include:

1. The Principle of Connexion of Elements: (320) Here Wundt concluded that the brain and its operations were made up of a

number of "elements," all of which were in "close connexion with the others." This principle, he asserted, held for anatomy, physiology, and psychology in his model.

2. The Principle of Original Indifference of Functions: (322) Here Wundt concluded that the parts of the central nervous system produced a particular experience not because of their own properties but because of their interconnections with other elements.
3. The Principle of Practice and Adaptation: (324) Here Wundt concluded that performance was perfected by its repeated performance. It is in this context that he (as did Hull a century later, see p. 133) also almost completely presages the ideas of Hebb (1949) despite the lack of nineteenth-century knowledge of the existence of synapses. Adaptation was also considered to be a result of practice, but one in which the performance declines rather than increases.
4. The Principle of Vicarious Function: (325) Here Wundt concluded that some learning can take place without explicitly related performance. We know this today as implicit learning.
5. The Principle of Relative Localization: (328) Here Wundt concluded that brain regions, although somewhat distinct, must overlap; otherwise there could be no modification of behavior. It is interesting to note that although Wundt rejected the phrenology of Gall, he did believe that the individual locales of the brain had specific functions. This commitment to a kind of limited localization supplemented the idea that conscious experience depends upon the interconnected nature of the parts of the brain more than upon the specific locales. He thus rejected the divisibility of psychical functions (a tenet of the old phrenology) while not denying a new phrenology of specialized, but interconnected, brain locales.

It is important to point out that Wundt's mid-nineteenth-century principles 1, 2, and 5 embody an idea that has become increasingly popular in recent years—the interconnectedness of brain regions.

However, he did not appreciate that this very interconnectedness is actually one of the greatest impediments to the development of a neurophysiologically reductive theory of the mind. The reason for the negative impact of this principle is that the interactions of such a system as Wundt described introduce the essence of the then-unknown concept of nonlinear complexity as a key player in debate over the possibility of the reducibility of mental processes to the mechanisms of the brain. Although undeniably a "principle of brain organization" (and, thus, also of behavior) widely accepted today, he did not realize at the time (nor do many psychologists of our time) that such interconnectedness led inexorably to intractable problems of analysis as discussed in chapter 3.

Wundt spelled out much more specific, and potentially much more useful, principles of mental processing per se in the less well-known but more accessible book *Outlines of Psychology* (Wundt 1897, 1969). These principles were derived from his earlier principles, but were much more specific and introduced some important new ideas for psychology. These laws were divided into two groups—laws of relation and laws of physical causality. Wundt's laws of relation were:[8]

1. The Law of Psychical Resultants: This law states that "every psychical compound" is influenced by the properties of the elements of which it is made but is not a simple sum of those properties.
2. The Law of Psychical Relations: This is the inverse of law 1. It states that "the psychical compound" influences that nature of the perception of the elements when the former can be analyzed into the latter.
3. The Law of Psychical Contrast: Otherwise known as the law of intensification through contrast, Wundt was expressing the idea that opposite qualities lead to an intensification of the one by the other.

Wundt's laws of physical causality, derived from the laws of relation, follow:

1. The Law of Mental Growth: This limited law worked only for processes that continue to change over time, according to Wundt. However, for those that did, this law expresses the continued development of mental processes both in the individual and in the social community.
2. The Law of Heterogeny of Ends: This law expresses the continuing emergence of new "psychical compounds" that act continuously to alter goals and motives. There is a teleological emphasis here that is somewhat unusual in the light of Wundt's other comments.
3. The Law of Development toward Opposites: This extrapolation of the law of intensification through opposites suggests further that the development of the individual goes through a series of oscillations because of the contrast effect. Opposite, but low-level, intensity "psychical compounds" can thus develop into strong ones as a result of this succession of enhancements.

Wundt's six laws, cryptic though they may have been, have within them the germ of an idea that has persisted into modern psychological thinking. Mental experiences were assumed throughout his system to be modular, that is, divisible into both mental components and localized brain regions. This kind of modularity plays an extremely important foundation role in much of today's research.[9]

The particular idea of contrast between perceived qualities was generalized by him to a kind of psychic contrast in which ideas could accentuate opposite ideas. Finally, we can also see in these laws an appreciation of the development through experience of the human mind as time goes by.

Wundt's somewhat obscure laws or principles represent one of the few examples in the literature of an explicit statement of general principles covering the whole of mental life. His contemporary William James (1890), who also utilized the "Principles" title, was much less prone to express such an orderly set of principles. Indeed, James often ranted against the very idea of extracting general principles. He was particularly critical of what he referred to as "metaphysical axioms," unverified relations such as "nature is simple and invariable" and "a thing can only affect another of its own kind" (2: 669). He also criticized what is considered to be a fundamental proposition of all science when he asserted: "The wildest postulate of rationality is that the world is rationally intelligible throughout, after the pattern of some ideal system" (2: 677). With a founding father with such a point of view, it is understandable why psychology has had such a hard time claiming to be a natural science in the usual sense. We reject the premise of a rational world at the risk of rejection of the scientific approach in general!

Concerning psychology itself, Wundt was able to go no further than the following generalities:

1. The mind has a native structure . . . that certain of its objects, if considered in together in certain ways give definite results; and that no other ways of considering, and no other results, are possible if the same objects be taken.
2. The results are 'relations' which are all expressed by judgments of subsumption and comparison.
3. The judgments of subsumption are themselves subsumed under the *laws of logic*.
4. Those of comparisons are expressed in *classifications*, in the sciences of *arithmetic* and *geometry*. (2: 676)

Beyond these very general principles (which can be thought of as statements comparable to Newton's "general rules"), it is difficult to find propositions or axioms that pertain to what might be considered to be a scientific psychology in James's influential book. Even then, we can never be sure exactly what he meant. Moreover, his meanings were further complicated by the fact that he was inconsistent in his writing about some of the most fundamental ideas. Like most other texts of his and earlier times, the precise meaning of much that was asserted is often obscured by linguistic difference between his time and ours. Many of the tentative steps he took toward laws or principles have within them the germ of a modern idea, but the antique writing style leaves little clue to their deep meaning in his thinking.

What a wonderful thing it would be to have a discussion with Wundt or James and to find out what they really meant. Unfortunately, such a thing is not possible, and probes from our time into their thought processes (as so inadequately expressed in writing under the best of conditions) often produce more confusion than clarity. What is clear is that, unlike Newton or Whitehead and Russell, neither of these two giants provided a well-ordered system in which well-established axioms could be manipulated to predict behavior. Instead, like most modern books, the chapters of James's book remain isolated documents capable of being read in any order with no eventual emergence of useful general principles.

4.4. THE GREAT LACUNA— THE SEARCH FOR MISSING PRINCIPLES OF PSYCHOLOGY IN THE MODERN LITERATURE

With few exceptions (e.g., Wundt and Hull), none of these older works (nor, as we shortly see, the innumerable current texts and treatises) ever made explicit attempts to identify basic principles, axioms, or fundamental assumptions that characterize psychology in the same manner Newton's did. Instead of discussions of the fundamental principles so frequently promised in its title, the standard modern textbook starts out with a few words attempting to define the range of topics taught within the domain of psychology and then presents a brief history of the field. A few of the great names of scientific history are then introduced, and relationships with other sciences such as genetics, sociology, and biology are sometimes highlighted.

It is also typical then to introduce a few of the great philosophical controversies (e.g., nativism versus empiricism; elementalism versus holism) that have continued to cause so much controversy in psychology over the years as speculation gave way to experimentation. This brief fling at issues is sometimes followed by a modicum of discussion about the various schools or different points of view of how scientific psychology might be pursued. The glaring absence, however, is of any explicit expressions of the axiomatic or even assumptive foundations that unite the material to be discussed in subsequent chapters.

To the contrary, modern psychology textbooks are then filled with data, phenomena, and results from the various areas packaged into chapters that rarely speak to each other. Thus, early chapters may discuss the nervous system, senses, perception, and learning. Later ones turn to the collection of other less well-defined subjects that make up so much of psychology's content, including personality, motivation, development, and social interaction.

For advanced books specifically aimed at some version of experimental psychology (e.g., a modern "cognitive" text) the discussion characteristically starts off with an introduction to the computer metaphor of "information processing stages."[10] Then individual chapters surveying topics such as learning, attention, recognition, categorization, and problem solving are presented with little to bind them together other than what is sometimes a common methodology and the bare fact that all are examples of observed behavior.

Unlike the situation in the physical sciences, there is no pyramiding of early material to produce a foundation for later materials in either the introductory or advanced psychological texts. In fact, it is entirely possible to read most psychology texts (including the classic works of Wundt and James) in virtually any chapter order, each being independent of the others.[11]

One area in which all textbooks fail without exception is in providing a functional or useful definition of the mind, the psyche, consciousness, or any of the other words that are or have been used to describe our mental processes. If psychology is the study of the mind, as both the classic mentalists and the modern cognitivists agree, the subject matter is certainly inadequately defined and remains a ghost in the background of later discussions. Instead, most modern psychology textbooks turn immediately to a more or less exhaustive listing of observed phenomena and experimental results, often with little explicit efforts to build bridges, seek general principles, or identify commonalities among the various phenomena. Each chapter is a topic unto itself, with research in learning, as one example, congregated in one chapter and sensory processes in another, perhaps reflecting the organization of psychological research itself.

It is almost as if the idea of generalizing across different observations is either repugnant to modern psychology textbook writers or impossible for them to deal with. This in itself is a significant piece of data. Why this should be so is not clear. Perhaps this situation is a result of psychology's long-term desire to sever connections with its predecessors—theology and philosophy. Perhaps it is a result of something about the historical push toward modularization of experimental designs. (Most experimental protocols are severely constrained by the need for rigid control of independent variables other than the one being manipulated.) Perhaps it is due to the resulting compartmentalization of mental events that might otherwise be considered to be similar if not identical. Perhaps it is a valid statement of the fundamental undefined and immeasurable nature of cognitive (i.e., mental) processing.

Another possibility is that there is resistance to explaining the mysteries of the mind in terms of classification, interaction, and a basic materialism because of a residual influence of theological and other prescientific ideas. Religions are generally dualistic, and philosophies of this ilk are often threatened by cognitive and neuroscientific ideas that strive to identify "mechanisms" of mind. From this perspective, the study of the mind-brain link specifically, and the origin of mental activity in general, is threatening to religious beliefs.

Whatever the cause, psychology is typically presented by its proponents as a grab bag of experimental results, fragmentary descriptions, and narrow descriptive (as opposed to explanatory) microtheories. The search for general principles, however often promised by the books' titles, is never brought to fruition. Nor is any attempt (with rare and failed exceptions) made to set up a formal system comparable to

Newton's that assumes axioms, derives theorems, and predicts behavior despite the ubiquity of psychological books titled with some version of *The Principles of*. . . Although many psychologists may find it unpalatable to accept the possibility that psychology is naturally fragmented and therefore recalcitrant to systemization, this hidden theme hangs like a dark cloud over the history of psychology.

Thus, there is an *almost* complete absence of psychological theories based on the axiomatic-deductive model that has done so much in other sciences to enhance our lives and the world. As we see later in this chapter, however, the absence of principles in the textbooks is not evidence of their absence. With a little bit of digging, a surprising number of putatively basic principles do emerge.

4.5. THE CATEGORIES

If no grand axiomatic-deductive theory of psychology is visible or even viable at the present time, it is still possible that a set of sometimes implicit and sometimes explicit "axiomatic" principles have emerged or are emerging in modern psychological thought. The main purpose of this section is to consider this possibility and to tabulate a list of categories that include related groups of foundation assumptions. Obviously, any such taxonomy must be designed to contain propositions of many different kinds.

I propose that the following major categories of basic assumptions or principles be used:

1. Ontological Principles
2. Epistemological Principles
3. Statistical and Measurement Principles
4. Methodological Principles
5. Pragmatic Principles
6. Empirical Laws

In the following sections, I spell out the meanings of these categories as I use them in this tabulation. This will then be followed by the tabulation of the assumptions themselves.

4.5.1. Ontological Principles

The first class of assumptions is designated as "ontological." Ontology is a branch of metaphysics, a major activity of philosophy dealing with the nature of reality, of what it means "to be." Ontological issues, such as the existence and reality of physical objects and mental processes, have long been controversial among philosophers. Issues of how we are to describe and delineate a "thing" from its environment have been considered since the time of Aristotle. Debates of great psychological import, such as the controversy between monism and dualism (e.g., are the mind and the brain expressions of the same kind of reality?), are still main topics of ontological speculation.

It is my conviction that, however important these ontological issues, psychological research will not be able to resolve them. There is little beyond speculation and a kind of belief-based hand-waving that can prove or disprove any ontological assertion. One or another position, especially when the contending sides are widely dichotomous, is almost certain to be true; however, neither is really open to empirical investigation. It is at this level that arguments between theologians and scientists can be expected to rage on into the unknowable future. My speculation is that millennia from now, to the extent that our species is still interested, these questions will be as unanswerable and controversial as they are today.

Sometimes this debate will continue because the basic strategy of science is just not relevant, and an objective resolution is, therefore, not possible. Prejudices arising from such deeply held concepts as the fear of death are likely to influence thinking about these ontological issues more powerfully than the presence or absence of empirical evidence (Uttal 2004). Sometimes, these ontological ideas will be unresolvable because they cannot be defined in the operational sense desired of science. Psychology has not converged on useful operational, noncircular definitions of the mind or the soul, much less a concept as elusive as "reality," and it does not seem likely that it will in the future. Without such definitions, it is clear that analytic, empirical answers to some of our most profound questions are not possible. Skeptics may lean one way and true believers (e.g., theological literalists) another without any possibility of definitive resolution. The latter may find the whole idea of applying objective empirical arguments to answer these deep ontological questions inappropriate. The former may not be able to find any objective means of answering them. What we are talking about in this section on ontological assumptions are "beliefs" that are not subject to test and verification. The adoption of the criteria of test and verification is itself a strong ontological principle that preempts any arguments from spiritualism or theology.

In sum, there are profound issues that transcend the power of science. Although many scholars may feel that science may in principle provide complete answers to great questions of nature, it cannot be overlooked that by far the majority of people who inhabit the world these days have come to a diametrically opposed answer.

4.5.2. Epistemological Principles

The second category—epistemological principles—is, like the ontological one, a subcategory of metaphysical philosophy. It is concerned with the nature of knowledge and how we can attain it. It is not too strong an assertion to suggest that psychology has been primarily concerned with epistemological issues from its very beginning.

Although epistemological issues are tremendously important for all scientific research, it seems especially so for psychology, which at least implicitly promises to provide empirical input into such questions. Many of the classic controversies in psychology (e.g., nature versus nurture) are intimately related to the epistemological question of how we gain knowledge.

Although I am sure that not all would agree with me, I contend that psychology is mainly involved in the elucidation and resolution of epistemological issues of the kind included in this category. This is not a new suggestion; others have also seen the close intellectual links between psychology and epistemology. The British empiricists originally accepted the close relationship with their emphasis on learning by experience. In recent years, Quine (1969) and Kornblith (1999) were among those who proposed a "naturalized epistemology" that essentially replaces epistemology with experimental psychology. Piaget's extensive studies of children's knowledge development (e.g., Piaget 1929, 1983) were labeled by him as "genetic epistemology," also clearly indicating his interest in what were originally epistemological issues. In all of these recent efforts, there was a hidden assumption, namely, that scientific psychology provided an objective means of attacking some of the previously unassailable problems of speculative epistemology. This topic is of such sufficient interest that I return to consider it in detail in the appendix to this book.

4.5.3. Statistical and Measurement Principles

The third class—statistical and measurement assumptions—incorporates a number of ideas about behavior that are more significant than simple methodological concepts but not as elusive as the ontological or epistemological ones. They speak to the nature of mental and behavioral processes including two of the most significant: (1) Is behavior fundamentally stochastic or is it fundamentally deterministic? and (2) Is mental activity sufficiently orderly and quantitative so it can be measured and the laws of mathematics applied to it in the same way as physics?[12] We will probably not make much progress in answering these two questions any more than has the field of physical sciences. Indeed, there is a substantial argument that this is an ontological argument that can no more be resolved than can the monism-dualism issue.

A number of far less profound issues are also included in this list that deal essentially with the methodology of statistics. Can we, for example, trust the null hypothesis significance test to provide insights into mental processes, or is it intrinsically misleading? As important as such issues are, to me they represent technological matters that do not rise to the level of the most important conceptual issues for psychology.

4.5.4. Methodological Principles

I have relegated the fourth category of fundamental principles of psychology to the class of methodological assumptions. These few general issues are practical aphorisms, some emerging from issues of complexity and numerousness (e.g., the inability to scale up toy problems) and some reflecting the experiences of those of us who have been frustrated in the laboratory by unstable results (e.g., the impact of small experimental design changes on findings). These subjects, no matter how important to good empirical order, are not, in my opinion, the intellectual core of a possible scientific psychology.

4.5.5. Pragmatic Principles

The fifth category, pragmatic principles, like the fourth, also consists of some useful and worldly advice to the psychologist-laboratory scientist. The guidance offered is useful only in the context of how to motivate or sell one's work instead of providing insights into underlying principles. These extrascientific assertions provide some strategic wisdom but not a substantive foundation defining the root principles of a science. It is here we encounter practical admonitions (e.g., "do applied work") or suggestions about letting "folk psychology" provide hypotheses for research. It is here that we also find general advice to work hard, be dedicated, be honest, and other admirable criteria that provide almost no help in answering the great questions of science.

4.5.6. Empirical Laws

Empirical psychological laws emerging from experimental research constitute the bulk of the sixth category. Unlike the empirical laws of the physical sciences, these psychological laws are, in the main, much less exact. No one would attempt to predict the behavior of an individual subject with the precision that the orbit of a missile would be computed. Empirical psychological laws are almost always loose estimations based on the accumulated behavior of groups; individual behavior is usually poorly represented by even the best of these empirical laws.

However, it must be acknowledged that, from one point of view, these empirical laws represent by far the best hope of developing an axiomatic-deductive system of the kind discussed in chapter 2. They are most likely to be the source of any axioms that might ultimately lead to formal theories. However, the variability problem remains an excruciating one for anyone hoping to model, predict, or control behavior. Unfortunately, no one has been successful in the development of an effective deterministic theory of behavior, and there is no promise of it on the horizon. Every practical application of empirical psychological laws must, of necessity, be framed in terms of probabilities and uncertainties. This will remain a major problem for the acceptance of psychology. No one can go into a court of law and state with assurance that a person did or will behave in a particular way.

4.6. A TABULATION OF IDENTIFIED PRINCIPLES

As I composed the following list, I tried to indicate those instances that represent major disagreements among psychologists (and others of similar interests) by expressing antithetical assumptions. I did this in two ways; first, by proposing the contrary view as a separate assumption; and, second, by simply using, when possible, the artifice of a parenthetical ("or is not") for those cases in which the two contending arguments are clear. Finally, as much as I have tried, I must acknowledge that this list is both incomplete and, at least partially, redundant. Redundancy is an unavoidable outcome because of the ambiguity of our language and the uncertain definition of many of the mental processes being considered here.

Incompleteness is an equally unavoidable outcome because no search strategies could ever fully incorporate every psychologist's unarticulated assumptions. Some researchers are just not aware that they are functioning in accord with dictates of the zeitgeist or covert principles and assumptions. Deep analysis of basic axiomatic assumptions is not usually encountered in the empirical journals of psychology. Furthermore, simple pragmatic concerns made it impossible to contact more than a handful of psychologists; many other perspectives, therefore, are sure to have been overlooked.

The principles incorporated into this taxonomy are enormously varied. Some will be grand issues and some will be of lesser import. We can be equally certain that any such list will contain propositions that are controversial and may be present in opposing versions that are antithetical to each other. This list has been prepared from a number of different sources. I searched through some of my previous writing and reviewed a number of other articles and books; I polled a number of colleagues,[13] asking for their advice and wisdom; and then I tried to integrate all of the suggestions into a reasonably coherent list of what I consider to be basic assumptions. Where I have used the exact wording of one of my correspondents, I have placed quotation marks around the comment. If no quotation marks are present, I am responsible for the exact wording. However, I want to acknowledge that the essence of the idea may have come from one or more of those who were courteous enough to have responded to my request. In a few instances, I have specifically identified a respondent. Most quoted comments, however, have not been so attributed; it seemed to me that each of the expressed "principles" had been stated so far out of any context that their authors might have preferred to remain anonymous. My task was to integrate and arrange all of this material and sometimes to rephrase a key idea that was only hinted at by my correspondents.

As I have already suggested, surprisingly few of these "principles" came from psychological textbooks or treatises. It seems that we do a very poor job of explaining to students, especially graduate students who plan to become researchers and teachers in this field, exactly what are the foundation principles and assumptions of a field to which they are about to dedicate their lives.

By no means should it be assumed at this point that inclusion of an item on this list represents my personal view (that task is left to chapter 5). This is, at best, intended to be a reasonable, but non-exhaustive, sampled tabulation of both sides of some controversial issues. I have tried to present both sides fairly to the maximum extent possible; however, I am sure that I could not remove all bias from the list completely.

Finally, I have limited the discussion in this book to what has generally been included in the rubric of experimental psychology. Although I touch on some topics relevant to other kinds of psychology, my coverage is of necessity limited to this part of the field. Nevertheless, I know of no other comparable lists and thus offer it as a first approximation to a plausible list of foundation principles for a scientific psychology. Others may well see fit to add issues or to challenge the significance of some that are included.

Ontological Principles

1. Mental processes are exclusively the result of complex neural activity in the brain. That is, the mind is a product of material actions. Without the material substrate there would be no mind. This principle has also been expressed in other forms including "There must be a corresponding and causal brain state for every mind state and every behavior" and "Material events provide a complete explanation of mental events." All are synonymous.
2. Mental processes represent a separate level of reality that can exist without the material substrate.

3. Mind is a real process, not a phantom or an illusion.
4. "Mind is a dynamic, self-organizing, complex system centered in the brain and extending throughout the nervous system to the periphery of the organism."
5. Cognitive behavior is determined by single causes.
6. Cognitive behavior is determined by multiple causes.
7. Mental life is fundamentally stochastic in the same way as quantum mechanics. Probability and randomness are realistic statements of the nature of the mind. "God does play dice with the universe."
8. Mental life is fundamentally deterministic in the manner believed in by Einstein. Probability and randomness are just expedients until we can identify all of the hidden variables. "God would not play dice with the universe."
9. The analogy from our own consciousness to "other minds" is the only evidence that we are not all automata. "How I perceive the basic sensory attributes and integrated objects should be similar to how others perceive the same stimulation under the same of very similar circumstance."
10. "All of mental life (including what the philosophers call raw feels as well as intentional acts) is, in its essence, overt behavior."
11. "All behavior, as far as we can now discern it, is composed of variations of a few basic themes [e.g., reflexes and classical and instrumental conditioning]" (Keller and Schoenfeld 1950, 401).
12. All behavior, as far as we can discern it, is the result of immensely complex neural and cognitive interactions possibly [probably, definitely] beyond our ken.
13. Human mental and neural development is guided by (a) innate genetic mechanisms (evolution), (b) learned processes, or (c) both interacting to an unknown degree.
14. "The feeling of free will is real."
15. "Free will is an illusion."

Epistemological Principles

1. The mind is such a complex, nonlinear entity that it can never be subject to the axiomatic-deductive model of the physical sciences.
2. Although complicated, inexact, and in an early stage of development, there is a possibility of psychology being described by an axiomatic-deductive model.
3. "It is possible (or not) and beneficial (or not) to set out formal explanations of events in terms of explanans and explanandum as in the Deductive Nomological Model outlined by Hemple (1965)."
4. "With properly defined and formalized systems, it is possible to reduce one theory or set of theories to another more fundamental theory or set of theories" (Wendroth and Latimer, 1978).
5. Mental processes can (or cannot), in principle, be reduced or explained in the language and concepts of neuroanatomy and neurophysiology.
6. "Phenomenal awareness can (or cannot) be directly reduced to specific neural components."
7. Mind is (or is not) encoded in the brain in the form of brain chunks, localized fields, single cells, or neural networks.
8. The neural networks underlying mental processes can (or cannot) be analyzed to determine how mind emerges.
9. "The subject matter of psychology must be 3rd person observable." That is, psychology can only deal with public behavior and not private thoughts.
10. "Consciousness [or any other word that signifies the mind] is (or is not) amenable to scientific examination."
11. The subject matter of psychology is our entire mental life, which can (or cannot) be inferred from behavioral observations or introspective reports.
12. Observations of behavior are in general valid. It is when we

attempt to infer or explain the processes accounting for that behavior that psychology goes astray.

13. "It is possible and beneficial to set out a vocabulary for studying psychological phenomena."
14. Psychology has not converged on a satisfactory vocabulary, much less a taxonomy of faculties, cognitions, or mental processes. Each generation suggests new mental activities that have no reality except as arbitrary definitions or the outcome of an experimental paradigm.
15. "Abstract-noun [hypothetical mentalist constructs] categories such as choice, timing, and risk represent real subject matters for psychology." Mental processes can be adequately defined for scientific examination.
16. "Abstract-noun [hypothetical mentalist constructs] categories such as choice, timing, and risk represent arbitrary phantoms that are not amenable to scientific examination." Mental processes cannot be adequately defined for scientific examination.
17. The fundamental mentalist epistemological assumption is that mental processes are accessible through introspective reports or inferences drawn from behavioral observations.
18. The fundamental behaviorist assumption is that mental processes are inaccessible and only overt behavior can be measured.
19. "Controversies among cognitive theoretical interpretations are rarely if ever resolvable by behavioral research."
20. Behavioral research can provide the basis for resolving controversies among cognitive theoretical interpretations.
21. Analogies can (or cannot) be a powerful means of understanding the nature of mental processes or mechanisms.
22. Isomorphism [same shape or time course] can (or cannot) be a powerful means of understanding the nature of mental processes and mechanisms.
23. Mathematics is the tool par excellence for unraveling how the mind works. Formal models of mental activity are possible.

24. Mathematics cannot go beyond description to reductively "explain" mental processes.
25. Because of the complexity of behavior, all formal models are either trivial or must ultimately fail.
26. Behavior and mathematics are neutral with regard to underlying processes and mechanisms.
27. Behavior and mathematics are powerful inferential tools that permit us to examine and understand underlying processes and mechanisms.
28. Introspection can (or cannot) provide a means of directly accessing mental processes.
29. Cognitive penetration contaminates all introspective reports.
30. "Only a small part of cognitive processing is revealed in consciousness."
31. We have no awareness of the neural or cognitive mechanisms that lead to our behavior.
32. There is no way to tell if different people (or animals) perceive basic sensory attributes and integrated objects in the same way.
33. "Other species experience consciousness."
34. Anthropomorphic projection of human consciousness onto lower animals is a gross logical and scientific error.
35. New technologies (such as the fMRI) provide "a real possibility of establishing direct relationships between behaviors and their neurobiological substrates *without mediating constructs*."
36. New technologies (such as the fMRI) do not "establish a direct relationship" between mental processes and their neurobiological substrate because of a host of conceptual and technical limitations.
37. Mind is complex but fundamentally a holistic, unified process.
38. Mind is complex but fundamentally made up of many separable components or modules.

39. "Mental processes can (or cannot) be analyzed into components (stages, elementary observations, etc.)."
40. The basic assumption of modular mental processes is based upon a series of corollary assumptions, most of which are not justified by modern psychological research. These *fallacious* corollaries were summarized by Pachella (1974) and can all be considered to be variants of the implausible idea of "pure insertion":[14]
    - A priori information is available that uniquely identifies the sequence of cognitive components that are involved in the process.
    - The cognitive components involved in a more complex process are independent of each other.
    - Each cognitive component carries out a specific and isolable operation.
    - It is possible to insert or delete a component process without changing the function of other components.
    - It is possible to insert or delete a component without changing the entire task posed to the subject.
    - So-called converging operations actually converge onto the same final cognitive process.
    - Cognitive components operate sequentially, that is, in serial order.
    - The duration of the cognitive components could be added together to determine the total duration of the process.
    - Psychological processes could be measured with a precision sufficient to carry out subtractions or to meaningfully determine the effects of adding factors.[15]
41. Some mental processes are serial in nature.
42. Some mental processes are parallel in nature.
43. All mental processes are partially serial and partially parallel.
44. It cannot be determined whether mental processes are serial or parallel in nature because serial processes can imitate parallel

ones and vice versa. No input-output analysis could resolve the matter in any event.

45. Mental modules are instantiated in particular localized brain regions. These brain regions perform separable functions that can be isolated from each other.
46. Mental processes "can be fruitfully examined in terms of networks of localized brain activity during the performance of appropriate tasks."
47. Mental processes are represented by networks of regions whose function can be understood.
48. Mental processes are represented by networks of regions whose functions are so interactive because of feedback and feed-forward mechanisms that we cannot determine their hierarchical organization. That is, it is indeterminate which regions are ascending, which are descending, and which are laterally interconnective (Hilgetag, O'Neil, and Young 1996, 2000).
49. Localization of brain regions encoding hypothetical mental modules does not work beyond the sensory, motor, and appetitive regions.
50. Mental processes can (or cannot) be studied by carrying out experiments in which all independent variables except one are held constant and one dependent variable measured.
51. Mental processes can (or cannot) have profound effects on the body's physiology. For example, placebos have (or do not have) positive effects on our responses.
52. Mental processes exert profound causal forces on our behavior.
53. The mind is epiphenomenal and does not have any profound effect on the body's physiology.
54. "Consciousness has no causally effective role in cognition, although we have an intuition or illusion that it does."
55. Perceptual experiences are represented in the nervous system by dimensionally congruent neural responses.
56. Perceptual experiences, at least in part, are represented by

symbolic representations whose dimensions have no isomorphic relations to the dimensions of the stimuli.

57. Memories validly replicate previous experiences.
58. Memories are highly flexible and are modified by time and relevance to the outlook of the subject.
59. "We learn about psychological processes by identifying dissociations and associations between phenomena."
60. Dissociation experiments do not provide proof of the necessity, sufficiency, or independence of cognitive processes.
61. "Progress in understanding mental processes and mechanisms is (or is not) possible."
62. "Psychological Science should work toward an understanding of underlying process mechanisms."
63. There are fundamental barriers to understanding psychology's underlying process and mechanisms.
64. "Recalcitrant problems are usually due to conceptual foundation errors."
65. There are some intractable problems that can never be solved for either practical (e.g., complexity) or in-principle (e.g., fundamentally ill-posed) reasons.
66. "Truth is not binary but a continuous variable."
67. "Models are a means of imposing comprehension on the real world. They are a projection onto a lower dimensional space."
68. "Results can be validated by converging operations."
69. No matter how many "converging results" may point in the same direction, there is no way to totally validate any reductive model of behavior.
70. Ockham's razor and Descartes' Methode can be useful criteria for choosing between competing psychological theories.
71. Ockham's razor and Descartes' Methode are irrelevant to the special problems posed by psychology primarily because of the great redundancy and available complexity of psychological and neural mechanisms that negate the value of the simplicity criterion.
72. "Hypothetical constructs" in the MacCorquodale and Meehl

(1948) sense are often polluted with "attributes that exceed their original defining operations."

73. "A science of behaviorism is not a science of psychology."
74. Behaviorism is all that psychology can ever be.

Statistical and Measurement Principles

1. Human behavior and, by inference, human mental processes are extremely variable and can only be meaningfully studied by statistical (pooled data) methods. Therefore, prediction of individual behavior is impossible.
2. "We can never have a complete, full understanding and description of mental processes at a level that would allow reliable forecast or prognosis of what will happen in human mind . . . only some statistical rules . . ."
3. The dimensions of the mind cannot be measured with the same effect as those of the physical sciences because of problems with ordinality and additivity (Michell 1999).
4. The dimensions of the mind can be measured with the same effect as those of physical sciences. This very highly questionable general principle actually has a very large number of statistical corollaries, previously summarized in Uttal (2003).
    - Highly variable cognitive processes can be adequately measured with psychophysical procedures.
    - The properties of cognitive processes are adequately quantitative and display regular scales and orderly, if not, linear superimposition.
    - Humans behave rationally.
    - The results from individual responses or observers can be pooled in a meaningful way.
    - Slight changes in an experimental protocol are essentially meaningless and without major effect on results.
    - Slight changes in an experimental protocol can produce totally (partially, somewhat) different results.

- A sample distribution always accurately reflects the total population distribution.
- A "case history" can be validly generalized to the total population.
- The outcomes of statistical analyses are immune from logical errors.
- The best explanatory theory is one that fits the data best.
- The rare occurrence of improbable and coincidental random events can be used as proof of equally unlikely theories.
- All data can be uncritically pooled or combined to give improved precision.
- Data from different populations or sampled according to different rules can be uncritically combined.
- Rounding errors are always insignificant in drawing final conclusions.
- Data can be extrapolated and interpolated to extend theories and fill in gaps.
- Discontinuities are unlikely to occur in what had been a continuously trending trajectory.
- Finally, and perhaps most notably, behavior and the brain can be dealt with as simple linear systems (174–75).[16]

5. A particular result of a null hypothesis test does (or does not) specify whether or not an effect is real. Despite the near universal ideal of statistical significance and the widely accepted .05 criterion, Killeen (2005), Nickerson (2000), and many others have reminded us such a rejection is not, in fact, appropriate and that we can never "reject the null hypothesis." As an example, Killeen notes that determining the probability of a coin toss resulting in a head is a direct inference (i.e., a "downhill process") and can fairly be done. However, when going from the observed behavior of the coin toss (e.g., that it resulted in eight heads and only two tails), there is no way to

determine the "fairness of the coin" without invoking other assumptions about its expected behavior. The problem is that it is not possible to go uphill from observation to inference; the logic is incomplete. Nevertheless, the acceptance of null hypothesis statistical tests as a basic assumption of scientific psychology is widely accepted throughout the psychological community. Corollaries of the assumption of the fallibility of null hypotheses testing include:

- "Statistical significance does not mean theoretical or practical significance."
- "The rejection of the null hypothesis does not establish the truth of a theory that predicts it to be false."
- A .05 significance test result is not a valid criterion for publication.
- The failure to achieve significance does not mean that an experiment has failed.
- "Experimental data and results set out clearly in terms of descriptive statistics and graphic should not be sacrificed for mere statistical significance."

6. Correlation Argues for Causation: Another widespread assumption among psychologists is that a demonstration of correlation implies causation. A close corollary of this principle is that analogous behavior implies homologous causation. Although it has been convincingly argued for years (Yule 1926) that "correlation does not imply causation," there is still a pervasive tendency to causally link two similar functions that may actually be independent results of a third invisible factor.
7. Psychological Processes Are Generally Normally Distributed: This near universal assumption is the basis of almost all psychological testing. Most psychological tests take for granted the assumption of normal or Gaussian distribution. However, it is almost certain that such an assumption is invalid and that deviations from Gaussian distributions are more the exception than the rule in complex human data.

8. The Ranks in Scaling Experiments Remain the Same from One Person or One Trial to Another: Rank orderings have no universal (i.e., cross-subject) meaning and can introduce major measurement errors (Bartoshuk, Fast, and Snyder 2005).
9. Necessity implies sufficiency. The specific neurophysiological corollary of this assumption is that activity in a region of brain tissue during a particular mental task does not mean that that region is the locus of that psychological function.
10. Subjects in experiments (or groups of subjects) do (or do not) exhibit stable behavior over time.

Methodological Principles

1. Small-scale (i.e., toy problem) solutions can (or cannot) be scaled up into practical large-scale solutions to mind-brain problems.
2. Similar behaviors in different species are (or are not) mediated by similar mechanisms.
3. Drugs may have multiple and unknown effects on the nervous system, thus making it difficult to assign causal relations.
4. "Control your conditions and order will emerge."
5. Adequate control in psychological experiments is hard to obtain.
6. Small changes in an experimental protocol may produce huge changes in the outcome.

Pragmatic Principles

1. Curiosity is a valid motivating force for scientific research, particularly for psychology.
2. "People's eternal questions about the nature of our mental life are important guides to what we should study in psychology."
3. "Folk psychology and common sense produce inadequate and potentially misleading explanations regarding causation."

4. "The value of psychology is in its scientific/statistical methodology."
5. The value of psychology is not in its methods but in the substance of its discoveries and understanding of the human condition.
6. Since controversies among cognitive theories cannot be adjudicated by behavioral data, it really is pointless to debate them.
7. "Time and effort are limited, so pick problems that advance science but with an eye toward application."
8. "The game of psychological research is to get other psychologists to accept your theories." This can be best achieved by "honesty, clarity, simplicity, and power to the greatest extent possible."
9. "The task of a scientist is to choose the hardest problem that is potentially solvable in one's lifetime."

Empirical Laws

It is obvious as one reads the literally hundreds of journals relevant to psychology and the thousands of contained articles that psychology has no shortage of empirical laws. Each and every experiment produces functional relationships between independent and dependent variables in the forms of equations, tables, and charts. Each of these findings is a potential contributor to some inductively arrived-at axiom or premise of some theoretical development. However, in fact, rarely is any part of this mass of observations cumulated into a form that could be used as an axiom in a comprehensive theory as can $f = ma$. Psychology, as we have seen, seems at the present to be made up of a collection of fragmentary observations that have only rarely been collected into common, synoptic laws by means of inductive processes.

It would be impossible to try to tabulate all of these findings. However, there are a few instances in which some attempts at integration have been made. The most expedient way of including them in this tabulation is to identify a few of the quasi-generalities that have come from a number of the best-developed fields of experimental psychology.

The important aspect of this category is that it is here where we are likely, if ever, to find the foundations for the axioms that are most similar to the one used by Newton and others who sought to develop axiomatic-deductive theories in other sciences. Unfortunately, it is only in the rarest instances that such a course has been attempted. Psychology's empirical laws remain fragmentary and isolated. Therefore, there are no well-defined, quantitative axioms that can provide the basis for an axiomatic-deductive theory. No grand theory is yet at hand or even contemplated. Some of the best-known empirical laws include:

From the Study of Learning

Not too surprisingly, given the history of scientific psychology in the past few centuries, a special burst of empirical laws has emerged in the field of learning. They are specific enough to deserve special consideration, particularly because they come close in some cases to the assumptions of a future axiomatic-deductive theory of psychology. These learning principles include:

1. Learning occurs because of association of stimuli and responses. This is the fundamental assumption of the associationist or empiricist tradition. This assumption has been particularized in the forms of certain laws that describe the conditions that optimize the associative process.
2. Law of Similarity—learning proceeds best when the stimuli and the response are similar.
3. Law of Contiguity—learning proceeds best when stimuli are close together in space or time.
4. Law of Contrast—learning also occurs when stimuli are opposites of each other.
5. Law of Effect—learning proceeds best when there is some effect (either positive or negative) of what you are practicing.
    - A widely held modern corollary of the law of effect is that learning proceeds best when the process is positively rewarded. This is often called the principle of hedonism.

    - Another corollary is that punishment tends to weaken learned responses.

6. Law of Repetition or Exercise—learning is enhanced by repetition. This has been formalized by Teichner and Krebs (1974) for reaction times in the form

$$\text{Reaction Time} = a \text{ Log}_{10} \text{ Number of Trials} + b$$

(where a and b represent more or less arbitrary constants required to fit the data). Furthermore, there is another similar, overlapping, but quite different set of approximately twenty-five laws offered by Skinner (1938). He classifies them into three broad classes:

- **Static Laws:** For example, "the magnitude of a response is a function of the intensity of a stimulus" (3).
- **Dynamic Laws:** For example, "the strength of a reflex may be increased through presentation of a second stimulus which does not itself elicit the response" (16).
- **Laws of Interaction:** For example, "the response of one reflex may constitute or produce the eliciting or discriminative stimulus of another" (32).

It should be pointed out that these "laws" are qualitative, only suggesting general trends, unlike the strict numerical equality implied by the symbol = of physical axioms and theorems. Furthermore, Skinner (1938) made no attempt to integrate them into a formal, quantitative theory. Indeed, he was very specific about the limits of how these laws were to be used: "[The system] is positivistic. It confines itself to description rather than explanation. Its concepts are defined in terms of immediate observations and are not given local or physiological properties. [Its terms] are used merely to bring together groups of observations, to state uniformities, and to express properties of behavior which transcend single instances. They are not hypotheses to be proved or disproved, but convenient representations of things already known" (44).

Thus, although they sound very much like Newton's axioms, Skinner's "laws" represent something quite different. They are the end product of his system, not the initial conditions. Many empirical laws observed in psychology are of this kind and do not provide the foundation for the development of a formal theory.

From the Study of Perception

Sensory and perceptual research, anchored as it is to familiar and well-defined dimensions of the physical world, has generated large numbers of empirical laws, at least some of which are genuinely and fully quantitative.

1. Among the most familiar are the dozen or so laws of gestalt grouping exemplified by the "law of similarity." This law asserts that components that are similar in shape (or motion or virtually any other dimension) will be grouped together.
2. Similarly, Grassman's four laws of chromatic color mixing have long been established as approximately true in the same general sense as Skinner's laws.[17] For example, one of the Grassman laws asserts that "[a]ny chromatic mixture, no matter how it is composed, must have the same appearance as some mixture of a pure spectral color and white." Grassman's laws have been applied to the development of the well-known chromaticity diagram, which is a close approximation to a formal descriptive theory of color vision. It (and the equivalent equations that it represents) can be used to predict and control color mixing in a way that emulates Newton's theory of mechanics.
3. There are other similar models scattered throughout the sensory sciences that also exhibit some of the properties of a formal theory. Unfortunately, once one proceeds beyond the sensory (and, with an equivalent degree of success, motor) topics to higher-level cognitive processes, models with this degree of precision are hard to locate.

From the Study of Information Processing and Motor Performance

Motor performance and the mental information processing that presumably underlies it have also generated a number of general, well-established empirical, but not precise, quantitative laws.

1. Fitts's (1954) law (Movement Time = a + b × Accuracy), where a and b are constants describing the compensatory relation between speed and accuracy, is one of the oldest.
2. The Hick-Hyman (1952, 1953) law (Reaction Time = a + b × Information Load) indicating the increase of response times as a function of the information content of the stimulus is another universally accepted relationship between the stimulus and the time it takes to process information. Other laws of performance, especially from the applied human factors field, exist in abundance.
3. In summary, it should be pointed out that virtually every experiment in which an independent variable is varied and a dependent variable is measured produces an empirical law. We have a huge and increasing number of such relationships, most of which speak only to the conditions of the particular experiment whence they came and which are mainly statistical summaries. Thus, they do not serve well as the general axiomatic principles for which we are searching.

4.7. INTERIM CONCLUSION

What emerges from this review of the search for psychological principles and the dream of applying the axiomatic-deductive approach to psychology is the realization that the dream has not been and probably cannot be fulfilled. In its place has emerged a plethora of microtheories, highly specialized but indeterminate empirical laws, philosophical (i.e., ontological and epistemological) points of view, and qualitative generalities that do not yet provide a foundation for anything approximating an axiomatic-deductive model of psychological science.

We may gain some insight into the possibility of some future axiomatic-deductive model in psychology by briefly summarizing the overall significance of the principles uncovered in this search. At the grandest levels are ontological principles collectively adhered to by all except the most inconsistency-tolerant psychologists. That the mind is real (and not an epiphenomenal illusion) and a product of the activity of a material nervous system is, thus, virtually universally accepted by every scientist working in the field. Without this primary belief in both a functional and a material reality, much of psychology, especially the neuroreductive part of the enterprise, would become nonsensical.[18]

Beyond that basic monistic assumption of a single kind of reality, there are great differences in the ontological beliefs of psychologists that have profound implications on their day-to-day work. Some psychologists see a basic simplicity while others see a basic complexity. Whichever side of the argument one accepts, these are likely to be empirically untestable assumptions about the basic nature of the mind. As much as any principle, however, this materialism guides modern psychology. Unfortunately for anyone hoping for a rational, logical, scientific world, this basic monist, materialist principle is not held by the overwhelming majority of humans alive today.

One major basic principle of neural reality—that learning takes place because of the dynamic changes in synaptic conductivity—is widely, if not universally, accepted by cognitive neuroscientists (Hebb 1949). Nevertheless, there is *at present* no demonstration of the validity of this principle. No direct link between the level of synaptic activity and human learning has yet been established.

Furthermore, as I argued in Uttal (2005), the computational complexity of the brain may make it impossible to ever show this kind of direct relationship between behavioral change and the ensemble of variable neural interactions. We accept the neural network principle, as we do Hebb's synaptic assertion, by default because there is no plausible alternative, and it is unlikely that it can be resolved empirically. Everything suggests that much of human behavioral change is due to synaptic efficiency changes, but nothing confirms it.

Whatever the difficulties in determining their validity, these ontological principles are the bedrock on which our science is built. In a sense, they are the *qualitative* root assumptions, otherwise known as beliefs, on which we base our work. They are rarely explicitly discussed but exert a profound influence on the kind of work that we do in the laboratory. Unfortunately they do not provide the quantitative specificity to serve as the functional axioms of a deductive theoretical system.

Other categories in this tabulation are "merely" methodological, within which I would include the special considerations of statistics and measurement. I choose the word *merely* here not in the pejorative sense but only to emphasize that these principles are guides to how we should conduct our experiments rather than fundamental postulates of the mind-brain-behavior relationship. These methodological principles are almost independent of the foundation ontological or epistemological doctrines of our science. One would carry out identical statistical analyses to describe human behavior if one was a materialist or if one believed in some version of an independent, nonmaterial soul.

Empirical laws represent another important category. These expressions sum up the observations of psychological research. As such, they represent the outcomes of the science, not the driving motivational inputs. Although they come closer to the initial needs of an axiomatic-deductive scientific system, most are not quantified, precise, or universal enough to the degree that would be necessary to deduce specific theorems.

Then there are the pragmatic principles. I must admit to being somewhat surprised to have encountered this kind of principle in my survey. However commendable and practical, these are not the kinds of principles that can be used to guide the intellectual development of a science. Pragmatic concerns should never constrain or distort scientific concerns!

I argue here that the category of epistemological assumptions represents the crux of modern psychological science. It is in this category that we find arguments about what can and cannot be known about brain, behavior, and mind and the means of achieving that knowledge. It is here that we are likely to find the heart of the future of scientific psychology. It is here that the problems, the challenges, and the most fundamental controversies are located.

Now, having made what must be appreciated as a very preliminary effort to identify the issues, I turn to another task—to detail my personal view of those principles that should guide a modern psychology.

NOTES

1. I must anticipate one criticism at this point. A critic of what I have just written might well see an inconsistency between the proposed reality of mind and my frequently expressed contention that it is inaccessible. This is a serious problem because of the mixture of ontological and epistemological issues that I hope will be clarified later in this chapter.

2. John Reich's comments were also previously listed in Uttal 2003, 170–71.

3. Amazon.com lists nearly one hundred books in which principles of psychology are promised in their titles.

4. My selection of the protopsychologists is incomplete, of course. Many other philosophers, scholars, and, theologians have concerned themselves with the problems of the soul cum mind for millennia. I have concentrated here on those who specifically promised psychological principles. Unfortunately, even these scholars have more often offered principles by suggestive title rather than by substance.

5. Spencer was such a committed atheist that he is reputed to have entered a church only once in his life—for the funeral of Charles Darwin!

6. Twenty years later, however, psychology was flourishing in the United States with many laboratories and both a society (the American Psychological Association founded in 1892) and active journals (the *Psychological Review*, for example, was founded in 1894 and is still a premier psychological journal).

7. All page references to Wundt are from the 1910 translation by Titchener.

8. In expressing each of these laws, I have made a best guess of their meanings from the often complex language that characterizes translations from Wundt's original German. I apologize if my interpretations differ from his original intent and invite my readers to do better.

9. Wundt's ideas on brain localization are also transparent here.

10. It is at this point that certain assumptions are covertly injected into the text. These include (a) the idea of modularity and (b) the supposed functional independence of these modules from the addition or subtraction of others by manipulation of the stimulus environment or selective surgery.

11. It should not go unremarked, as a number of psychologists have pointed out, that most modern and classic texts use essentially the same outline that Aristotle used in his groundbreaking *De Anima* of roughly twenty-four hundred years ago.

12. It should not be overlooked that the physical sciences wrestle with this same issue. The debate between probabilistic quantum physics and a more conventional deterministic physics continues, although the idea that there is an essential uncertainty concerning matter and its properties seems to have more proponents today.

13. Colleagues who directly contributed to this survey include Talis Bachman, Mary Lou Cheal, Jeffery Cochran, Jean-Claude Falmagne, Anthony Greenwald, Alexander Guiora, John Jonides, Peter Killeen, Roberta Klatzky, Cyril Latimer, Barry Leshowitz, George Mandler, Sergio Masin, Tadasu Oyama, Irwin Pollack, Michael Posner, Karl Pribram, Howard Rachlin, Richard Schuster, John Staddon, and Arnold Tannebaum.

14. The idea of pure insertion has been attributed to Sternberg (1969). It is defined as the assumption that components in a system may be added or subtracted from the system without any effect on the other components of the system.

15. It is important to appreciate that all of the assumptions in Pachella's list are also paralleled by their antitheses. Many of them lie at the heart of cognitive psychological thinking. Various forms appear throughout this list of epistemological assumptions.

16. Once again, it is important to remind my readers that each of these corollaries is paralleled by antithetical principles that represent the intellectual core of empirical research in psychology.

17. Although Grassman is given credit for organizing these laws of color mixing, the actual empirical study was carried out by other visual scientists in the nineteenth century.

18. I cannot resist telling one personal anecdote concerning the influence of this kind of ontological assumption. Some years ago, I was a visitor at an eclectic study center. Among my colleagues were two theologians. We had long and wonderful conversations in which there were almost no disagreements about the mysteries of life. It was only when we arrived at the most basic foundation assumption that our points of view diverged. The theologians attributed the mysteries to the workings of a personified God. I attributed them to the complexity and randomness of a material world. At that point there was no way to resolve our final fundamental differences. Each of us had our own basic ontology. No argument to evidence (from me) or belief (from them) could change the other's view. The point of this little anecdote is that there are some basic ontological assumptions that cannot be resolved but that can have profound effects on our worldviews. This influence can be either explicit or cryptic. For a discussion of one exemplar—dualistic thinking and how it arises from a primordial fear of death—see Uttal (2004).

Chapter 5

CREDO PSYCHOLOGICA

One Psychologist's View of His Science

5.1. INTRODUCTION

It is in this context of uncertainty and argument expressed so far that I attempt what is clearly one of the most reckless writing tasks of my career. So far, I have tried to present, to the maximum extent possible, an even-sided account of the issues in evaluating the scientific status of psychology. I have sought to tabulate the great conceptual principles that both divide and unite psychologists. I also inquire into the disturbing question of whether or not psychology is a science in the usual sense of the word.

In this final chapter, I propose a "credo"—a selection of those principles that define my personal psychological perspective. My purpose in doing so is to sharpen the discussion about what psychologists believe and what they do not believe about the status of their science. I am sure that not everyone will agree with every principle I enunciate here. That is fine, but perhaps it will provide the beginning of a framework so that what has become a collection of isolated observations can become a more widely accepted natural science. To those who disagree, I send a general invitation to detail their personal points of view.

5.2. FUNDAMENTAL ONTOLOGICAL PRINCIPLES

1. The primary monistic assumption without which cognitive neuroscience could not survive is that all mental activity is a function of or is equivalent to some brain activity. Without the brain (or in some unlikely future, a totally unexpected brain prosthesis) the mind ceases to exist. This means that any hopes for a life after the physical termination of brain activity are futile.
2. There is only one kind of reality—a material and rational world driven by regular physical laws and principles. All of science must be based on natural and material concepts, not supernatural and spiritual or irrational ones. The material world, in principle, provides a full account of all psychological phenomena, events, and principles, even if these are not achievable in practice.
3. The primary mental assumption without which psychology could equally well not survive is that mental processes are real. Unfortunately, the only evidence we have for this assumption is our firsthand experience of our own mind. By analogy, however, everybody else is also sentient and not an automaton. William James put it especially well when he said: "All people unhesitatingly believe that they feel themselves thinking, and that they distinguish the mental state as an inward activity or passion, from all the objects with which it may cognitively deal. I regard this belief as the most fundamental of all of the postulates of Psychology, and shall discard all curious inquiries about its certainty as too metaphysical for the scope of this book" (1: 185).
4. Mental activity is at its most fundamental level deterministic. Unfortunately, the interactive neural mechanisms and

processes underlying it are so complex and numerous that we are not able to either describe it at that level or determine exactly how consciousness is generated. Stochastic methods hide this essential determinism by substituting multiple observations of quasi-random processes (statistical inference) for elucidation of the "hidden" causal factors.

5. It is not known (and may not be knowable) whether or not mind is epiphenomenal. That is, do mental processes affect the activity of the brain or do mental states simply passively follow brain states? This is the conundrum of psychosomatic influence.[1]
6. "Truth is not a binary but a continuous variable." Most dichotomous controversies eventually end up as compromises between the two original extreme positions.

5.3. THE EPISTEMOLOGY OF MIND

1. Observations offered as scientific evidence must be "third-person" publicly observable by anyone with the appropriate instruments. That which is private to special "gifted" individuals such as prophets or psychics falls outside of the range of science.
2. Scientific knowledge that can be publicly shared must also be to at least a substantial degree reliable and replicable. That which is ephemeral falls outside of the realm of science.
3. Empirical evidence always takes priority over speculation.
4. The effort to scientifically study human behavior and cognitive processes should be guided by the age-old admonitions of scholars as far back as Aristotle, Descartes, and Newton and as recent as Whitehead and Russell. These admonitions include:
    - A critical, indeed, skeptical point of view about existing ideas is necessary for progress.
    - Simplicity is a virtue but not an end-all in scientific thinking.

- A single kind of reality should be assumed to underlie all of our thinking about the world, its parts, and its inhabitants. In particular, the laws of the mind must be in agreement with the laws of matter. Any mental events that violate or contradict the laws of material nature must be a priori rejected. Laws that work in one context must be assumed to work in another.
- Nature must be actively wrestled with by experimentation to achieve understanding.
- Speculation is not a substitute for logic. "Idle fantasies" cannot substitute for observation.
- The establishment of axioms by inductive thinking is a necessary but fragile approach to scientific thinking.
- Deduction does not discover new knowledge. It uncovers already known truths embedded in our observations and suggested by our inductively generated axioms. To the extent that deduced theorems agree with observations, the axioms are supported.

5. The mind, also known as consciousness, sentience, ego, soul, or self-awareness, is a personal sense of being. It is private and known only to the individual. It seems to accompany and motivate behavior but can be active without overt behavior.
6. Direct knowledge of our own personal consciousness is limited to ourselves. Although it seems likely that other people have the same private experiences, there is no way to tell for sure. At best, we reason by analogy from our perceived nature of our minds to the nature of other minds. At worst, we all commit what William James referred to as the "psychologist's fallacy"—projecting our meaning, thoughts, and logic onto the words of others.
7. Whether or not animals have a similar or reduced form of consciousness is also impossible to determine.
8. Unfortunately, psychologists have never been able to adequately define mental processes. The vocabulary of mentalism

is totally inadequate to provide a solid foundation for the scientific study of mental processes. Ill-defined mental entities represent hypothetical constructs, intervening variables, or post hoc theories rather than objectively and operationally defined entities. From our very beginning James (1890, 1: 194) acknowledged that the "first source of error in psychology" was the "misleading influence of speech."

9. The processes studied in psychological research laboratories are often the instantiated results of our experimental designs rather than true psychobiological realities.
10. It is not possible to answer a fundamental question of mental activity—Are our thoughts represented by isomorphic or symbolic representations? Similarly, there are many other specific "structural questions" (e.g., do mental processes operate in serial order or in parallel?) that are not answerable with psychological experiments. Serial processes can mimic parallel processes and vice versa.
11. Given the complexity of mind and the failure of all modern neuroreductionist theories of mental processes, it is very unlikely (to the point of impossibility) that eliminativist theories of mind will ever be accomplished. That is, psychology will never be replaced by neuroscience.
12. Mental processes are inherently inaccessible through either introspection or experimental assay methods. Current research that specifically attempts to infer mental processes from behavior is a priori invalid. "No cognitive debates can ever be resolved by behavioral data." In fact, we have no more insight into or awareness of the cognitive logic of our own mental activity than we do into the neural mechanisms of those mental processes.
13. Therefore, the only plausible form of psychology is one that concentrates on the description of publicly observable and measurable behavior—the approach to psychology called behaviorism.

14. Observations of behavior are in general valid regardless of one's theoretical orientation. It is only when we attempt to infer the mental mechanisms (i.e., generate hypothetical constructs or reductively explain the processes accounting for that behavior) that psychology deviates from generally acceptable scientific standards.
15. There is a fundamental psychological "uncertainty principle" that prevents us from examining mental processes without altering them. This raises serious questions about the objectivity of the data of psychology and the control that experimenters actually have in their laboratory studies.
16. Behavior and mathematics are neutral with regard to underlying mechanisms and processes.
17. Therefore, "Controversies between neural or cognitive mentalist theories cannot be resolved by behavioral research."
18. Mental processes are intrinsically holistic and cannot be analyzed into constituent modules. The reason for this is not that modules may not exist; instead it is because of the "one-to-many problem." That is, there is an innumerable number or possible modular structures that can account for behavior and no way to distinguish between them with psychological research methods. Furthermore, modularity is based on a number of implausible assumptions regarding mental processing that cannot be justified by empirical methods.
19. Since mental modules are so difficult to verify and are so poorly defined, efforts to localize them in the brain are also likely to be unfulfillable despite some suggestive evidence that mental faculties are influenced by broadly demarcated brain regions. The confusion of regions that are necessary with those that are sufficient is among the main sources of the illusion of localization.
20. Unlike physics and mathematics in which the standard paradigm is to start from primitive axiomatic principles and then derive general theories and theorems in a "bottom-up" style,

the prototypical paradigm in psychology is to observe the whole—behavior—and then to attempt in a "top-down" style to infer what are the primitives. Although the former is valid in principle, if not always in practice,[2] the latter is a priori invalid in that it can never lead to a unique explanation. This is why neural and cognitive module reduction is an inappropriate approach in psychology.

21. "Psychology is not just something to do until the biochemist [or neurophysiologist] comes" (attributed to Ulrich Neisser 1967). This aphorism is loaded with practical importance for psychology as a science regardless of what school or approach one is comfortable with. It asserts that psychology unto itself is a worthy effort and that it does not depend on any further reduction to other sciences. In fact, if reduction and analysis of cognitive processes turn out to be infeasible, psychology may be our only entrée into understanding human nature. We diminish it at our own peril.

5.4. THEORIES

1. Psychology has no primitive axioms of a kind comparable to Newton's $f_a = f_b$ from which to work from the bottom up.
2. For a number of reasons, and in a number of different fields,[3] scientists and philosophers have distinguished between strong and weak theories. Although there are many ways to make this distinction, I shall use the one suggested by Kim (1982.) A weak theory is defined as one that works within the confines of a narrowly defined field, whereas a strong theory is one that has broad applicability to a wide range of topics. The weak-strong dimension is anchored to the idea of underdetermination. For this reason and many of the others discussed in chapter 4, most of the theories of psychology must be classified as weak and underdetermined.

3. The putative measurability of mind, a basic foundation for the applicability of mathematical methods to mental processes, remains a serious problem for the application of all kinds of mathematics in psychology. Quantifiability depends on three properties of that which is being measured—ordinality, additivity, and linear causality. Many mental phenomena do not exhibit these properties. Therefore, it seems likely that mental processes are not measurable in the same manner as are most physical properties. This results in meaningless expressions that are sometimes cloaked in mathematical formalisms.
4. Most mathematical models in psychology are stochastic in nature, substituting probability and randomness for a complete determinist description of the many forces and effects that control behavior. Those simple laws that assert some specific relation between a stimulus and a response are typically gross approximations that promise much but are not useful for the prediction of individual human behavior. Psychological hypotheses are more conjectures of loose relationships between stimuli and responses than equations.
5. Some of the most venerable methods for choosing among competing theories (e.g., the principle of parsimony or Ockham's razor) may be irrelevant to the study of psychology simply because redundancy and complexity may trump simplicity. Nevertheless, one of the hallmarks of good science has been the ability to explain the most with the least.
6. There are many pitfalls on the road to theory building. We can be misled by functional similarities and isomorphisms that appear superficially to be homologs but are actually only analogs. Semantic properties can be simulated by syntactic relationships as was the case in such theoretical approaches as list processing.
7. At the present time, it does not appear that psychology has any general empirical laws or primitive axioms that would permit the development of a theory of either mind or behavior

comparable to Newton's *Principia*. Psychological laws do not justify the use of the equal symbol (=). Instead, = means "is related to" or "is approximated by."

8. The quest for a unified theory of cognitive processes is probably hopeless. Psychology seems to be an aggregate of microtheories, each of which is specific to a particular research topic. There has been no convergence toward a set of universal laws or principles. We cannot even agree on the necessary and sufficient conditions to designate a unified theory. There have been some theories that claim to be "universal" (e.g., Anderson 1996, Newell 1990), however, neither of these efforts accomplishes the task of unifying even the narrowly defined domain of cognitive psychology. What Anderson and Newell did do was to provide a pair of programming languages that could be generally used to describe cognition. Neither, however, is an explanatory or reductive theory.
9. The hypothetical-deductive method of theorem proving that has proven so useful in the physical sciences and mathematics has not proven to be a satisfactory method of psychological theory building. Indeed, it is not yet established what the primary axioms of such an effort would be. Some of the reasons that the classic method may not be applicable include:[4]
   - The questionable quantifiability of mental activity.
   - The fact that psychological laws are situation-specific and not general.
   - The hypothetical constructs of psychology are capacities, not structures.
   - The language (including the vocabulary and the syntax) of mental events differs from the language of mathematics.
10. Most theories of psychological processes and behavior are little more than descriptions of observed phenomena or names attached to them. None are satisfactory reductive explanations either to basic cognitive processes or to neural mechanisms that go beyond "just so stories," distant analogs, or "possible inferences."

11. There are, of course, other models cum theories of human behavior including computer-based simulations. However, simulations of this kind are only designed to reproduce behavior including such impressive abilities as problem solving and pattern recognition. In most such simulations, the underlying principles are not, however, defined by putative psychological mechanisms but rather by the abilities and properties of the computer and its program. It is very easy to confuse simulations of this kind with theories of the mind. For many reasons, systems that behave alike may be doing so for very different reasons. Even the best artificial intelligence (AI) computer program need not be a good explanation of the behavior it imitates, since quite different mechanisms might produce identical results.
12. Mental processes are almost certainly represented or encoded by networks of putative cognitive and neural networks that are so heavily interactive by feed forward, feed backward, and lateral mechanism that we cannot even unravel their hierarchical relationships, much less determine how they produce mental activity.
13. Computer network theories or models, although probably closer to the truth than any other explanation of how the mind is made by the brain, are generally incapable of being scaled up to psychologically significant levels. Those that do successfully simulate some behavior do so by methods based on the proclivities and abilities of computers rather than by those of any plausible neural processes. In general, modern connectionist models are no longer "neural net" theories but elaborate "boxologies" (flowcharts of arrows and boxes) incorporating functional modules much more complex than neurons.
14. One of the most common modern approaches to theory is to develop a simulation or analog of the behavior under examination. The algorithms used by a computer to produce the desired behavior are then assumed to be the same (in some

logical sense) as the processes used by the brain to implement cognitive processes. This is a classic error! Analogous behavior is never a sufficient proof of equivalent (i.e., homologous) mechanisms. Mammals, birds, insects, and even some fish can navigate in the air. However, the mechanisms that permit these different creatures to accomplish this task need not, and typically do not, arise from the same embryological sources. Each creature has evolved a mechanism for moving through the air from its own special heritage. These are examples of convergent evolution, not homologous mechanisms. In the same sense, however similar the behavior generated by a computer program may be to human behavior, there is no assurance that the program arrived at the final outcome by means of the same logic, mechanisms, processes, or procedures that underlie superficially similar human behavior.

15. Many of the tasks undertaken by psychological theorists are actually the equivalent of what are already known to be intractable mathematical problems.
16. Theories cannot be validated by converging operations. Imprecision perpetuates imprecision.
17. However well it may represent the ideal of scientific method, the axiomatic-deductive approach described in earlier chapters is not, of course, the only means of carrying out scientific activities. Some scientific activities are merely explorations based on a question as simple as "I wonder what is over the next mountain?" or "What would happen if I mixed these two substances together?" Some of the most important scientific discoveries have been the result of pure accidents and a receptive serendipity. However, as sciences mature, many gradually evolve into a more and more formal version that ever-more closely approximates the axiomatic-deductive model of the ideal. Information is acquired by one means or another, and generalizing theories are propounded that identify general principles that may themselves become axioms of other levels

of analysis. At least this is the fiction; scientific reality is a far less-organized process than these few words might suggest, with prejudices, prejudgments, philosophical and theological convictions, and various kinds of other vested and subjective interests also forcing the development of a field of inquiry.

5.5. BEHAVIORISM

1. Most of the findings obtained in psychological research studies are valid and even potentially useful data (excluding any obvious or subtle flaws in the methodology). It is only when these data are used to infer unique mental mechanisms and processes that psychologists are attempting to do the impossible.
2. Behavior is determined by multiple causes interacting in complex ways.
3. Behavior consists of third-person observable events and may include motor, verbal, endocrine, and other physiological responses. Private mental events are not behavior and are inaccessible. Replication and verification beyond the original observer (using, for example, a double-blind control) is also required. This does not mean that mental events without behavior cannot occur but rather that such behavior-free thoughts are fundamentally unobservable.
4. It is not possible to infer mental states from introspective reports. Many of the results of psychological experiments are heavily contaminated by what may generically be called "cognitive penetration." That is, logical order, secondary motives, and personal needs often unrelated to the purpose of the experiment, as well as simple ignorance of one's own logical and motivational processes, confound and confuse first-person reports. People are not aware of the causes of their behavior.
5. It is not possible to infer mental states from behavior. The

problem is made intractable by the "one (behavior)-to-many (explanations)" problem.

6. It is not possible to infer mental states from mathematical analyses or models. Mathematics is primarily a descriptive method that is neutral with regard to the mechanisms whose outcome is being described.
7. A modern scientific psychology must be behaviorist and be characterized by the following properties:[5]
    - Psychophysical anchoring: Classical psychophysics has provided us with excellent methods for scientific investigation in which stimuli and responses are anchored to physical dimensions and parameters. Psychophysics has been enormously effective because it has developed a system of standardized procedures (e.g., the method of limits, forced choice procedures, signal detection theory, etc.) that helped to avoid or, at least, to understand some of the biases that can creep into interpretations of empirical findings. In this manner it is possible to characterize the transformations between stimuli and responses and to determine which attributes of a stimulus are salient; that is, which have effects and which do not. We can also measure the transformations that characterize the relationships between stimulus and response relationships. Beyond that kind of descriptive, transformational behaviorism, psychology is on treacherous grounds when it attempts to infer neural and mental processes and mechanisms from behavior.
    - Simple responses: Responses must be restricted to as simple judgments as possible. The idea is the class A judgment (Brindley 1960) characterized by nothing more complicated than the responses of "same" or "different." Anything more complicated runs the danger of allowing cognitive penetration effects to distort the actual functional relationships.

- Operational: Psychology must define its concepts in terms of procedures, not in terms of unverifiable, ad hoc, hypothetical mentalist constructs.
- Mathematically and behaviorally descriptive: Since reductive explanations are constrained if not prohibited by epistemological concerns, we must appreciate that all theories and models can, at best, only describe the behavior of a complex system of as great complexity as the brain. The best way to accomplish this description is by the use of mathematics with its tight rules and logic. However, all mathematical theories (including computational and neural net versions) are in fundamental principle incapable of determining the underlying mechanisms that account for the observed behavior. Leaps of inference from behavioral data to reductive explanation, no matter how ingenious, cannot be verified. Goodness of fit of a mathematical model with empirical observations, likewise, does not verify the existence of its inferred hypothetical constructs. In short, mathematics, computer simulations, and behavior are all *neutral* concerning the specific nature of underlying mechanisms.
- Neuronally nonreductive: Because the brain is a vast matrix of many neurons multiply and idiosyncratically interconnected; because the organization of this neuronal matrix is the ultimate psychoneural equivalent of mental activity; and because complexity theorists have taught us about the intractability of NP-complete problems (of which the brain is likely to represent a valid example), the hope of reductively explaining any behavioral observation by a neural model cannot be fulfilled. This does not mean that neural nets cannot be made to simulate some aspects of cognitive processes, but rather that such a simulation cannot validate the separable neurophysiological assumptions of a mathematical model.

Nevertheless, no reductive theory can ever be singled out from the many possible ones as the "true" explanation. This does not mean that some of the tentative "theories" may not be amusing, interesting, or serve some useful purpose such as intellectual stimulation. It just means that we should not take them seriously.

- Experimental: No science can be pursued in the absence of a regular, continual, and rule-constrained grappling with nature or, more specifically, the kind of nature with which that science is concerned. The major means for testing ideas for scientific psychology is controlled experimentation. This does not mean that all observations are unequivocal or that all questions can be answered by laboratory or naturalistic methods of investigation. Nevertheless, like democracy, this is the best we have.
- Molar: Because of the epistemological limits on reduction to either neurons or cognitive modules, the main approach of any scientific psychology should be a molar one. Of course, in the peripheral world of sensory and motor functions, some early-level analyses are possible. However, when it comes to higher level cognitive processes, a holistic, unified approach is the proper one.
- Empiricist$_1$ and nativist: Throughout the history of behaviorism, one of the heaviest and least sustainable intellectual burdens it carried was the overwhelming emphasis on the learning (empiricism$_1$) as opposed to the innate (nativist) determinants of behavior. Clearly, modern developments in the genetic sources of human development make it clear that the nature-nurture issue is far more complicated than any simplistic and exclusionary theories of this genre would suggest. The appropriate resolution of this age-old controversy almost certainly has to be an eclectic one in which both factors are

acknowledged to be important in the determination of behavior. However, it is unlikely that we will ever be able to determine the exact degree of influence of either, given the complex, nonlinear manner in which the two influences interact.

- Empiricist$_2$ and rationalist: The debate between champions of direct, stimulus-determined behavior (empiricism$_2$) and those who believe it is mediated by active processes in the organism (rationalism) has also bedeviled traditional behaviorist approaches. This debate has also been exacerbated by humanistic ideals of "free will." There is sufficient evidence of nonveridical processing in the visual system resulting in distortions and misinterpretations of the incident stimulus pattern to support the hypothesis of an active, mediated cognitive system. However, even though both direct and mediated factors must be at work, this question probably cannot be resolved. These doubts are based on the assumption that there is no way to determine the underlying mechanisms from the psychophysical reports. In other words, it is possible, perhaps even likely, that an ultra-complex "direct" system could produce responses that are indistinguishable from the most complex, mediated behavior. Indeed, this issue is the prototypical example of the fragility of any attempt to "explain" underlying mechanisms from external observations. What is clear is that, whether it is direct or mediated, the organism plays a powerful dynamic and transformational role in determining how we behave. In summary, we are not driven by stimuli alone.
- Antipragmatic: Throughout the history of American psychology in particular, from the pragmatism[6] of Charles Sanders Pierce and William James to the therapeutically and humanistically oriented modern applied psychologies,

practical values have dominated much too much of our science. This has happened to the detriment of psychology as a pure science rather than as a putative contributor to the "well-being" of society and of the individual. It is virtually impossible to argue against such noble practical goals, but all too often psychologists have substituted criteria of "social value," "affirmative action," or "political correctness" for scientific objectivity and the quest for truth and basic understanding. (How few of us are willing to study the differences in abilities between races or genders these days?) I propose to leave these otherwise noble and desirable goals to those social engineers among us. In return, I ask them to leave to scientific psychology the quest for long-term goals of understanding and knowledge for their own sakes. The applied mentalists who, for one reason or another, choose to defend both accessibility and cognitive reductionism, are welcome to proceed, but in the final analysis, any success psychotherapy is able to demonstrate is more likely to be attributable to inspired intuition or the special empathy enjoyed by certain gifted individuals than to the results of rigorous scientific investigation.[7] Theories of the nature of psychobiological nature should remain unpolluted by social needs or trends, but, to the contrary and to the maximum extent possible, should be based on an objective and independent evaluation of natural observations by unbiased observers.

5.6. MIND-BRAIN RELATIONSHIPS

1. At the present time, we have no idea how the brain functions to produce the mind. There is at least an argument that the classic question—How do the macro properties of the mind emerge from the micro properties of the brain?—cannot be answered.

All major neural theories of the mind are deeply flawed. Field theories are based on an analogy that the global electrical effects are comparable to mental processes. Single-cell neural theories are based on vastly undercontrolled experiments in which it is not known what is happening at neurons other than the few from which responses are recorded. Neural net theories are based on toy computer models that cannot be upwardly scaled. Brain chunk or locale theories are based on the outdated assumption that well-defined psychological processes are mediated by equally well localized and demarcated regions of the brain. (See Uttal 2005 for a complete discussion of this topic.)

2. It seems likely at this point that the goal of eliminativism—a complete mind-brain neuroreductionism—can never be achieved.
3. Any neural theory of the mind is challenged by the following properties of the brain:
    - Combinatorial explosion due to the large number of neurons involved in even the simplest thought.
    - Nonlinearity of the interactions in the brain.
    - Chaotic (apparent) randomness of neuronal components.
    - The "Black Box problem" asserting that internal structure cannot be determined by input-output mechanisms.
    - Fragile database of neurophysiology and experimental psychology.
    - Elusive and incomplete definitions of cognitive processes and the resulting uncertain meaning associated with them.
    - Mental processes can be encoded by the nervous system in many different ways, producing equivalent behavior. It is unlikely that brains are wired in the same way. Instead, as a result of change and experience, our brains use different mechanisms to produce similar mental experiences. The neural mechanisms underlying a given thought or behavior may also vary from time to time.
4. It has been fashionable recently to ask, How are actions of the

different regions of the brain coordinated? This is known as the "binding problem" and is based on the idea that cognitive and neural modules exist. It is likely that this is a false question that needs no answer. Instead, the brain may be operating as a global and unified mechanism in which any allusion to a putative binding is superfluous.

5. We know of many drugs that affect the activity of the brain, the mind, and behavior. In general, the action of all of these chemicals is known only in terms of their effects on brain synapses as mediated by their transmitter substances. However, no truly explanatory theory of how these effects produce changes in mental processes is known. In the main, the "science" of psychochemistry is atheoretical.
6. Because of the enormous success in identifying the neural transmission codes of the sensory and motor pathways, a mistaken impression has developed that the answer to the codes for ill-defined hypothetical constructs (e.g., "abstract-noun categories such as choice, timing, and risk") is at hand. In fact, without the anchors to the physical world enjoyed by the peripheral neural mechanisms, these mentalist terms are unlikely to be neurally decoded—ever.
7. Cummins (2000) sums up the problem of neuroreductionism as follows:

> Even if we are convinced that the mind is the brain, or a process going on in the brain, physical observation of the brain seems to give us data in the wrong vocabulary; synapses rather than thoughts.

5.7. EMPIRICAL LAWS AND OBSERVATIONS

1. Despite the problems with theory building and reductive explanation, psychology, neurophysiology, mathematics, and com-

puter science—the fields collectively known as cognitive neuroscience—have much to discover and offer to a modern scientific outlook of the world. The discovery of empirical laws and novel relationships, even if not rigidly adhering to strictly quantitative relationships, is exceedingly important and helps us to understand how we behave, if not why we do so.

2. Psychology's empirical laws, however, are highly specific to the situation in which they are observed. Most psychological research is aimed at observing and collecting data. Most of modern psychology's educational effort is aimed at how to do that; little education is aimed at critical analysis of underlying concepts, assumptions, and principles.
3. Unfortunately, cognitive neuroscience is so complicated and so multidimensional that it is currently characterized as a collection of isolated empirical results and narrowly defined "theories" that at best describe restricted empirical topics.
4. Many of the most interesting observations in traditional psychology are nonveridical, that is, there are discrepancies between the dimensions of the physical world and those of the perceived world. It is the main purpose of the empirical research to determine the nature of these discrepancies and the transformations that describe them. Because of the inaccessibility of the cognitive process and mechanisms, the description of these transformations must be the main activity of an empirical scientific psychology. There is no hope of unraveling the details of the internal logic, processes, or mechanisms of the "mind" that account for these transformations.
5. This goal does not preclude the identification of peripheral neural coding mechanisms for sensory and motor processes that are adequately anchored to both external physical measurements and relatively simple neurophysiological observations. It does preclude the identification of the neurophysiological equivalents of poorly defined cognitive processes and such problems as whether we see by means of gestalt organization or

local features. Although there have been many studies that purport to have resolved such issues, in fact, they remain controversial and unresolved. The most likely explanation is that many factors influence how we perceive and that none is unique.

6. Many fields of psychology have a rich history of empirical observations. We know that people learn best when they practice and when the stimuli and responses are closely related in time and space. It is likely that learning can be optimized for different skills.
7. However, we do not know what the underlying processes and mechanisms of learning are. Many of the classical questions (e.g., Do we learn by associating micro-components or by encoding configurations? Are some behaviors, for example, speech, innate or must everything be learned? How many different kinds of memory exist? Where does memory reside? How do we recall?) are probably not answerable. Answers proposed to these questions are speculative inferences and are not amenable to empirical analysis.
8. Such strengths and limits also hold for all other fields of psychology. Great progress can be made in observing behavior in various areas of performance and cognitive processes such as problem solving. We can study reaction times, risk estimation, and decision times under conditions of time sharing and forced divided attention. However, unique and definitive *reductive explanations* concerning how the mind accomplishes these wonderful tasks are unobtainable. The most important conclusion is to remember that "empirical observations are not theories." It requires a number of inferential, logical, and integrative leaps to make observations into reductive theories. Unfortunately, the conceptual and technical barriers to making these leaps are enormous and probably insurmountable.

5.8. APPLIED PSYCHOLOGY

1. Applied psychology can be divided into main divisions (as can the rest of psychology). The first division includes those subfields of inquiry that are based primarily on behavioral observations and is exemplified by forensic human factors research. The second division is exemplified by clinical psychotherapy that seeks (with the exception of a few behavioral therapies) to interpret past, present, and future mental states and to "cure" abnormal behavior by manipulating those mental states.
2. Human factors research is a pure form of behaviorism. No effort is made to infer internal mental mechanisms. All that matters is the raw performance data. With the exceptions of choice of threshold criteria and applicability to particular instances, there is usually little controversy over the data obtained.
3. Clinical psychotherapy is a pure mentalism. It is based on the assumption that the mind is accessible and manipulable. Psychotherapists are in constant conflict about methods, theories, and especially about their ability to predict human behavior.
4. Clinical (or psychotherapeutic) psychology is aimed at the alleviation of what now is appreciated as a poorly differentiated family of mental disorders that vary from minor neuroses to major psychotic behavior. The standard manual of mental aberrations is the *Diagnostic and Statistical Manual of Mental Disorders DSM-IV*, published by the American Psychiatric Association (Anonymous 1992, Anonymous 2000). This document is an ambitious, extraordinarily convoluted, but ultimately failed effort to provide a coherent classification system for mental disorders. Its ultimate goal was to develop taxonomy of mental illness similar to the Linnaean classification system used in biology or the Mendeleyev system used to classify the chemical elements. This goal was not achieved by the psychologists who put this document together, and there is good reason to

believe that it cannot be achieved by anyone else (Spiegel 2005, Kirk and Kutchins 1992).

5. Most tests of psychotherapeutic effectiveness have not been validated (Lilienfeld 2002).
6. Most studies of the effectiveness of psychotherapy indicate that it does seem to work but that no method (other than a slight advantage accruing to behavioral methods) seems to work any better than any other (Anonymous 1995, 2004; Shapiro and Shapiro 1982; Lipsey and Wilson 1993). There is a strong suggestion, therefore, that any positive effect is largely attributable to a placebo and that there is no scientific foundation for any of the specialized theories. Mentalistic psychotherapy, therefore, is largely outside of the bounds of standard science, along with other even less well-documented attempts to "read people's minds."

5.9. PSYCHOLOGY AS A SCIENCE OF THE USUAL KIND

1. Psychology is a science in the usual sense of the word to the degree that it is behaviorist and characterized by the following propositions:
    - Behavior is available to public observation and, thus, is available to third-person verification.
    - Behavior is quantifiable and orderly and, thus, measurable.
    - Behavior is anchored to the physical world by a common set of measurements and dimensions.
    - Although not without its difficulties and differences with other sciences, behaviorist psychology meets many of the criteria of a standard science. It is accurate, consistent, orderly, somewhat fruitful, testable, and linguistically and methodologically based on natural and material foundation assumptions. Unfortunately, behavioral theories are plagued by the absence of any convergence

onto an ever-reducing (i.e., pyramiding) set of synoptic (i.e., broad-based) laws.[8]

2. Psychology is not a science to the degree that it seeks to infer internal mental mechanisms from behavioral observations or introspections.
    - Mentalisms deal with intangible, immeasurable, imprecisely defined, inferred hypothetical constructs, whose existence is private to the individual.
    - Mental phenomena, although real, are not measurable or quantitative because they are not anchored to a system of units and dimensions that meet criteria for measurability.
    - A major difficulty is that mental phenomena often operate in violation of other laws of physical science.
    - Inferred mental processes and mechanisms are nonunique because of the one-(phenomenon)-to-many (explanations) problem.
    - Mentalisms meet few of the criteria that define a normal science. Mentalist theories, including modern cognitivisms, suffer from fragile and inconsistent observational data, a lack of taxonomic order and linguistic naturalism in the definition of mental constructs, testability, and fruitfulness. Furthermore, they share with behaviorism the absence of breadth and convergence on a set of synoptic concepts, laws, and principles.
3. Psychology as an aspiring theoretical science, in general, suffers from continued acceptance of the challenges that led to Hull's noble failure to develop a formal model in the spirit of Newton. In the still-relevant words of Koch (1954), psychological theories do "not adequately meet concrete problems of empirical definition, of measurement, of quantification, of intervening variable function construction, and various subspecifications of all of these" (161).
4. Mathematics is a powerful tool in science, and psychology is no exception. However, the role of mathematics in psychology

is not explanatory or reductive; it is only descriptive. In many instances, mathematical expressions give the false impression of precision and explanation. However, many of these applications are meaningless because of the absence of quantifiable mental dimensions.

5. Because of the great complexity and variability of the activities involved in even the simplest kind of mental responses, mathematical psychology is mainly structured in terms of probability and randomness. It does poorly at predicting individual behavior even though it can effectively summarize group trends.
6. To an arguable degree, psychology is more akin to applied engineering than to theoretical physics. Psychology and engineering are both mainly descriptive; psychology does poorly at the kind of explanation that theoretical science holds as its holy grail. Psychology, at its best, describes behavior but has so far failed to explain why it works as it does.

5.10. GENERAL CONCLUSIONS

1. The main purposes of this book have been to develop a taxonomy of psychological principles and to ask, Is psychology a science in the usual sense of the word? We now know that this is not an easy question to answer. Conclusions proposed here are dependent, not unexpectedly, on a set of assumptions that are ontological and epistemological as well as an examination of the criteria that define science in general.
2. It seems clear that psychology is not a standard or normal science. The expectation and desire to emulate physics ("physicophilia") is fatally flawed. Psychology and physics differ substantially in terms of their methodology as well as their subject matters. These differences are based on differences in complexity and accessibility as well as the historic degree to which they have pyramided into coherent synoptic theories. Although

it is true that both psychology and physics deal with inaccessible entities (distant stars and the nearby mind), psychology has a much more severe problem in interpreting its kind of behavioral data. The mind is much more complex and variable than a distant star. Even more important is that physics can assume that its laws work as well here as at the limits of the universe. The laws of the ultra-small and the ultra-distant are likely to be the same. Psychology cannot make this same claim, since its laws of space and time and the laws of the mind do not seem to follow those of the physical universe.

3. Mentalist psychologies share many characteristics with organized religion. Both mentalism and religion invoke inaccessible, unverifiable, hypothetical entities with no possibility of verification and innumerable plausible alternative instantiations. Belief and acceptance rather than critical disbelief and skepticism are their standard modi operandum. Modest correlations and coincidences between events dominate thinking in both fields rather than compelling demonstrable verification. The act of inferring mental structures, processes, and mechanism from overt behavior or introspection has much in common with ancient religious beliefs about the soul.
4. The history of psychology is confounded with theological constructs (e.g., mind-brain dualism) that continue to this day to affect its standing as a science. (See Uttal 2004 for a fuller discussion of this topic.)
5. Nevertheless, by concentrating on the observation and analysis of publicly observable behavior and eschewing mentalistic hypotheses, psychology can be considered to be a natural, if undeveloped, science.
6. If psychology is to survive, it must evolve from its current mentalism to a revised and rejuvenated behaviorism. At present, experimental psychology is having a crisis because of inroads from analytic mentalism and other reductionist theoretical approaches such as cognitive neuroscience.

7. This rejuvenated behaviorist psychology must survive because the alternatives (neural and cognitive reductionism) are not tenable. Therefore, if psychology is lost as a science, we lose hope of ever answering some of the most profound questions about human nature.
8. Many of the principles and assumptions that I have listed here as a part of personal credo are probably not verifiable. For many there are no "killer arguments" that would quickly convince one side or the other to change favorite assumptions. However, the most important message of this book is that our initial assumptions exert a powerful influence on our theoretical thinking and experimental protocols. If this book reminds my readers to occasionally check to see what their own fundamental assumptions are, it will have served its purpose.

NOTES

1. At the present time, most research tends to show that prayer or humor does not affect medical outcomes.

2. Complex systems behave in ways that make them appear to be chaotic, random, and unpredictable. So many small influences can determine their ultimate behavior that it is usually impossible to predict a future outcome or reconstruct the path the system took to arrive at its current state.

3. This includes such diverse fields as religion (e.g., strong versus weak versions of agnosticism), evolution, astronomy, artificial intelligence, and geometry.

4. With appreciation to R. Cummins (2000) for making some of these properties especially clear.

5. This is my most recent version of a statement of what I believe must be the core of a modern scientific behaviorism. It is expanded and adapted from pp. 230–32 of Uttal (2002) and is used with the permission of the original publisher, Lawrence Erlbaum Associates Inc.

6. The main theme of American pragmatism is that scientific value is to be found in its practical utility. This is in contrast to the more esoteric idea that

the value of a science should be knowledge and truth for their own sake. Pragmatism is an almost anti-intellectual idea, but a profoundly American one.

7. See Dawes (1994) for a much richer and fuller treatment of this assertion.

8. Definitions and elaborations of the meanings of these terms can be found in chapter 1. A fuller development is given in Uttal (2005).

Appendix

EPISTEMOLOGICA PSYCHOLOGICA

The Confluence of Psychology and Epistemology

A.1. INTRODUCTION

In chapter 4, I proposed a minitaxonomy consisting of six different kinds of assumptions, postulates, and principles that characterized psychology.

1. Ontological Principles
2. Epistemological Principles
3. Statistical and Measurement Principles
4. Methodological Principles
5. Pragmatic Principles
6. Empirical Laws

As one looks over the list of what I have labeled Epistemological Principles, it is clear that most of the principles encountered there are concerned with what we can know and how we go about knowing. Furthermore, most of them are nearly synonymous with many of the problems that challenged psychological researchers and their predecessors for centuries. The history of psychology is filled with controversial dichotomies including holism versus elementalism, accessibility versus inaccessibility, nature versus nurture, and serial versus parallel that map directly onto the epistemological vocabulary. This then raises the question of the relation between scientific psychology and epistemology in its baldest form: Can experimental psychology replace epistemology?

An affirmative answer to this question has considerable merit, and there are distinguished philosophers (e.g., Quine 1969) who leaned in this direction when they proposed what came to be called "naturalistic epistemology." However, there are a considerable number of others (e.g., Stroud 1984, Shatz 1993) who feel that there are fundamental distinctions between the two endeavors that suggest that, in the long run, it is to our advantage to keep them separate. One of these distinctions is that epistemology is considered by some philosophers to be exclusively a study of knowledge that depends on a priori concepts; that is, knowledge based on reason alone.[1] Psychology as a putative science, however, is concerned with knowledge that is based on a posteriori concepts; that is, knowledge that emerges from experience and empirical research.

Whichever side of this controversy one falls on concerning psychology's putative replacement of epistemology is not so much a matter of debate as it, too, is a matter of the basic assumptions under which one labors. Accepting the rational assumption that knowledge can be validated by reason alone places one firmly and irrefutably in the a priori and, thus, separateness camp. Experimental psychology, from this perspective, is simply a modest adjunct or even unnecessary. Assuming that evidence is required to convert a belief into knowledge, to the contrary, suggests that psychology may well be a replacement for epistemology or may unify the two fields by removing any differences between them.

If it is not yet clear what my views are, I state them now for clarity's sake. I argue that rational, speculative, logical, or a priori approaches can never resolve issues of the truth or verification of our foundation assumptions; there is simply too much that can be taken for granted; too much to accept as being "self-evident"; too much left to intuition. The criteria of logical consistency and speculative coherence by themselves will usually leave even relatively simple issues unresolved.

A priori arguments, therefore, have the negative effect of permitting unsupportable assumptions simply because they can be imagined. It is analogous to the problem of "possible worlds," a fallacious strategy used by some philosophers to provide an entrée into otherwise unsupportable speculations. In this manner, what is "just possible" all too easily becomes reified as a real entity worthy of some nonzero probability, even though it may have no other empirical foundation.

There is no better example of how this can happen than in the "possibility" (i.e., "hope") that our consciousness can exist after our bodies have ceased to function. The ramification of the mere "possibility" of an afterlife into the enormous and complex theological enterprise that dominates thinking in the modern world is an example of how far one can go with logical if misleading consistency once a "possibility" has been accepted. In a more materialist and psychological context, a priori beliefs also tend to incorporate ideas such as the validity of introspective reports and the accessibility or the modularity of mental functions, all of which, to say the least, are open to question and remain possibilities rather than established facts.

Thus, many of the highly questionable assumptions of mentalist psychology are implicit in the strategies of a priori epistemology. A priori epistemology can lead to the same kind of unresolvable controversies that afflict mentalist psychologies and that are only partially ameliorated by sticking to a purely behaviorist approach to the study of human nature. Furthermore, the a priori method, devoid of empirical anchors to the world of public observation and measurement, offers a doorway into consideration of the supernatural, the occult, or the "intuitive," simply because they invoke propositions that can be realized in the form of what appear to be meaningful sentences but that in fact are meaningless.

My position is quite different; it is composed of two parts that are the usual standards on which most other scientific endeavors depend. First, truth (or our closest and best approximations to it) can only be verified if there are measurable connections to the material world. Second, empirical results are the most robust kind of evidentiary anchors to that material world. Although a strictly a posteriori approach of this kind may leave many important questions unanswered, it provides a sounder foundation for verification than the most logical, internally consistent, speculative epistemology ever can. Having a psychology with a much heavier commitment to conceptual and normative issues would, in my opinion, be a step in the right direction. In this context, the answer to the rhetorical question asked previously is that it is likely that a properly thoughtful psychology can replace epistemology or at least the parts we wish to preserve.

A.2. TOWARD SOME CRITICAL DEFINITIONS

To appreciate the complexity of some of what may at once seem to be simple and arcane issues, it is important to be as clear as possible about the meaning of some key terms. Among the most relevant to present discussion are knowledge, epistemology, and verification. Furthermore, we may be able to approach a clearer idea of what is meant by a scientific "psychology" by expanding on the idea of how closely it is related to epistemology.

A.2.1. Knowledge

The best place to start is with the word *knowledge*. As we see, the word appears explicitly throughout all of the definitions of epistemology. To achieve a precise definition of knowledge, I first consider a somewhat restricted and widely accepted meaning framed in a scientific vocabulary; namely, that knowledge is potential information that has been verified by evidence. Unsubstantiated or unverifiable ideas that arise out of subjective needs (e.g., the fear of death) do not rise to the levels of knowledge. Nor, for that matter, do the proposed solutions to some of the great ontological arguments about the nature of "reality" and "existence." These unproven or unprovable convictions are far better connoted by the word *belief*. Knowledge has a more specific denotation—*proven* speculations or *verified* ideas as opposed to *just possible* or *hypothetical*, but *unsubstantiated*, beliefs.

It would be inappropriate to indicate that beliefs in the existence of a particular god or an afterlife represent knowledge in the sense I use here. The same is true of private revelations reported by an individual that cannot be subject to empirical test and replication. Information about the geography of the United States (measured and remeasured as it has been by surveyors for centuries and anchored to independent measures on the other hand) represents knowledge, even if it has not been directly experienced by the observer.

A distinction can, therefore, be drawn between information that has been directly experienced by at least one person and can be publicly shared with others (knowledge), on the one hand, and speculative beliefs about events that have never been directly experienced, on the other.[2] Mere recitation of what an individual reports has been experienced cannot transform a hallucination or "private revelation" into knowledge. The private reports of prophets have no place in verifying knowledge.

It is crystal clear that any such definition of a word such as *knowledge* is going to be subject to as much uncertainty and debate as are the mentalist terms of psychology. Philosophers have long debated just how complete the verification must be for it to be accepted. Indeed, it was Plato who first offered the traditional definition of knowledge as "justified true belief."

Recent arguments about the meaning of knowledge have been concerned with just how certain (or uncertain) the verification must be. Given what we have already encountered concerning the stochastic nature of people and the universe, it can be reasonably argued that it may never be possible to produce perfect verification. Particularly in psychology, dominated as it is by statistical and probabilistic considerations, it is not at all certain what would constitute universally acceptable "knowledge."

Some recent arguments concern the logic of what constitutes knowledge. The issue is framed in the context of the necessity and sufficiency for knowing that a proposition represents true knowledge. This standard argument for what constitutes knowledge as a "justified true belief" was stated in the following form by Gettier (1963).

An observer (O) "knows" (i.e., has knowledge) a proposition (P) is true IF

1. P is true.
2. O accepts P.
3. O has justification for believing in P.

Gettier (1963) challenged this traditional form of an argument for knowing a proposition (P) is true (i.e., represented knowledge as opposed to belief). He pointed out that there are situations in which all of the steps in this argument are true, and, yet, P is not true because of some additional information or intuition not included in these formal steps. Simply put, Gettier was arguing against the classic definition of knowledge being "justified true belief" because of the potential incompleteness of virtually any solely logical argument. A justified true belief, thus, may be necessary but may not be sufficient to be considered "knowledge" in the strict sense proposed here. Gettier's argument is now considered a major problem for philosophers who are attempting to define knowledge.

Another major problem with loose and controversial definitions of knowledge occurs when philosophers contend with "possible worlds" (e.g., the zombie worlds of Chalmers 1996). In those debates, there is no foundation for verifying beliefs. All that is available is the rawest form of speculation about what may be possible, that is, what can be put into words. The probability of the possible world is usually not considered, nor is our ability to measure or evaluate those probabilities. Premises based on what is possible, not on what has been substantiated or verified, are a fragile foundation on which to build a hope that some otherwise intractable issues could be resolved.

The limited meaning of *knowledge* is also closely bound up with the constraints on inductive reasoning. I have already pointed out that inductively proven axioms are not always compelling arguments in the same way that deductive proofs are. Axioms, then, are not only subject to the possibility of the "next available" observation being contradictory, but they also suffer from the same fundamental illogic illustrated by the Gettier problem. There is some possibility, in this context, that the "Gettier problem" is logically interconnected with Gödel's incompleteness proof. Both speak to the incompleteness of the information necessary to substantiate belief as knowledge or to prove the internal consistency of a deductive system, respectively.

A.2.2. Epistemology

Now let's turn specifically to a search for the meaning of epistemology. One useful initial effort to determine the meaning of a word is to examine its entry in a standard dictionary. The *Encarta Online Dictionary*, for example, offers the following definition. "The branch of philosophy that studies the nature of knowledge, in particular its foundations, scope, and validity." The Principia Cybernetic Web article includes a definition of epistemology that defines it as "the branch of philosophy that studies knowledge. It attempts to answer the basic question: what distinguishes true (adequate) knowledge from false (inadequate) knowledge?" Wikipedia, the Free Encyclopedia, goes into a little more detail: "Epistemology, from the Greek words episteme (knowledge) and logos (word/speech) is the branch of philosophy that deals with the nature, origin and scope of knowledge. It has historically been one of the most investigated and most debated of all philosophical discourses." Schmitt (2004) provides an especially good definition: "epistemology [is defined] in the traditional way, as the conceptual and normative study of knowledge. Epistemology inquires into the definition, criteria, normative standards, and sources of knowledge and of kindred statuses like justified belief, evidence, confirmation, rational belief, perceiving, remembering and intelligence" (841). Finally, one of the most scholarly dictionaries of philosophy (Blackburn 1966) gives the following definition: "Epistemology (Gk., *epistenie*, knowledge). The theory of knowledge. Its central questions include the origin of knowledge; the place of experience in generating knowledge, and the place of reason in doing so; the relationship between knowledge and certainty, and between knowledge and the impossibility of error; the possibility of universal skepticism; and the changing forms of knowledge that arise from new conceptualizations of the world. All of these issues link with other central concerns of philosophy, such as the nature of truth and the nature of experience and meaning" (123).

These quotations add further credibility to the idea that many of the epistemological questions that philosophers have traditionally asked are either identical to or contained within those asked by psychologists. "How we acquire knowledge" is newly reformulated in the experimental psychologist's vocabulary of learning, perception, and cognition. For example, the history of learning theory has been characterized by the antagonism between the alternative means by which we learn and thereby gain knowledge. This psychological framework is a particular form of the general epistemological question, What methods of acquiring knowledge are valid and effective?

Two very different points of view dominate this controversy in both epistemology and psychology. On the one hand are the associationists or empiricists who claim that we learn by putting together sensed elements into knowledge. These empiricists believe that knowledge is accumulated on the "blank slate" of what is initially a totally inexperienced mind. On the other side of the controversy are the rationalists who believe that not only is some knowledge innate, but that it can be verified as a result of its inherent reasonableness and logical consistency.

An important field of epistemology and, likewise, psychology, therefore, is aimed at examining the methods by which we convert beliefs (a word that can be closely associated with the inductive generation of axioms and basic assumptions) into knowledge (a word that is closely associated with truths "proven" or "verified" by deductive methods). Indeed, much of technical logic is aimed at providing a firm basis for justifying the transition of unverified beliefs into knowledge.

Thus, a fundamental question of epistemology concerns the possibility of acquiring knowledge through speculation or reflection alone. For most of human history, speculation was the only method available. There now exists an alternative means—empirical (i.e., scientific) exploration. In spite of the fact that empirical evidence seems far better able to define and verify knowledge, there is still a strong propensity on the part of many people, laypersons and philosophers alike, to give undue credulity to pure speculation. Some see this as a conservative vestige of the past. Others see a commonality of speculative discourse and mathematical proofs.

A new question thus arises: Is mathematics analogous to speculation and reflection or is it another form of empirical research? Speculation has many features in common with inductive reasoning, and, of course, the essence of mathematics is deductive. We are thus led to other conundrums: Is induction scientific and able to provide a basis for converting beliefs into knowledge? Does deduction uncover new ideas or merely provide us a means of verifying some ideas on the basis of previously verified knowledge? Questions like these continue to perplex both psychologists and epistemologists.

It does not take too much of a lexicographic leap, therefore, to see that psychology comes very close to being defined in very much the same way as philosophy. It only takes a few transposed words to make epistemology into psychology and vice versa.[3] Furthermore, it can be argued that knowledge is fundamentally a mental process, and, by both its historic intent and current mentalistic bent, psychology is, purportedly, the study of mental processes. From my own point of view, psychology seems to be the main entrée to even beginning to resolve some of the epistemological issues in a scientific manner.

Others (e.g., Schmitt 2004) have noted the similarity of cognitive science (i.e., psychology) and epistemology. Schmitt suggests that they differ only in terms of their "aims, interests, and methods" (841). Psychology was declared by him to be an approach to understanding how we acquire knowledge using empirical laboratory methods; epistemology, he suggests, is a more speculative approach using tools of logic and conceptual analysis. Again the relationship between epistemology and psychology is clear: any differences are mainly methodological, not substantive. Both are attempting to understand how we verify knowledge as well as to establish its nature.

In the light of comments made in chapter 1 about one of the great deficiencies of modern psychology—its deficient and inadequate use of conceptual analysis, it may be that the distinction made by Schmitt misses a critical point. Psychology and epistemology, representing two different approaches, are not identical but are tied together far more intimately than he suggests; psychology without conceptual (i.e., epistemological) analysis would become the sterile activity of a bunch of thoughtless laboratory mechanics. Conceptual analysis without empirical validation would permit an unending number of beliefs to encumber our search for understanding.

A.2.3. Certainty and Verification

Another property of epistemology that should play a much greater role in contemporary psychology is skepticism concerning the verification of inferences drawn from behavioral findings. The rich array of statistical uncertainties, observer variabilities, and methodological mishaps that are involved in even the best-designed experimental protocol should raise red flags concerning the degree of confidence placed in the internal mechanism and processes inferred from what is at best a fragile database.[4]

Epistemologists distinguish between two broad attitudes toward certainty—skepticism and dogmatism. The first-order meaning of these two words is obvious, and only a brief comment need be made. In science, as in philosophy, the opportunity for obfuscation and illogic is always great. This simple fact means that skepticism must be a sine qua non of any science, psychology included. Dogmatism, on the other hand, should be eschewed at all costs simply because it inevitably leads to an unwillingness to drop earlier untenable ideas and to incorporate new evidence into a revised world model. Unfortunately, much of what passes for psychological research these days is beset by an illogical, unreasonable dogmatism in which uncertainty is promoted to certainty with abandon.

Skepticism has a deeper meaning, however, in the epistemological literature. Skeptics come in many kinds, but the near-universal assumption is that some (or many or all) propositions cannot be proven beyond doubt. Depending upon the particular form of skepticism, only certain types of beliefs or propositions can become knowledge. At one extreme end of the skeptical spectrum are those who would challenge even the empirical evidence produced by our senses. Because we do not contact the real external world directly and can only reconstruct that world on the basis of coded neural signals, we can never be absolutely sure that those signals have not been generated artificially, however unlikely this may be.[5] This extreme kind of skepticism throws doubt on the very existence of the real world and our ability to know anything. Whether true or not, we have to behave as if it were not true and take for granted the basic facts of the reality of the external world. Other closely related skeptical issues concern our limited ability to know other minds and to verify "intuitions" about the nature of the supernatural.

At the middle of this skeptical spectrum are those who believe that we can have knowledge about some things but not others. Traditional "Academic" and "Pyrrhonian" skepticism fall into this middle category, both of which, to a greater or lesser degree, reject reason as a means of converting beliefs into truths. The most obvious examples of how we can be deceived even by our senses in some instances are visual and auditory illusions. The most obvious examples of how our senses are useful are evident in those cases in which our percepts are congruent or coherent with other measures of the same thing.

Near the other end of the skeptical spectrum are those who accept almost everything, but even here there are major differences. Rationalists, to a very significant degree, are antiskeptical, since they believe that various kinds of speculation and rational logic can verify and authenticate our beliefs. So, too, are the empiricists who, as we have seen, attribute great trust to the evidence of our senses and the results of our experiments. The other extreme end of the skeptical spectrum houses the antiskeptics—the dogmatists—the theologically and supernaturally oriented who accept beliefs in the absence of evidence, logic, and reason.

Skeptics, therefore, come in various grades. There are some who demand such high levels of justification or verification that all progress would come to a grinding halt if we accepted their criteria. Others impose only the slightest limits on what is acceptable as psychological knowledge. In between are some (myself included) who feel that we must examine the logical and conceptual foundations of psychology, filter out the bad from good, and, perhaps most important, apply known limits and constraints from the material world to the verification and certainty of knowledge. Included among these limits must be advisories from other sciences and from mathematics. Some such beliefs or hopes have already been shown to be unverifiable; these include perpetual motion, specific hierarchical organization, and solving certain combinatorial problems. To continue a fruitless search for verification of speculative assumptions for issues that have already been definitively shown to be unobtainable is a fruitless quest and an enormous waste of resources. Only by continuing to maintain a substantial portion of skepticism can psychologists avoid some of the serious pitfalls that await the overly enthusiastic.

How do we practice an enlightened skepticism? Skeptics have three ways of dealing with unverified beliefs. One is to demand that the scientific method be applied to verify or reject a belief. If a belief cannot be demonstrated to be third-person public and sharable, then it is to be rejected. The second is to simply assert that beliefs based on supernatural criteria—and, therefore, not compatible with the laws of the material world—must be rejected a priori. The third is to demonstrate logical inconsistencies or conflicts within the "rational" arguments used to verify by means of reflection or speculation alone. Whatever the strategy, skeptics reject the idea that there are a priori foundational assumptions that must be accepted a priori.

These arguments against a facile acceptance of "knowledge" as true are rejected by dogmatists who would accept beliefs as knowledge on several, much less robust, grounds. One of the most common is a kind of spiritualist dogmatism in which the scientific criteria are rejected as being irrelevant to the conversion of a belief into knowledge. Supernatural concepts are accepted, not rejected, a priori. Science, it is asserted, has no capability to examine issues that transcend the material world. All of the logical or evidentiary means of establishing validity are rejected. A typical counterargument is "If you do not know what spiritual means, there is no way I can tell you!" The meaning of this phrase is that the scientific method is simply not applicable to matters of faith and spiritualism.

It has to be acknowledged that there is little one can do to counter these kinds of dogmatism; the principles being enunciated are typically ontological rather than epistemological. As I noted earlier, our deepest and most profound ontological principles are not subject to test and verification but depend upon arbitrary beliefs. These beliefs are usually driven by social, historical, and theological forces rather than by the application of the scientific method.

Perhaps the most formidable counterargument to a scientifically sound skepticism is the logical argument against proving a negative; that is, proving that there is not a "monster in the closet." Such a proof would be the intellectual equivalent of accepting a null hypothesis—a statistical and methodological prohibition. Thus, there really is no limit or constraint on the generation of beliefs in the invisible or untestable.

Furthermore, no means of collecting evidence can completely exclude the possibility of a critical observation or event being verified sometime in the future. Science has been reminded many times over the years that animals unobserved for years may suddenly appear. Fossils such as the coelacanths, long thought to be extinct, suddenly appear in a fisherman's net; new species of even relatively large animals such as the giant shark Megamouth or the okapi are discovered after the list of species was essentially closed.[6] However, none of these were so improbable that they created a revolution in science—a surprise, yes, but a revolution, no.

Beyond this conceptual discussion of skepticism, however, it is clear that many psychologists, like most scientists, are regularly functioning as good skeptics. Studies of sensory and perceptual distortions (i.e., experiences that are not veridical with the stimuli) are dealing with problems of the limits of knowledge in ways that differ little from epistemological concerns. For example, it is clear that the inability of observers to detect massive changes in the stimulus scene (e.g., change blindness as studied by Simons and Chabris 1999; Johansson, Hall, Sikstrom, and Olsson 2005) is an example of a very important epistemological topic—the limits of acquiring knowledge. Our inability to fully process all of the information with which we are confronted, a behavioral fact, sets strong limits on the means that we have to acquire full knowledge of the world in which we live.

Clearly, any separation of epistemology and psychology is an arbitrary distinction based mainly on their respective methodologies. Both fields are already closely integrated; psychology cannot flourish without deep conceptual analysis including public examination of its basic epistemological principles. Equally certainly, a purely rational epistemology would do poorly without some empirical evidence to support its "conceptual analyses."

The key question is, Are experimental psychology and epistemology just complements of each other or are they, in a more fundamental sense, just two methodological sides of the same activity? Given the weakness of any nonempirical, purely rational approach, we can further ask, Can (or should) experimental psychology replace epistemology?

My personal answers to questions like these convince me that any purely rational (i.e., speculative) strategies leave the door open for supernatural, extraphysical, and theological intrusions into the proper monistic, materialistic interpretation of the world. Therefore, it seems desirable that experimental psychology pick up the tasks previously assigned to epistemology. Perhaps this kind of empirical psychology should be designated as "Applied Epistemology." Much of the especially active fields of learning and sensory perception are explicitly concerned with how we acquire knowledge and what are the limits of that knowledge. Furthermore, most of the great debates of modern psychology map directly onto the classic questions of epistemology. It is in epistemology, more than any other field of philosophy, that the older speculative strategies can be seen to be so deeply flawed and for which modern alternatives exist.

A.3. INTERIM CONCLUSION

It should now be clear that many of the historical questions about what constitutes truth are mired in a pre-empirical morass. Yet, some of the questions raised here have now become amenable to evaluation, proof, and verification by means of experimental analysis. Other classic questions about the nature of knowledge have receded into the background as it became clear to an informed and appropriately skeptical modern audience that they were methodologically unanswerable. With the rise of modern scientific psychology has come the realization that its methods offer the opportunity to completely revolutionize epistemological studies of the past and to answer some of the questions pondered by humans from the dawn of cognition.

NOTES

1. A priori beliefs are closely related to a school of epistemology known as foundationalism. The basic premise of foundationalism is that some

beliefs have to be taken as true regardless of any kind of justification. These foundational beliefs represent basic ideas from which other, more complex ideas can be derived. Of course, the problems of arbitrary and unjustifiable intuitions, prejudices, and the absence of evidence raise serious questions for this point of view. Foundational beliefs may be compared to axioms, but the inductive (i.e., collective or synoptic) attribute of an axiom is not mirrored in the basic idea of a priori beliefs in foundationalism.

A related argument for justifying a priori belief is that a belief is true if it is coherent with other beliefs and acts in concert rather than in conflict with them. "Coherence" epistemology of this genre unfortunately shares many of the same difficulties as foundational epistemology. It adds a further difficulty; false assumptions can emerge when invalid beliefs mutally support each other.

2. The report of one individual, as just mentioned, is not sufficient to verify a belief or convert a belief into knowledge. Knowledge depends upon publicly shared experience, not private revelation. This usually means that there must be at least an available third observer who can verify the observation.

3. One might also consider the distinction made by Wittgenstein between philosophy as linguistic clarification and science as discovery. On this point of view, neither can assume the role of the other. However, much of epistemology is presented as a means of discovery, and so this argument does not wash.

4. Although I previously argued that all findings from psychology are valuable as behavioral observations, we cannot deny the fact that many empirical findings do not do well when replicated. This is what I mean by "fragile data."

5. This perspective was developed into the science fiction movie *The Matrix*. Everything was an illusion driven by a giant computer system that was hidden from the characters.

6. Recently (December 2005) a new species—a carnivorous mammal—was discovered in the jungles of Borneo for the first time in more than a century.

BIBLIOGRAPHY

Abbott, E. A. 1884, 2002. *Flatland: A Romance of Many Dimensions*. Introduction and notes by I. Stewart. Cambridge, MA: Perseus.

Anderson, J. 1996. *The Architecture of Cognition*. Mahwah, NJ: Erlbaum.

Anonymous. 1992. *Diagnostic and Statistical Manual of Mental Disorders DSM-IV*. Washington, DC: American Psychiatric Association.

———. 2000. *Diagnostic and Statistical Manual of Mental Disorders DSMV-IV-TR*. Washington, DC: American Psychiatric Association.

———. 2004. "Drugs vs. Talk Therapy." *Consumer Reports*, October, 22–29.

———. 1995. "Mental Health: Does Therapy Help?" *Consumer Reports*, November, 734–39.

Arrow, K. J. 1953. "The Role of Securities in the Optimal Allocation of Risk Bearing." *Review of Economic Studies* 31: 91–96.

———. 1951. *Social Choice and Individual Values*. New York: Wiley.

Bain, A. 1859. *The Emotions and the Will*. London: John W. Parker and Son.

———. 1855. *The Senses and the Intellect*. London: John W. Parker and Son.

Bartoshuk, L. M., K. Fast, and D. J. Snyder. 2005. "Differences in Our Sensory Worlds." *Current Directions in Psychological Science* 14: 122–25.

Bechtel, W. 2002. "Decomposing the Mind-Brain: A Long-Term Pursuit." *Brain and Mind* 3: 229–42.

Bentham, J. 1780, 1907. *An Introduction to the Principles of Morals and Legislation*. Oxford: Clarendon.

Bitterman, M. E. 1988. "Vertebrate-Invertebrate Comparisons." In *The Evolutionary Biology of Intelligence*, edited by H. J. Jerison and I. Jerison, 251–76. Berlin: Springer.

Blackburn, S. 1966. *The Oxford Dictionary of Philosophy*. Oxford: Oxford University Press.

Bornholdt, S. 2005. "Less Is More in Modeling Large Genetic Networks." *Science* 310: 449–51.

Brindley, G. S. 1960. *Physiology of the Retina and the Visual Pathway*. London: Edward Arnold.

Bush, R. R., and F. Mostellar. 1951. "A Mathematical Model of Simple Learning." *Psychological Review* 58: 313–23.

Carpenter, W. B. 1877. *Principles of Mental Physiology: With Their Applications to the Training and Discipline of the Mind, and the Study of Its Morbid Conditions*. London: H. S. King.

Chalmers, D. J. 1996. *The Conscious Mind: In Search of a Fundamental Theory*. New York: Oxford University Press.

Cohen, I. B., and A. Whitman. 1999. *Isaac Newton: The Principia (Mathematical Principles of Natural Philosophy): A New Translation Preceded by a Guide to Newton's Principia by I. Bernard Cohen*. Berkeley: University of California Press.

Combe, G. 1822. *Essays on Phrenology; Or an Inquiry into the Principles and Utility of the System of Drs. S. Gall and Spurzheim, and into the Objections Made against It*. Philadelphia: H. C. Carey and I. Lee, 1822.

Conant, J. B. 1951. *Science and Common Sense*. New Haven, CT: Yale University Press.

Coombs, C. H. 1984. "Psychology and Mathematics." In *Psychology and Its Allied Disciplines: Volume Iii: Psychology and the Natural Sciences*, edited by M. H. Bornstein. Hillsdale, NJ: Erlbaum.

Couvillon, P. A., and M. E. Bitterman. 1988. "Compound-Component and Conditional Discrimination of Colors and Odors by Honeybees: Further Tests of a Continuity Model." *Animal Learning and Behavior* 16: 67–74.

———. 1991. "How Honeybees Make Choices." In *The Behaviour and*

Physiology of Bees, edited by L. J. Goodman and R. C. Fisher, 116–30. Oxford: C-A-B International.

———. 1980. "Some Phenomena of Associative Learning in Honeybees." *Journal of Comparative and Physiological Psychology* 94: 878–85.

Couvillon, P. A., T. P. Ferreira, and M. E. Bitterman. 2003. "Delayed Alternation in Honeybees (*Apis Mellifera*)." *Journal of Comparative Psychology* 117, no. 1: 31–35.

Cummins, R. 2000. "'How Does It Work?' vs. 'What Are the Laws?' Two Conceptions of Psychological Explanation." In *Explanation and Cognition*, edited by F. Keil and R. Wilson. Cambridge, MA: MIT Press.

———. 1983. *The Nature of Psychological Explanation*. Cambridge, MA: MIT Press.

Darwin, C. 1859. *On the Origin of the Species by Means of Natural Selection or the Preservation of Favoured Races in the Struggle for Life*. London: J. Murray.

Dawes, R. M. 1994. *House of Cards: Psychology and Psychotherapy Built on Myth*. New York: Free Press.

Dayanand, S. 1999. "Surface Reconstruction." In *Computational Modeling of Vision: The Role of Combination*, edited by W. R. Uttal. New York: Marcel Dekker.

Debreu, G. 1991. "The Mathematization of Economic Theory." *American Economic Review* 81: 1–7.

———. 1959. *Theory of Value: An Axiomatic Analysis of Economic Equilibrium*. New Haven, CT: Yale University Press.

Descartes, R. 1677, 1912. *A Discourse on Method*. Translated by J. Veitch. London: J. M. Dent.

———. 1927. *The Meditations and Selections from the Principles of René Descartes*. Translated by J. Veitch. Chicago: Open Court.

———. 1649, 1989. *The Passions of the Soul*. Translated by S. Voss. Indianapolis: Hackett.

———. 1644, 1988. *Principia Philosophiae*. Translated by B. Reynolds. Lewiston, NY: Edwin Mellen Press.

Eltis, W. 2002. "How Quesnay's Tableau Economique Offered a Deeper Analysis of the Predicament of France." *Journal of the History of Economic Thought* 24: 39–53.

Eriksen, C. W., and J. F. Collins. 1968. "Sensory Traces versus the Psychological Moment in the Temporal Organization of Form." *Journal of Experimental Psychology* 77: 376–82.

Estes, W. K. 1950. "Toward a Statistical Theory of Learning." *Psychological Review* 57: 94–107.

Euclid. 1714. *The Elements of Euclid; with Select Theorems out of Archimedes*. Translated by A. Tacquet. London: William Whiston.

Falmagne, J-C. 2004. "Meaningfulness and Order—Invariance: Two Fundamental Principles for Scientific Laws." *Foundations of Physics* 34: 1341–84.

Feyerabend, P. K. 1975. *Against Method.* London: Verso.

Finkelstein, I., and N. A. Silberman. 2002. *The Bible Unearthed: Archeology's New Vision of Ancient Israel and the Origin of Its Sacred Texts.* New York: Free Press.

Fitts, P. M. 1954. "The Information Capacity of the Human Motor System in Controlling the Amplitude of Movement." *Journal of Experimental Psychology* 47: 381–91.

Fodor, J. 1983. *The Modularity of Mind: An Essay on Faculty Psychology.* Cambridge, MA: MIT Press.

Frank, M. 2003. "Are There Rationally Undecidable Arguments?" *Common Knowledge* 9: 119–31.

Frege, F. L. G. 1893, 1964. *The Basic Laws of Arithmetic: Exposition of the System.* Translated by M. Furth. Berkeley: University of California Press.

———. 1879, 1967. "Begriffsschrift: A Formula Language, Modeled on That of Arithmetic, for Pure Thought." In *From Frege to Gödel*, edited by J. van Heijenoort. Cambridge, MA: Harvard University Press.

Gettier, E. L. 1963. "Is Justified True Belief Knowledge?" *Analysis* 23: 121–23.

Gibson, J., D. J. Mascord, and G. A. Starmer. 1995. "The Effects of Caffeine on the Development of Fatigue in a Prolonged Driving Task." In *Alcohol, Drugs, and Traffic Safety*, edited by C. N. Kloeden and A. McLean, 92–97. Adelaide: National Health and Medical Research Council Road Accident Research Unit.

Gödel, K. 1931. "Uber Formal Unentscheidbare Satz Der Principia Mathematica Undverwandter Systeme I " [On Formally Undecidable Propositions in Principia Mathematica and Related Systems]. *Monatshefte fur Mathematik und Physik* 38: 173–98.

Greenwald, A. G. 2004. "The Resting Parrot, the Dessert Stomach, and Other Perfectly Defensible Theories." In *The Yin and Yang of Social Cognition: Perspectives on the Social Psychology of Thought Systems*, edited by J. Jost, M. R. Banaji, and D. A. Prentice, 275–85. Washington, DC: American Psychological Association.

Hagen, M. 1997. *Whores of the Court: The Fraud of Psychiatric Testimony and the Rape of American Justice*. New York: Regan Books.

Hammond, K. R., R. M. Hamm, and J. Grassia. 1986. "Generalizing over Conditions by Combining the Multitrait Multimethod Matrix and the Representative Design of Experiments." *Psychological Bulletin* 100: 257–69.

Harley, T. A. 2004. "Does Cognitive Neuropsychology Have a Future?" *Cognitive Neuropsychology* 21: 3–16.

Hartline, H. K. 1940a."The Receptive Field of Optic Nerve Fibers." *American Journal of Physiology* 130: 690–99.

Hatfield, G. 1994. "Remaking the Science of Mind: Psychology as Natural Science." In *Inventing Human Science*, edited by C. Fox, R. Porter, and R. Wokler, 184–232. Berkeley: University of California Press.

Hebb, D. O. 1949. *The Organization of Behavior. A Neuropsychological Theory*. New York: Wiley.

Hemple, C. G. 1965. *Aspects of Scientific Explanation and Other Essays in the Philosophy of Science*. New York: Free Press.

Herbenick, R. M. 2005. *Aristotle and Mathematical Ethics for Happiness*, http://www.Bu.Edu/Wcp/Papers/Teth/Tethherb.htm2005. Accessed March 10, 2007.

Hick, W. E. 1952. "On the Rate of Gain of Information." *Quarterly Journal of Experimental Psychology* 4: 11–26.

Hilgetag, C. C., M. A. O'Neil, and M. P. Young. 2000. "Hierarchical Organization of Macaque and Cat Cortical Sensory Mechanisms Explored with a Novel Network Processor." *Philosophical Transactions of the Royal Society of London* B, no. 355: 71–89.

———. 1996. "Indeterminate Organization of the Visual System." *Science* 271: 776–77.

Holth, P. 2001. "The Persistence of Category Mistakes in Psychology." *Behavior and Philosophy* 29: 203–19.

Hopfield, J. J. 1982. "Neural Networks and Physical Systems with Emergent

Collective Computational Abilities." *Proceedings of the National Academy of Sciences, USA* 79: 2554–58.

Hull, C. L. 1952. *A Behavior System: An Introduction to Behavior Theory*. New Haven, CT: Yale University Press.

———. 1943. *Principles of Behavior: An Introduction to Behavior Theory*. New York: D. Appleton-Century Company.

Hull, C. L., C. I. Hovland, R. T. Ross, M. Hall, D. T. Perkins, and F. B. Fitch. 1940. *Mathematico-Deductive Theory of Rote Learning*. New Haven, CT: Yale University Press.

Hume, D. 1888. *A Treatise of Human Nature*. Oxford: Clarendon.

Hyman, R. 1953. "Stimulus Information as a Determinant of Reaction Time." *Journal of Experimental Psychology* 45: 423–32.

James, W. 1890. *The Principles of Psychology*. New York: Holt.

———. 1892, 1948. *Psychology: The Briefer Course*. New York: Holt.

Johansson, P., L. Hall, S. Sikstrom, and A. Olsson. 2005. "Failure to Detect Mismatches between Attention and Outcome in a Simple Decision Task." *Science* 310: 116–19.

Jonsen, A. R., and S. Toulmin. 1988. *The Abuse of Casuistry: A History of Moral Reasoning*. Berkeley: University of California Press.

Judd, J. S. 1991. *Neural Network Design and the Complexity of Learning*. Cambridge, MA: MIT Press.

Kahneman, D., and A. Tversky. 1972. "Subjective Probability: A Judgment of Representativeness." *Cognitive Psychology* 3: 430–54.

Kant, I. 1965. *Critique of Pure Reason*. Translated by N. K. Smith. New York: St. Martin's.

Kantor, J. R. 1971. *The Aim and Progress of Psychology and Other Sciences: A Selection of Papers by J. R. Kantor*. Chicago: Principia.

Karp, R. M. 1986. "Combinatorics, Complexity, and Randomness." *Communications of the Association for Computer Machinery* 29: 98–108.

Kauffman, S. A. 1971. "Articulations of Parts Explanations in Biology." In *Boston Studies in the Philosophy of Science*, edited by R. C. Buck and R. S. Cohen, volume 8, 257–72. Boston: Reidel.

Keller, F. S., and W. N. Schoenfeld. 1950. *Principles of Psychology: A Systematic Text in the Science of Behavior*. New York: Appleton-Century-Crofts.

Keynes, J. M. 1936. *The General Theory of Employment, Interest, and Money*. New York: Harcourt, Brace.

Kiang, N. Y-S. 1965. *Discharge Patterns of Single Fibers in the Cat's Auditory Nerve*. Cambridge, MA: MIT Press.

Killeen, P. R. 2005. "An Alternative to Null Hypothesis Significance Tests." *Psychological Science* 16: 345–53.

———. 2005. "Tea Tests." *The General Psychologist* 40: 12–15.

Kim, J. 1982. "Psychophysical Supervenience as a Mind-Body Theory." *Cognition and Brain Theory* 5: 129–47.

Kirk, S. A., and H. Kutchins. 1992. *The Selling of the DSM: The Rhetoric of Science in Psychiatry, Social Problems, and Social Issues*. New York: A. de Gruyter.

Koch, S. 1954. "Clark L. Hull." In *Modern Learning Theory*, edited by A. T. Poffenberger, 1–176. New York: Appleton-Century-Crofts.

———. 1959b. "Epilogue." In *Psychology: A Study of a Science*, edited by S. Koch, volume 3. New York: McGraw Hill.

———. 1981. "The Nature and Limits of Psychological Knowledge: Lessons of a Century Qua 'Science.'" *American Psychologist* 36: 257–69.

———. 1959a. *Psychology: A Study of a Science: Study I. Conceptual and Systematic*. Volume 1. New York: McGraw Hill.

———. 1969. "Psychology Cannot Be a Coherent Science." *Psychology Today* 3: 66–68.

———. 1993. "'Psychology' or 'the Psychological Studies.'" *American Psychologist* 48: 902–904.

———. 1992. "Psychology's Bridgman vs. Bridgman's Bridgman." *Theory and Psychology* 2: 261–90.

Kornblith, H. 1999. "In Defense of a Naturalized Epistemology." In *The Blackwell Guide to Epistemology*, edited by J. Greco and E. Sosa, 158–69. Malden, MA: Blackwell.

Leeuwenberg, E. 1971. "A Perceptual Coding Language for Visual and Auditory Patterns." *American Journal of Psychology* 84: 307–49.

Levins, R. 1966. "The Strategy of Model Building in Population Biology." *American Scientist* 54: 421–31.

Lilienfeld, S. O. 2002. "The Scientific Review of Mental Health Practice: Our Raison d'Être." *Scientific Review of Mental Health Practice* 1: 1–10

Lipsey, M. A., and D. B. Wilson. 1993. "The Efficacy of Psychological, Educational, and Behavioral Treatment: Confirmation from Meta-Analysis." *American Psychologist* 48: 1181–1209.

Locke, J. 1690, 1967. *An Essay concerning Human Understanding*. Edited and with an introduction by J. W. Yolton. London: Dent.

Loftus, G. R. 1996. "Psychology Will Be a Much Better Science When We Change the Way We Analyze Data." *Current Directions in Psychological Science* 5: 161–71.

Luce, R. D. 1959. *Individual Choice Behavior: A Theoretical Analysis*. New York: Wiley.

———. 1995. "Why Should Mathematics Play a Role in Psychology?" *Annual Review of Psychology* 46: 1–26.

Luce, R. D., and S. S. M. Mo. 1965. "Magnitude Estimation of Heaviness by Individual Subjects: A Test of Probabilistic Response Theory." *British Journal of Mathematics and Statistics* 18: 159–74.

Lykken, D. T. 1991. "What's Wrong with Psychology Anyway?" In *Thinking Clearly about Psychology: Volume 1: Matters of Public Interest. Essays in Honor of Paul E. Meehl*, edited by D. Cicchetti and W. M. Grove, 3–39. Minneapolis: University of Minnesota Press.

MacCorquodale, K., and P. E. Meehl. 1948. "On a Distinction between Hypothetical Constructs and Intervening Variables." *Psychological Review* 55: 95–107.

Machado, A., O. Lourenco, and F. J. Silva. 2000. "Facts, Concepts, and Theories: The Shape of Psychology's Epistemic Triangle." *Behavior and Philosophy* 28: 1–40.

Marx, K. 1867, 1992. *Das Capital (Capital: A Critique of Political Economy)*. Edited by C. J. Arthur. London: Lawrence and Wisehart.

Marx, K., and F. Engels. 1848, 2004. *The Communist Manifesto*. Edited and translated by L. M. Findlay. Peterborough, ON: Broadview Press.

Massaro, D. W. 2004. "From Multisensory Integration to Talking Heads and Language Learning." In *Handbook of Multisensory Processes*, edited by G. Calvert, C. Spence, and B. E. Stein, 153–76. Cambridge, MA: MIT Press.

McClelland, J. L., and D. E. Rumelhart. 1986. *Parallel Distributed Processing: Explorations in the Microstructure of Cognition*. Volume 1: *Foundations*. Cambridge, MA: MIT Press.

———. 1986. *Parallel Distributed Processing: Explorations in the Microstructure of Cognition*. Volume 2: *Psychological and Biological Models*. Cambridge, MA: MIT Press.

Medawar, P. 1964. "Is the Scientific Paper a Fraud?" In *BBC Talk*.

Mendel, G. 1865. "Versuch Uber Pflanzen-Hybriden" [Experiments on Plant Hybridization]. *Verb. Naturf.-Ver. Brunn* 4: 3–47.

Meyer, A. R., and L. J. Stockmeyer. 1972. "The Equivalence Problem for Regular Expressions with Squaring Requires Exponential Space." Paper presented at the Proceedings of the Thirteenth Annual IEEE Symposium on Switching and Automata Theory, 125–29, Los Alamitos, CA.

Michell, J. 1999. *Measurement in Psychology: Critical History of a Methodological Concept*. Cambridge: Cambridge University Press.

Mill, J. S. 1843, 1874. *System of Logic, Ratiocinative and Inductive Being a Connected View of the Principles of Scientific Investigation*. New York: Harper and Brothers.

Miller, G. A., E. Galanter, and K. H. Pribram. 1960. *Plans and the Structure of Behavior*. New York: Holt.

Minsky, M., and S. Papert. 1988. *Perceptrons*. Expanded edition. Cambridge, MA: MIT Press.

Moore, E. F. 1956. "Gedanken-Experiments on Sequential Machines." In *Automata Studies*, edited by C. E. Shannon and J. McCarthy, 129–53. Princeton, NJ: Princeton University Press.

Moore, G. E. 1903. *Principia Ethica*. Cambridge: Cambridge University Press.

Motte, A. 1729. *The Mathematical Principles of Natural Philosophy. By Sir Isaac Newton. Translated into English by Andrew Motte. To Which Are Added, the Laws of the Moon's Motion, According to Gravity. By John Machin*. London: Printed for B. Motte.

Muotri, A. R., V. T. Chu, M. C. N. Marchetto, W. Deng, J. V. Moran, and F. H. Gage. 2005. "Somatic Mosaicism in Neuronal Precursor Cells Mediated by L1 Retrotranscription." *Nature* 435: 903–10.

Neisser, U. 1967. *Cognitive Psychology*. New York: Appleton-Century-Crofts.

Newell, A. 1990. *Unified Theories of Cognition*. Cambridge, MA: Harvard University Press.

Newton, I. 1704. *Opticks, or, a Treatise on the Reflexions, Refractions, Inflexions and Colours of Light: Also Two Treatises on the Species and Magnitude of Curvilinear Figures*. London: S. Smith and B. Walford.

———. 1687. *Philosophiae Naturalis Principia Mathematica* [Mathematical Principles of Natural Philosophy]. London: S. Pepys, Reg. Soc. Praeses.

Nickerson, R. S. 2000. "Null Hypothesis Significance Testing: A Review of an Old and Continuing Controversy." *Psychological Methods* 5: 241–301.

Nihm, S. D. 1976. "Polynomial Law of Sensation." *American Psychologist* 31: 808–809.

O'Donohue, W., and J. A. Buchanan. 2001. "The Weaknesses of Strong Inference." *Behavior and Philosophy* 29: 1–20.

Orponen, P. 1994. "Computational Complexity of Neural Networks: A Survey." Egham, England: Espirit Working Group in Neural and Operation Learning.

Pachella, R. G. 1974. "The Interpretation of Reaction Time in Information Processing Research." In *Human Information Processing: Tutorials in Performance and Cognition*, edited by B. H. Kantowitz, 41–82. Hillsdale, NJ: Erlbaum.

Palmer, S. E. 2001. "Babies and Bathwater: Reduction in Perceptual Science." *Journal of Mathematical Psychology* 45: 189–204.

Parberry, I. 1994. *Circuit Complexity and Neural Networks*. Cambridge, MA: MIT Press.

Piaget, J. 1929, 1983. *The Child's Conception of the World*. Translated by J. Tomlinson and A. Tomlinson. Totowa, NJ: Rowman and Allanheld.

Platt, J. R. 1962. *The Excitement of Science*. Boston: Houghton Mifflin.

———. 1966. *The Step to Man*. New York: Wiley.

———. 1964. "Strong Inference." *Science* 146: 347–53.

Popper, K. R. 1959. *The Logic of Scientific Discovery*. New York: Basic Books.

Quesnay, F. 1767. "Maximes Generales Du Gouvernment D'un Royaume Agricole." *Institut National d'Etudes Demographiques*: 949–76.

———. 1758, 1972 "Tableau Economique." In *Quesnay's Tableau Economique*, edited by M. Kuczynski and R. L. Meek. London: Macmillan.

Quine, W. V. O. 1975. "On Empirically Equivalent Systems of the World." *Erkenntnis* 9: 313–28.

———. 1970. "On the Reasons for the Indeterminacy of Translation." *Journal of Philosophy* 67: 178–83.

———. 1969. *Ontological Reality and Other Essays*. New York: Columbia University Press.

———. 1936. "Truth by Convention." In *Philosophical Essays for Alfred North Whitehead*, 90–124. New York: Longmans, Green.

Rapp, B., ed. 2001. *The Handbook of Cognitive Neuropsychology: What Deficits Reveal about the Human Mind*. Philadelphia: Psychology Press.

Rashevsky, N. 1948. *Mathematical Biophysics*. Chicago: University of Chicago Press.

Ratliff, F., and H. K. Hartline. 1959. "The Response of Limulus Optic Nerve Fibers to Patterns of Illumination on the Retinal Mosaic." *Journal of General Physiology* 42: 1241–55.

Reid, T. 1764. *An Inquiry into the Human Mind, on the Principles of Common Sense*. Edinburgh: A. Millar.

Rescher, N. 1969. *Introduction to Value Theory*. Englewood Cliffs, NJ: Prentice-Hall.

———. 1984. *The Limits of Science*. Pittsburgh: University of Pittsburgh Press.

Rescorla, R. A., and A. R. Wagner. 1972. "A Theory of Pavlovian Conditioning: Variations in the Effectiveness of Reinforcement and Nonreinforcement." In *Classical Conditioning Ii: Current Research and Theory*, edited by A. H. Black and W. F. Prokasy, 64–99. New York: Appleton-Century-Crofts.

Ricardo, D. 1817. *On the Principles of Political Economy and Taxation*. London: John Murray.

Rieping, W., M. Habeck, and M. Nildes. 2005. "Inferential Structure Determination." *Science* 309: 303–306.

Rosenblatt, F. 1958. "The Perceptron: A Probabilistic Model for Information Storage and Organization in the Brain." *Psychological Review* 65: 386–408.

———. 1962. *Principles of Neurodynamics*. Washington, DC: Spartan.

Rousseau, J. J. 1755, 1797. *Discours sur L'economie Politique*. First English edition. Albany: Barber and Southwick.

Rumelhart, D. E., and J. L. McClelland. 1986. *Parallel Distributed Processing: Explorations in the Microstructure of Cognition*. Volume 1: *Foundations*. Cambridge, MA: MIT Press.

Russell, B. 1945. *A History of Western Files, and Its Connection with Political and Social Circumstances from the Earliest Times to the Present Day*. New York: Simon and Schuster.

———. 1937. *The Principles of Mathematics*. New York: Norton.

Sarton, G. 1952. *A History of Science: Ancient Science through the Golden Age of Greece*. Cambridge, MA: Harvard University Press.

Scharf, H. E. 1973. *The Computation of Economic Equilibria*. New Haven, CT: Yale University Press.

Schlinger, H. D. 2004. "Why Psychology Hasn't Kept Its Promises." *Journal of Mind and Behavior* 25: 123–44.

Schmitt, F. F. 2004. "Epistemology and Cognitive Science." In *Handbook of Epistemology*, edited by I. Niniluoto, M. Sintonen, and J. Wolenski, 841–918. Dordrecht: Kluwer.

Shallice, T. 1988. *From Neuropsychology to Mental Structure*. Cambridge: Cambridge University Press.

Shapiro, D., and D. Shapiro. 1982. "Meta-Analysis of Comparative Therapy Outcome Studies: A Replication and Refinement." *Psychological Bulletin* 92: 581–604.

Shatz, D. 1993. "Skepticism and Naturalized Epistemology." In *Naturalism: A Critical Appraisal*, edited by S. J. Wagner and R. Warner. Notre Dame, IN: University of Notre Dame Press.

Simons, D. J., and C. F. Chabris. 1999. "Gorillas in Our Midst: Sustained Inattentional Blindness for Dynamic Events." *Perception* 28: 1059–74.

Skinner, B. F. 1983. *Behavior of Organisms*. New York: Appleton-Century-Crofts.

Slife, B. D., and R. N. Williams. 1997. "Toward a Theoretical Psychology: Should a Subdiscipline Be Formally Recognized." *American Psychologist* 52: 117–29.

Smith, A. 1776, 1976. *The Wealth of Nations*. Chicago: University of Chicago Press.

Smith, R. 1997. *The Human Sciences*. New York: Norton.

Spencer, H. 1862. *First Principles*. London: Williams and Norgate.

———. 1864. *The Principles of Biology*. London: Williams and Norgate.

———. 1892. *The Principles of Ethics*. London: Williams and Norgate.

———. 1855, 1892. *The Principles of Psychology*. London: Longmans.

———. 1896. *The Principles of Sociology*. New York: Appleton.

Spiegel, A. 2005. "The Dictionary of Disorder: How One Man Revolutionized Psychiatry." *New Yorker*, no. 3, January, 56–63.

Staats, A. W. 1999. "Unifying Psychology Requires New Infrastructure, Theory, Method, and a Research Agenda." *Review of General Psychology* 3: 3–13.

Sternberg, S. 1969. "The Discovery of Processing Stages: Extension of Donder's Method." *Acta Psychologica* 30: 276–315.

Stevens, S. S. 1951. "Mathematics, Measurement, and Psychophysics." In *Handbook of Experimental Psychology*, edited by S. S. Steven. New York: Wiley.

———. 1961. "The Psychophysics of Sensory Function." In *Sensory Communication*, edited by W. A. Rosenblith, 1–34. Cambridge, MA: MIT Press.

Stockmeyer, L. J., and A. K. Chandra. 1979. "Intrinsically Difficult Problems." *Scientific American* 240: 140–59.

Stockmeyer, L. J., and A. R. Meyer. 2002. "Cosmological Lower Bound on the Circuit Complexity of a Small Problem in Logic." *Journal of the Association for Computing Machinery* 49: 753–84.

Stroud, B. 1984. *The Philosophical Significance of Skepticism*. Oxford: Oxford University Press.

Suppes, P. 1959. "Measurement, Empirical Meaningfulness, and Three Valued Logic." In *Measurement: Definition and Theories*, edited by C. W. Churchman and P. Ratoosh. New York: Wiley.

Suppes, P., and J. L. Zinnes. 1963. "Basic Measurement Theory." In *Handbook of Mathematical Psychology*, edited by R. D. Luce, R. R. Bush, and E. Galanter, volume 1. New York: John Wiley and Sons.

Tanner, W. P., Jr., and J. A. Swets. 1954. "A Decision Making Theory of Visual Detection." *Psychological Review* 61: 401–409.

Teichner, W. H., and M. J. Krebs. 1974. "Laws of Visual Choice Reaction Times." *Psychological Review* 81: 75–98.

Titchener, E. B. 1899. *An Outline of Psychology*. New York: Macmillan.

Turing, A. M. 1937. "On Computable Numbers, with an Application to the Entscheidungsproblem." *Proceedings of the London Mathematical Society* (series 2) 42: 230–65.

Tolman, E. C. 1932. "Purposive Behavior in Animals and Man." New York: Appleton-Century-Crofts.

Tversky, A. 1969. "Intransitivity of Preference." *Psychological Review* 76: 31–48.

Tversky, A., and D. Kahneman. 1973. "Availability: A Heuristic for Judging Frequency and Probability." *Cognitive Psychology* 5: 207–32.

———. 1974. "Judgment under Uncertainty: Heuristics and Biases." *Science* 185: 1124–31.

Uttal, L. 2002. *Making Care Work: Employed Mothers in the New Childcare Market*. New Brunswick, NJ: Rutgers University Press.

Uttal, W. R. 1975. *An Autocorrelation Theory of Form Detection*. Hillsdale, NJ: Erlbaum.

———. 2004. *Dualism: The Original Sin of Cognitivism*. Mahwah, NJ: Erlbaum.

———. 2006. *Human Factors in the Courtroom: Mythology versus Science.* Tucson, AZ: Lawyers and Judges Publishing.

———. 2005. *Neural Theories of the Mind: Why the Mind-Brain Problem May Never Be Solved.* Mahwah, NJ: Erlbaum.

———. 2001. *The New Phrenology: The Limits of Localizing Cognitive Processes in the Brain.* Cambridge, MA: MIT Press.

———. 1988. *On Seeing Forms.* Hillsdale, NJ: Erlbaum.

———. 2003. *Psychomythics: Sources of Artifacts and Misconceptions in Scientific Psychology.* Mahwah, NJ: Erlbaum.

———. 2000. *The War between Mentalism and Behaviorism: On the Accessibility of Mental Processes.* Mahwah, NJ: Erlbaum.

Valenstein, E. S. 1998. *Blaming the Brain: The Truth about Drugs and Mental Health.* New York: Free Press.

Wallace, A. R. 1858. "On the Tendency of Varieties to Depart Indefinitely from the Original Type." Paper presented at the Special Meeting of the Linnaean Society, July 1, 1858, London.

Ward, J. 1920. *Psychological Principles.* Cambridge: University of Cambridge Press.

Watson, J. B. 1914. *Behavior: An Introduction to Comparative Psychology.* New York: Holt.

Watson, J. D., and F. H. C. Crick. 1953. "Molecular Structure of Nucleic Acids." *Nature* 171: 737–38.

Weber, E. H. 1834, 1942. "De Puksa, Resorptione, Auditu, et Tactu: Annotationes Anatomicae et Physiologiae." Cited in *In Sensation and Perception in the History of Experimental Psychology*, edited by E. G. Boring, 513. New York: Appleton-Century-Crofts.

Wendroth, P. M., and C. R. Latimer. 1978. "On the Relationship between the Psychology of Visual Perception and the Neurophysiology of Vision." In *Festschrift in Honour of W. M. O'Neil*, edited by J. P. Sutcliffe. Sydney: University of Sydney Press.

Westfall, R. S. 1973. "Newton and the Fudge Factor." *Science* 179: 751–58.

Whitehead, A. N., and B. Russell. 1910–1913. *Principia Mathematica.* Cambridge: Cambridge University Press.

Wiles, A. 1995. "Modular Elliptic Curves and Fermat's Last Theorem." *Annals of Mathematics* 141 (series 2): 443–551.

Wimsatt, W. C. 1974. "Complexity and Organization." In *Proceedings of the 1972 Biennial Meeting of the Philosophy of Science Association.* Volume

20 of the Boston Studies in the Philosophy of Science, edited by K. F. Schaffner and R. S. Cohen. Boston: Dordrecht-Holland.

Wittgenstein, L. 1958. *Philosophical Investigations*. Englewood Cliffs, NJ: Prentice-Hall.

———. 1921, 1947. *Tractatus Logico-Philosophicus*. With an introduction by Bertrand Russell. New York: Harcourt, Brace.

Wolfs, F. Appendix E. *Introduction to the Scientific Method*, http://teacher.nsrl.rochester.edu/phy_labs/AppendixE/AppendixE.html. Accessed March 10, 2007.

Wright, R. J. 1875, 1974. *Principia or Basis of Social Science*. New York: Arno Press.

Wundt, W. M. 1874, 1910. *Grundzuge Der Physiologischen Psychologie* [Principles of Physiological Sychology]. Translated by E. B. Titchener. Leipzig: W. Engelmann.

———. 1897, 1969. *Outlines of Psychology*. Translated by C. H. Judd. St. Clair Shores, MI: Scholarly Press.

Yule, G. U. 1926. "Why Do We Sometimes Get Nonsense-Correlations between Time Series? A Study in Sampling and the Nature of Time Series." *Journal of the Royal Statistical Society* 89: 1–64.

Zipf, G. K. 1935, 1965. *Psycho-Biology of Languages*. Cambridge, MA: MIT Press.

NAME INDEX

SUBJECT INDEX